Craig Steiner

MOVING
FORWARD

BY LOOKING BACK

EMBRACING FIRST-CENTURY PRACTICES IN YOUTH MINISTRY

ADORATION

COMMUNITY

TRUTH

SERVICE

ZONDERVAN®

ZONDERVAN.com/
AUTHORTRACKER
follow your favorite authors

youth
specialties

youth
specialties

Moving Forward by Looking Back
Copyright 2009 by Craig Steiner

Youth Specialties resources, 300 S. Pierce St., El Cajon, CA 92020 are published by Zondervan, 5300 Patterson Ave. SE, Grand Rapids, MI 49530.

ISBN 978-0-310-28250-1

Web site addresses listed in this book were current at the time of publication. Please contact Youth Specialties via email (YS@YouthSpecialties.com) to report URLs that are no longer operational and replacement URLs if available.

Cover design by Toolbox Studios
Interior design by Mark Novelli, IMAGO MEDIA

Printed in the United States of America

09 10 11 12 13 14 • 18 17 16 15 14 13 12 11 10 9 8 7 6 5 4 3 2 1

DEDICATION

To My #1 Youth Group:

Jonathan, Micah, and Hannah

ACKNOWLEDGMENTS

I didn't create this book sitting alone in a room with a laptop computer. Rather it was shaped through many personal experiences and the influence of many people in my life. I want to thank several who've been extremely helpful in the process of writing this book.

First, I want acknowledge the profound influence that my pastor, James MacDonald, has on my life, my ministry, and has had on this book. I'm blessed to serve in a church where the senior pastor is so passionate about students and student ministry. While I was writing this book, Pastor James was preaching a series at Harvest Bible Chapel from the book of Acts. He was gracious to allow me to pass along some insights that I gained about the early church in his series. You can obtain the sermon series "Church on a Mission" through walkintheword.com.

God has blessed me with a wonderful staff team in Harvest Students including DP, Mark Z., Luke Mac, Dustin, Ed, Josh, Kegel, TQ, Jenny, Colizza, Steph, and Sarah. It's a joy to serve together and sharpen one another. You're some of my favorite people.

I'm grateful to Joe for his leadership and encouragement in my life.

Sonlife Ministries has deeply impacted my 15 years of student ministry, especially the training from Dann Spader, the mentoring from Mark Edwards, and more recently the sharpening from Chris Folmsbee. Sonlife gave me a vision for a disciplemaking ministry and was the first to expose me to the priorities of adoration, community, truth, and service. I'm forever grateful for the ministry of Sonlife.

I'm grateful to Chris Hudson for being the first to believe in this book.

Jay Howver and the whole YS team have been wonderful to work with on this project. Many thanks to Dave Urbanski for his thoughtful feedback and helpful assistance during the whole editorial process, and to my friend, Mark Novelli, for sharing his incredible creativity in designing the interior of this book.

I owe a huge debt of gratitude to Dan Luebcke and Eric Leichty for reading every word of my manuscript and commenting on most of them. I'm honored by your friendship and the hours you devoted to helping to craft this book. You guys are the best.

Thank you to my bride, Camille, for your steadfast encouragement and friendship over this long journey and to my dad and mom, Kent and Deanna, and Keith and Lynsey for cheering me on toward the finish line.

CONTENTS

INTRODUCTION

Ever feel as if you pour yourself into ministry, but all your efforts produce so very little? It's not as though you're not trying—anybody can see that. You develop your programs, then you ask God to bless your programs. Seems fair enough. But still something isn't quite right.

Here's a thought: Rather than asking God to bless your program, why not get on God's program? Instead of asking God to be part of what you're doing, why not be part of what God's doing?

Specifically, transforming lives. Clearly, while only God can transform lives, God also invites us into that process—we have roles to play. And as youth workers, our roles can (and should) be about creating youth ministries that transform lives.

If you desire to engage in ministry God empowers, God works through, God blesses—a ministry where God is transforming lives—then this book is for you. A student ministry that transforms lives stirs up students to follow Jesus passionately. But how do we help students become and grow as followers of Jesus?

The book of Acts describes how Jesus' disciples got on God's program and embraced their mission to make disciples. And God empowered their ministry. As a result, lives were transformed.

My conviction is that the priorities that brought about spiritual transformation in the first-century New Testament church still apply in our 21st-century student ministries. If we're going to move forward, we must first look back.

Getting into Acts

Before ascending into heaven, Jesus called his first disciples to a mission. The book of Acts picks up the account, describing how they lived out their mission, how God empowered their ministry, and how God transformed lives through their acts. The following snapshot of the early church in Acts 2 will serve as the foundation for this book:

> They devoted themselves to the apostles' teaching and to the fellowship, to the breaking of bread and to prayer. Everyone was filled with awe, and many wonders and miraculous signs were done by the apostles. All the believers were together and had everything in common. Selling their possessions and goods, they gave to anyone as he had need. Every day they continued to meet together in the temple courts. They broke bread in their homes and ate together with glad and sincere hearts, praising God and enjoying the favor of all the people. And the Lord added to their number daily those who were being saved.
> (Acts 2:42-47)

No question about it: The Acts believers had an all-out devotion to each other and to their common mission. The early church gathered together in the temple and in homes. They valued times of worship, small group fellowship, and ministry outside the walls of the church.

Now you're probably wondering what all the symbols stand for. Here goes: The highlighted phrases are what God did; the boxes and circles show what the believers did—the ministry contexts; and further, the circles indicate things they were devoted to: The apostles' teaching, fellowship, breaking of bread, prayer, being together, selling belongings to distribute proceeds to meet needs, and praising God. Although the Acts church was devoted to many things, we can summarize them in four broad priorities:

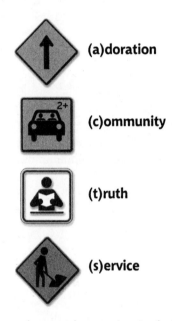

(a)doration

(c)ommunity

(t)ruth

(s)ervice

Adoration was what was happening in the midst of the breaking of bread, prayer, and the praising of God. *Community* was occurring in fellowship, being together, and sharing with each other. *Truth* was observed in their commitment to the apostles' teaching. *Service* was being experienced in their reaching out and meeting people's needs.

God empowered the Acts believers' devotion to these ministry priorities. God was transforming lives. People were filled with awe of God. No, the religious establishment didn't like what they were doing, but they experienced favor with many others. God was redeeming lives and growing their body daily. Luke makes it clear that life transformation wasn't merely a result of human efforts. The apostles

moving forward > by looking back

didn't convene a strategic planning meeting for church growth. Rather God was adding to their numbers. The early church simply got on God's program and was engaged in ministry God was empowering.

Since God is the same "yesterday and today and forever" (Hebrews 13:8), I believe that the God who was transforming lives in the Old and New Testaments still wants to transform lives today. Again, my conviction is that the priorities that brought spiritual transformation in the first-century church still apply today in our 21st-century student ministries. *If we're going to move forward, we must first look back.*

Format of This Book

This book isn't a new ministry model that prescribes one correct way to program student ministry. Instead this book is about developing deeper biblical convictions to guide your leadership and your student ministry—because much more than a *philosophy* of student ministry, we need a *theology* of student ministry. Therefore, the focus of this book is on the Acts priorities for ministry that transforms lives. It's divided into four primary sections:

(a)doration > engaging students with God

(c)ommunity > engaging students with God's people

(t)ruth > engaging students with God's Word

(s)ervice > engaging students with God's world

Each section has four chapters. The first chapter in each section is *looking back* at the ministry priority in the book of Acts and establishes a biblical theology of the priority. The last three chapters in each section are devoted to *moving forward* as practicing theologians in today's student ministry. Each chapter ends with questions for personal reflection and leadership team discussions. The order of the book follows the Acts outline, but you're free to start reading the sections that resonate most with you and then go back and read the rest. However, it's helpful to read the first chapter in a section before any other chapters in that section because the first chapter explains underlying principles.

A Biblical Framework

Many things are built upon frames. Cars. Skyscrapers. Even the chair you're sitting on. An eyeglass frame holds a lens in place. A picture frame sets a photograph in place. Our country is built on the framework of the Constitution. Frames are essential for providing necessary structure.

This book offers ideas for application in student ministry, but it's more than a book of ideas. This book offers a biblical framework for ministries transformed by God based on the biblical priorities of the early church in the book of Acts. Then it moves forward with practical applications for student ministry today.

Previewing the Priorities

The Acts priorities are not programs. Because these are priorities and not programs, it's possible to experience multiple (sometimes all four) priorities in one ministry program. These priorities can be experienced in the context of a large group or a small group or on a ministry trip or in any other ministry context.

The Acts priorities are not program elements. Think with me on this one.

Let's consider *adoration*. Most student ministry leaders believe worship is an important aspect of student ministry. However, a natural tendency is immediately to jump to the application of scheduling time each Wednesday night for worship (i.e., singing) and developing a worship band. But do we have biblical convictions of what worship really is? Isn't there more to worship than merely singing? And just because students are singing and clapping doesn't mean worship is really happening, right?

This book provides a holistic perspective of worshiping God with our lips and our lives. The first section offers dozens of adoration ideas that don't involve singing (not that there's anything wrong with singing). It encourages allowing students to be contributors to the worship experience rather than simply being spectators or participants or an audience looking up at a worship leader. Also, it addresses how to create a culture of prayer.

How about *community*? Most of us agree fellowship is essential in student ministries, and we tend to view small groups as the solution for fellowship. But just because you offer small groups doesn't mean students are experiencing Christian fellowship, right? And isn't there more to small groups than fellowship? And conversely, many small groups are nothing more than prearranged times for students to talk about whatever. So can't we experience fellowship in settings other than in small groups? The reality is that community should be developed in every ministry setting.

This book calls student ministry leaders to move their youth groups beyond being relational communities to forming spiritual communities that embody the "*one anothers*" and are concerned with connecting the disconnected.

Now consider *truth*. Most student ministry leaders agree the Bible must have an essential role. But when, where, and how? Just because 20 or 30 minutes a week is set aside to teach the Bible doesn't mean students are engaged, right? What's the role of the Bible in large-group times and in small groups? And shouldn't our goal be much more than just teaching the Bible? What about training students to think biblically? Are there effective ways to encourage students to memorize, meditate with, or study the Bible?

This book encourages a rethinking of our standard (and oftentimes boring) approach to teaching by offering practical ways to engage students with God's truth through interactive teaching. It works with groups of 12, 40, or hundreds of students—with a clear emphasis on helping students discover God's Word for themselves.

Finally, let's consider *service*. Most student ministry leaders don't need convincing that getting students to serve others is pleasing to God. But should we be content with getting some students to show up twice a year for a service project day? People have physical and spiritual needs. How can we motivate our students to serve these needs holistically? Since students have spiritual needs, including a relationship with God, how can we engage our students in reaching out? And what is the ministry's role in providing events for reaching out?

This book encourages becoming a missional community to mobilize students to engage compassionately with the physical, relational, and spiritual needs of people in God's world—in their schools, their communities, and around the globe.

I invite you to join me on a journey as we consider answers to these questions and more. Let's begin *moving forward > by looking back*...for the glory of God.

(a)doration
engaging students with God

1.0 LOOKING BACK
@ (a)doration

A TV is designed to be...watched.

A car is designed to be...driven.

Tortilla chips are designed to be...eaten.

Clothes are designed to be...worn.

A video game is designed to be...played.

You are designed to...＿＿＿＿＿＿.

How would you fill in the blank? How would your students fill in the blank? Be happy? Do good to others? Make a difference in the world? What's the answer to this fundamental question?

Our Creator declares, "The people I formed for myself that they may proclaim my praise" (Isaiah 43:21). The Westminster Shorter Catechism begins with these words: "Man's chief end is to glorify God and to enjoy him forever." Peter writes, "You are a chosen people...belonging to God, that you may declare the praises of him who called you out of darkness into his wonderful light" (1 Peter 2:9). You are designed to worship God.

I love what worship leader and theologian Don Williams writes: "The greatest truth of God is that he is worthy of our worship, and the deepest truth about ourselves is that we have been created to worship him. When we actually do this, we find the real and eternal end, or *telos*, of our existence."[1] *Telos* comes from the Greek word for "end," "purpose," or "goal." The purpose of your existence is to glorify God. In other words, you are designed to worship God.

As youth leaders, we have the incredible privilege of helping students know their Creator. This ought to fire all of us up. Let's not forget: We offer much more than games, devotional lessons, and hang-out time. We get to engage students with the God of the universe.

(a)doration in Acts

The Acts church was theocentric. The book of Acts shows God-centered believers devoted to the priority of adoration through their commitment to prayer and worship.

Our Acts 2:42 snapshot shows that the early church was devoted to prayer. I find it interesting that the original Greek language contains a definite article ("the") and a plural form ("prayers"). The literal translation is, "They were devoted to...the prayers." This implies the early church had common prayers that were written and then repeated verbally. Unscripted, freestyle prayers are valuable expressions of faith. But we also receive great benefit from meditating on and reciting the thoughtful prayers of our church fathers and mothers. It seems to me we should strive for a balance of both.

The devotion to prayer in the early church doesn't surprise me because it was a priority of their Master. The disciples never said to Jesus, "Lord, teach us to do miracles." Nor did they say, "Lord, teach us to teach." Or "teach us to love." But they did ask, "Lord, teach us to pray." Jesus' prayer life was contagious. They longed to pray like Jesus. After all, quoting from the book of Isaiah, Jesus said, "My house will be called a house of prayer for all the nations" (Mark 11:17).

There were no worship wars in the early church because worship wasn't about music; worship was about God. The early Christians weren't limited to a certain worship style—instead they engaged with God in a variety of forms. It's important we, too, understand the difference between form and function as it relates to worship. The function of worship is to glorify God by declaring his praises. We should never compromise the function of worship. But as with the church in Acts, we should be open to various forms of worship. The Acts believers praised God together in the temple. They praised God intimately in their homes. Their lives overflowed with gladness and gratitude to the Lord. They were filled with awe of God. And they routinely broke bread in remembrance of Christ. Worship took forms other than music.

Let's consider a few examples from the book of Acts on the priority of adoration—first in prayer and later in worship.

Priority of prayer

Prayer was central to the life of the early church. The believers engaged in a tremendous amount of prayer throughout the book of Acts. Through a quick word search at BibleGateway.com, I discovered that "prayer" is mentioned twice as many times in Acts as in any other New Testament book. Prayer is a major theme of Acts starting in the first chapter (1:14) and continuing through to the final chapter (28:8).

Acts 4 records one of the most incredible prayers in the history of the church. The religious leaders were ticked that the apostles were teaching the people and proclaiming in Jesus the resurrection of the dead. So they seized Peter and John and threw them in the slammer. The next day Peter and John stood trial for their faith in Christ. Even under the duress of persecution and interrogation, they didn't back down from their faith. In fact, they were more emboldened. After threatening them and ordering them to stop preaching about Jesus, the Sanhedrin released them. Peter and John immediately went back to the community of believers.

After hearing the details about Peter and John's persecution, the believers "raised their voices together in prayer" (Acts 4:24). Don't you love this? This was the first thing they did. Prayer was a priority—not a last resort. They *raised their voices*. In other words, they cried out to

moving forward > by looking back

God. They boldly and confidently called out to God. This was not an in-the-quietness-of-the-moment-silently-talk-to-God gathering. They weren't whispering prayers in small groups. They weren't tentative in their prayers. No. I'm sure the volume of their prayers matched the intensity of their prayers. They approached the throne of God with confidence. They were literally crying out to God.

And they raised their voices *together*. They were united in their prayer. They were in it together. Perhaps they were audibly crying out to God all at the same time. Why are our group prayer times often passive, unemotional, and formulaic (e.g., "Dear God, thank you for tonight. Thank you for bringing us together. Please help us to live for you better. In Jesus' name, Amen.")? When was the last time your group truly raised their voices together in prayer"?

And the focus of the Acts 4 prayer was powerful. They didn't ask God for protection or for the peaceful ceasing of persecution. Instead they launched out by praising God for his sovereignty. Then they begged God to enable them to speak with boldness: "After they prayed, the place where they were meeting was shaken. And they were all filled with the Holy Spirit and spoke the word of God boldly" (Acts 4:31). Wow! God is always eager to answer this kind of prayer. God's presence filled the room and filled their lives.

I love what British theologian Michael Green says about the believers in Acts: "When people pray, the Spirit comes, the place where they pray is shaken, prison doors break open, and people dare to die with radiance."[2]

The early church believed firmly in the power of prayer. They were persistent in prayer. Expectant in prayer. Fervent in prayer. Unified in prayer. Bold in prayer. Scripture-filled in prayer. Passionate in prayer.

Prayer was central to the life of the early church. Is prayer central in your ministry?

PRIORITY OF WORSHIP

The second focus of the priority of adoration is worship, and one of the greatest worship services in the book of Acts didn't occur in the temple. Nor did it occur in a house church. Nor in a large public gathering in a city square. Instead it was in the confines of a dark and damp prison cell.

Acts 16 records a bad day Paul and Silas had in Philippi—one that surpasses Alexander's *Terrible, Horrible, No Good, Very Bad Day.*[3] It started a few days before as they were going to the place of prayer. (The religious law required 10 Jewish males in order to establish a synagogue in a town. Because Philippi didn't have a quorum, the Jews gathered as a small community beside the river just outside the city gates. This was called "the place of prayer.") At this place of prayer they came across an enslaved girl. This girl was enslaved in two ways— by human owners and by an evil spirit. Because of her demonic possession she was able to tell the future. These abilities made her a cash cow for her owners. Can you say, "Cha-ching!"? This demon-possessed girl followed Paul's entourage of missionaries for several days and proclaimed them to be "servants of the Most High God, who are telling you the way to be saved" (Acts 16:17). All this was absolutely true, but she was causing harm to the cause of Christ because others were associating her with the message.

Paul grew weary of the way the girl was harassing them and of the way the demon was harassing the girl. He ended both by turning toward the girl and boldly speaking to the evil spirit. With authority he demanded, "In the name of Jesus Christ I command you to come out of her!" (Acts 16:18). And immediately she was liberated.

As you might imagine, this didn't go over well with her owners. Outraged about their loss of revenue, they made a citizen's arrest. They dragged them to Philippi's central public square to stand trial before the magistrates on trumped-up charges of disturbing the peace.

A guilty verdict was handed down. The sentence included a mob beating and prison time. First Paul and Silas were attacked, stripped, and flogged. The flogging was similar to the punishment of caning still practiced in some countries.

Paul and Silas' flesh was ripped off their bodies in the flogging. Beaten and bloodied, they were thrown into jail—but not in an ordinary cell. Instead they were thrown into maximum-security lockdown in the extreme depths of the prison with their feet fastened in stocks. And the stocks weren't the like the ones from the early days of the Pilgrims. Rather the stocks were instruments of torture, pulling their legs as far apart as possible.

moving forward > by looking back

If I were Paul or Silas, I'd have been angry about the injustices committed against me. I'd have been demanding my personal rights and complaining about my unfair treatment. It would've been easy to turn my anger toward God, too. I could've rationalized, "I was just trying to serve you and be faithful. And this is what I get? If you loved me, you wouldn't let this happen." I might even have groaned, "Woe is me," and drowned in depression. How about you?

Paul and Silas had a remarkable response. They turned their terrible, horrible, no-good, very bad day into an amazing worship service. One must have asked the other, "Now what?"

And the other replied, "Let's pray and sing together."

"Okay!"

Because "About midnight Paul and Silas were praying and singing hymns to God, and the other prisoners were listening to them" (Acts 16:25). If Matt Redman's "Blessed Be Your Name" had been written in the first century, perhaps they would've sung:

On the road marked with suffering

Though there's pain in the offering

Blessed be Your name

You give and take away...

Lord, my heart will choose to say

blessed be Your name.

(Beth Redman & Matt Redman, from *Where Angels Fear to Tread* © *2002 Kingsway's Thankyou Music*)

Listen. Can you hear them singing a joyful cry from a suffering heart?

Remember their feet were in devices of torture. They were in a stinking dungeon cell. Their backs were bleeding. Yet they were praising God!

How did they turn their persecution into praise? Paul and Silas understood this truth: God is good in the good times, but still good in the hard times. This reminds me of a statement from Tony Dungy, the head coach of the Indianapolis Colts, shortly after his son's suicide: *Our situations change for better or worse, but God's worth never changes.* Isn't this an awesome statement?

Our students need to understand this important truth: Our situations change for better or worse, but God's worth never changes. It's easy to worship God when life is good. But what about when the storms of hardship, tragedy, and discouragement wreak havoc in our lives? What about when life is draining and our emotions are numb? What about when life seems to be falling apart? What then? When life doesn't feel good, are we able to still sing, "You are good"? We don't want students to ignore their circumstances, nor do we want them to fake their emotions, but we do need to encourage them to worship God in the center of their circumstances. Regardless of what happens in our lives, God was, is, and always will be worthy of our worship.

In referring to God's propensity to show up at midnight, my senior pastor James MacDonald has said several times, "God never comes late. But he rarely comes early." And this was certainly the case in Acts 16 with Paul and Silas in prison singing praises to God.

Suddenly, the jailhouse worship service was interrupted by an earthquake that rocked the prison, sending doors flying open and chains falling off. Make a note of this: When the God of the universe is rightly worshiped, powerful things happen.

Once the dust settled (literally), the first thing out of the jailer's mouth wasn't some expletive outburst. Consider all the questions he could've asked. Instead he rushed to Paul and Silas and asked, "Sirs, what must I do to be saved?" (Acts 16:30). He'd witnessed something incredible—two guys authentically praising God. Their worship was profoundly evangelistic even though that wasn't their motive. Their praise rocked the jailer's world. Their worship created a curiosity about the reality of God and convicted him about a need he had deep in his soul. The jailer was begging, "I want to have what you have."

God used the power of prayer and worship to transform the jailer, his family, and very likely the lives of the other inmates in the prison.

moving forward > by looking back

This wasn't only true in the first century; it's in our youth ministries today, too.

I remember attending some training seminars when I first started in student ministry that promoted using secular music instead of worship music to draw non-Christian students to God. The rhetoric was, "Let's be sensitive and not offend or make them feel uncomfortable." Regrettably, I followed the advice. I was able to draw a crowd, but students weren't drawn to God because of familiar songs.

I later discovered non-Christians are drawn to God as they observe other students engaged in authentic worship. Worship can create a curiosity about the reality of God and convict students of a need deep within their souls.

When our student ministries prioritize adoration by engaging students with God, powerful things happen. God-things happen. Lives are transformed.

A Biblical Theology of (a)doration

Are you fired up about worship? I hope so. But before you establish a worship band or service, you need to establish a biblical theology of worship. Too many worship teams don't have a clue about what worship is.

So...what *is* worship?

The definition I use with our students is: *Worship is responding to God's greatness and graciousness with our lips and through our lives.* This definition is rooted in Psalm 145:1-13. It's an amazing psalm of adoration that speaks to three truths about worship.

WE WORSHIP GOD (PERIOD).

I recently stood on the stage and yelled, "How's the audience tonight?" The students screamed in a crazy frenzy. Then I reminded students that they weren't the audience—God was the audience. We live for and worship an Audience of one. We worship God (period).

God must be the *object* and *subject* of our worship. God's desire for exclusive rights to our worship is clear in the first two commandments:

"You shall have no other gods before me. You shall not make for yourself an idol in the form of anything in heaven above or on the earth beneath or in the waters below" (Exodus 20:3-4).

We worship God, not a lesser god.

What are some things students tend to worship instead of God? Here are some of the things that come to my mind:

> Celebrities—our pop culture worships Hollywood stars and sports heroes.

> Money—we love all the stuff and status money buys.

> Activities—sports, clubs, and hobbies can become gods students worship.

> Boyfriend or girlfriend—romantic infatuation is often worship.

> Personal happiness—many students worship anything that brings personal pleasure.

> My image—most students are totally into themselves and the images they project.

We need to remind our students God deserves exclusive rights to our worship. We worship God (period).

I love Psalm 145 because God clearly is the object and subject of worship (period). I count 22 uses of the *you* and *your* pronouns in the first 13 verses, including, "your mighty acts...your majesty...your wonderful works...your awesome works...your great deeds...your abundant goodness...your righteousness..." Clearly, God was the object and subject of David's worship.

As in the psalms of David, our songs need to include more *you* and *your* pronouns than *I* and *me* words. Worship isn't about us. Worship is about God. We must contend for the centrality of God in our worship. Many of today's popular worship songs speak primarily about self and only vaguely of God. But worship isn't about what God does for us. Nor is it about what we do for God. This is human-focused worship. Worship is about God (period).

moving forward > by looking back

We must guard the content of the lyrics because students may get more theology from the songs they sing than any other source. Just as it's essential to have theologically correct teaching, we must also have theologically correct worship lyrics.

There is a place for response-type songs, but these shouldn't be the only kinds of songs we sing. Because we worship God (period), the pinnacle of our worship times shouldn't be proclaiming what we'll do for God, but who God is. We must regularly get our students to this point. But this takes intention.

We worship God, not the worship experience.

It's easy to forget we worship God (period) when we come together for our youth group worship times. When someone says, "I liked worship tonight," what is he likely saying? "I liked the song choice" or "I think the drummer is really cute" or "The guitar sounded sweet" or "I like how it made me feel." Worship isn't for our entertainment. Worship is about God.

Students tend to approach worship by thinking, "What's in it for me?" or "What can I get out of it?" I fear we're raising a generation of students who believe it's all about them and how they respond to God rather than understanding that worship is about God. We don't worship *to get*, but we worship *to give* God our adoration. We worship God, not the worship experience.

I'm not saying we shouldn't enjoy worship. God does want us to delight in him. And God created our voices and love for music. Surely God wants us to find delight in our worship. The Psalmist writes, "Then will I go to the altar of God, to God, my joy and my delight. I will praise you with the harp, O God, my God" (Psalm 43:4). Worship in its purest sense is when God is our joy and delight—and that's when we find delight in the act of worship.

Matt Redman remembers a time when his church lost focus in regard to the purpose of worship. He recounts there was "too much attention on outward things and not enough focus on the heart of our offerings." When this happened, his senior pastor took away the sound system, band, and worship props for a season of time. In his search to help his people rediscover worship, the song "The Heart of Worship" emerged:[4]

When the music fades,

And all is stripped away,

And I simply come,

Longing just to bring

Something that's of worth

That will bless your heart...

I'm coming back to the heart of worship.

And it's all about You...

(Matt Redman, from *The Heart of Worship* ©1999 Kingsway's Thankyou Music)

At a recent winter retreat, our camp experienced a power surge, and we lost all electricity on Sunday morning. This meant no heat, no toilets (because the water pumps couldn't work), no kitchen appliances, no lights...and no amplified music for our final morning session. It had been an incredible weekend of ministry, and some speculated the loss of power was part of spiritual warfare. Was the Devil attacking? Or was God providing? Maybe God was reminding us that worship wasn't about amplifiers and video screens.

It's all about God. We worship God (period).

WE WORSHIP GOD FOR HIS GREATNESS AND GRACIOUSNESS.

We respond to God, not to a song or a worship leader or a music note. Worship doesn't originate with us. Worship originates with God. Worship begins with seeing God and then responding to who God is and what God has done.

If you had to summarize God in two words, which two words would you use? Not an easy task, huh? It seems impossible to summarize our infinite God with two words. However, if I had to, I would suggest these two words: *Great* and *gracious.*

Recently, while speaking to our students, I pulled a whiteboard onto the stage and asked them to call out attributes of God. Within 60 seconds, I had scribbled these attributes on the board: *loving, sovereign, majestic, holy, goodness, omniscience, omnipotent, omnipresent, forgiving, patient, just, righteous, marvelous, unchanging, compassionate, glorious, eternal, jealous, mighty, faithful, awesome, wonderful, Creator,* and *Almighty.* This is the God we worship!

After reflecting on this brainstormed list of attributes, we tried to place each into one of two categories: God is great and God is gracious. I'll bet you're hard pressed to find an attribute of God that doesn't fall into one of these two categories. Go ahead and try.

Louie Giglio states, "When God is not greatly praised, it's only because we don't think he's that great of a God. When our worship is small, it's because our concept of God is small. When we offer God little-bitty sacrifices, it's because we've somehow reduced him in our hearts to a little-bitty God."[5]

This theme of God being great and gracious is all throughout Psalm 145. In fact, God's greatness is the theme of verses 3 through 7, starting with, "Great is the LORD and most worthy of praise; his greatness no one can fathom" (v. 3). The theme of God's graciousness is in verses 8 through 13, starting with, "The LORD is gracious and compassionate, slow to anger and rich in love" (v. 8).

God is great, but aren't you glad God is gracious, too? God is gracious, but aren't you glad God is great? God is worthy of our worship because God is equally great and gracious.

Christians have placed more emphasis in recent years on knowing God—not just knowing *about* God. I'm all for this shift. However, we must make sure we aren't just experiencing a God we know nothing about. If we want our students to truly know God, we must grow our students' knowledge about God. Too many students have a kindergarten understanding of God—and this leads to shallow, elementary worship. Make note of this: The depth of our worship can only be as deep as our knowledge of God. We must expand our students' vision of God.

Teaching students about God doesn't have to be done in a 12-week series on God's attributes. We can teach our students a lot about God through selecting theologically accurate lyrics, themes for a worship set, the depth of our prayers, personal testimonies that personalize an attribute (God's faithfulness, goodness, forgiveness, etc.), and teaching about God's character as we teach the Word. We must constantly weave the truth of who God is into the tapestry of our ministry gatherings. We worship God not only in spirit, but in the truth of who God is. When students leave your ministry gathering *each* week, they should have a greater vision of God.

If we are truly gripped by the greatness and graciousness of God, we can't help but respond to him with our lips and our lives.

WE WORSHIP GOD WITH OUR LIPS AND THROUGH OUR LIVES.

God is jealous for our words *and* our actions. Hebrews 13:15-16 says, "Through Jesus, therefore, let us continually offer *to God a sacrifice of praise*—the fruit of *lips* that confess his name. And do not forget to *do good* and to share with others, for with such *sacrifices God is pleased*" (emphasis added). When the singing ends, we're not done worshiping. Worship involves our lips, but it must include our very lives.

Throughout Psalm 145, David expresses his worship with his lips. He writes, "I will exalt you...praise you...extol your...meditate on your...proclaim your..." But David also worshiped God with his life: "Every day I will praise you and extol your name for ever and ever" (v. 2). We worship God with the whole of our lives when we *live for God* every day and *love God* with our entire being.

We worship God through living for God.

First Samuel 15:22 says, "Does the LORD delight in burnt offerings and sacrifices as much as in obeying the voice of the LORD? To obey is better than sacrifice." God prefers our obedience over sacrificing a lamb as an act of worship. Hypocrisy occurs when we have gaps between our private lives and our public lives.

In rebuking the Pharisees, Jesus quoted from Isaiah, "These people honor me with their lips, but their hearts are far from me. They worship me in vain; their teachings are but rules taught by men" (Matthew 15:8-9). The Pharisees got an "A" for public performance but an "F" for authenticity. Worshiping God in truth involves following God, not just singing to God. Obedience is an act of worship.

Have you noticed that many of the New Testament verses are about a worshipful lifestyle rather than musical expression?

> "Offer your bodies as living sacrifices, holy and pleasing to God—this is your spiritual act of worship." (Romans 12:1)

> "So whether you eat or drink or whatever you do, do it all for the glory of God." (1 Corinthians 10:31)

> "And whatever you do, whether in word or deed, do it all in the name of the Lord Jesus, giving thanks to God the Father through him." (Colossians 3:17)

We worship God through our actions and interactions with people. When we do the right thing, God is worshiped—even if no one notices or cares. We need to help our students understand that God can be worshiped through the way they talk to their parents, treat siblings, love the lonely at school, or show genuine care for someone else in youth group. Students need to worship God in their schools, in their hang-out places, in their conversations with friends, on their sports teams, in their times at Starbucks, in their entertainment choices, in their spending habits, in their hidden thoughts, and in their joys.

And part of living for God involves serving others—"Do not forget to do good and share with others" (Hebrews 13:16). The main Greek word used for *worship* in the New Testament is *latreuo*, which actually means "to serve" (see Acts 7:42 and 24:14). Therefore, we should not limit the term "worship service" in our vocabulary to a corporate gathering. Instead *worship service* also describes how God is worshiped through our service to others.

We worship God by loving God.

When Jesus was asked about which was the greatest commandment, he replied without hesitation by quoting the Old Testament: "'Love the Lord your God with all your heart and with all your soul and with all your mind.' This is the first and greatest commandment" (Matthew 22:37-38, quoting Deuteronomy 6:5). Some scholars and pastors emphasize the distinctions between the three facets of the heart, soul, and mind. While there's some value to this, I believe Jesus' main emphasis was that we love God with the totality of our being.

"Put your heart in the game!" I remember when my high school soccer coach directed these words at me after being subbed from the field. In a similar way, we need to coach our students to put their hearts into worship. Our worship of God should not be half-hearted. Worship is more than giving lip service to words on a screen. We are to worship God with *all* our being, including with emotion. God is spirit, and we need to worship God with our spirits (see John 4:23). Worship should always involve our emotions—while avoiding emotionalism because we worship God (period), not the worship experience.

God is much more concerned with the attitude of worship than the activity of worship. God doesn't want our motions but longs for our emotions. God wants us to enter into worship in spirit and in truth. Worship is something to enter into with your entire heart, soul, strength, and mind.

David worshiped with the totality of his being. Look at the poker term for when a player moves all his chips to the middle of the table: "all in." David was "all in" with his worship. I long to see a generation of students who are "all in" and worship God's greatness and graciousness with their lips and through their lives.

Imagine If...

Imagine if we approached each ministry gathering as an opportunity to engage students with the living God. Imagine if we were truly dependent on and devoted to prayer. Imagine if prayer was central to our student ministries. Imagine if our students were gripped by the greatness and graciousness of God. Imagine if our students entered into worship to give to God instead of to get from God. Imagine if we expanded our practice of worship to include elements beyond singing and music. Imagine if our students embraced a lifestyle of worship through living for God and loving God.

Would our ministries be any different? Might we see God transforming lives?

If one descriptive statement could be made of Harvest's student ministry, I would want it to be: "God is there." Is that your desire, too?

moving forward > questions

Questions for personal reflection and team discussion:

1. What is worship?

2. What strikes you about the role of adoration—prayer and worship—for the early believers in the book of Acts?

3. How would you describe the difference between the form and function of worship?

4. How would you describe the prayer and worship temperature of your group? Hot? Cold? Lukewarm?

5. How can you teach some of the content in this chapter? What will you teach?

6. Would your ministry be any different if you were to renew your commitment to the priorities of prayer and worship? If so, in what ways?

7. What aspects of this chapter do you want to discuss with others on your leadership team?

1. Matt Redman, ed., *The Heart of Worship Files* (Ventura, CA: Regal, 2003), 122.

2. Michael Green, *Thirty Days That Changed the World* (Grand Rapids, MI: Eerdmanns, 1993/2002), 269.

3. Judith Viorst (New York: Aladdin, 1987).

4. Matt Redman, *Inside Out Worship* (Ventura, CA: Regal, 2005), 99.

5. Louie Giglio, *The Air I Breathe* (Colorado Springs, CO: Multnomah, 2006), 55.

"What's the first thing that comes to your mind when you think of worship?"

It doesn't matter if I ask this question of students or student ministry leaders, the response is always the same. Without any prompting, each person calls out in what sounds like a single voice: "singing." I'm not surprised. Are you?

Most student ministries are one-dimensional with respect to worship. We say, "Are you ready to worship? If so, please stand and sing..." The people who play instruments are part of the worship team. The collection of songs is the worship set. After singing some songs, the worship leader (the person with the guitar who's leading others in singing) says, "Wasn't worship great tonight?"

Music is a huge part of worship, but worship is more than music. Even the early church in Acts recognized this.

I'm deeply concerned that we're raising a generation of students who believe worship is only about standing, singing, clapping, and occasionally raising hands. Maybe we, as youth leaders, are part of the problem because we put so much emphasis on music—even to the point of *worshiping* worship music.

Since worship is more than singing, we must model other forms of adoration. We must expand our practice of worship. Since there are many ways to engage students with God, this chapter offers some creative adoration expressions. Perhaps you can adapt some of these ideas for your ministry. Or better yet, these ideas may inspire you to consider even more ways to engage students with the living God.

And don't get lost worrying about the size of your student ministry. You might think, "I only have a dozen students. My annual budget is $500. I don't have the people or the financial resources to do worship." That's not true. You might not be able to have a worship band, but you can worship. Regardless of the size of your group, you can engage students in worshiping God.

Worship Stations

The term "freedom of expression" is most often associated with First Amendment rights. But it can also apply to worship. The apostle Paul teaches in 1 Corinthians 11 about orderly worship, and we must not neglect these instructions. Worship should never be a chaotic free-for-all, but there are various ways to allow students to engage with God in sacred spaces.

A worship station can be incorporated into your regular worship time or by having a special evening dedicated to worship with many stations. Some student ministries dedicate the first Sunday night of the month as a worship night. Others do a special worship night if there is a fifth week in the month. We seek to incorporate a special worship night once a year in our middle school ministry and once a semester in our high school ministry.

I introduced some worship stations by giving students a guided tour. Before giving them 25 minutes to rotate among the stations, I briefly explained each station while I stood in front of it. Perhaps you can picture the stations and room setup through the following "tour."

Station 1: Wall of Psalms. I explained, "Perhaps one of the greatest worshipers to ever live on Planet Earth was David. The majority of the Psalms were written by David as he reflected on who God is

moving forward > by looking back

and what God has done. The Psalms are copies of David's inspired worship journal. This wall has dozens of posters with printed verses from various Psalms. You can worship God at this station by reading and pondering these verses."

Station 2: Letters to God. "As David worshiped God in the Psalms through journaling, you can worship God by writing letters to God using markers and this wall of paper. Some of you may choose to worship God by writing a letter starting 'Dear Heavenly Father' and ending by signing your name. Or you may simply want to write out attributes of who God is. This wall of paper is dedicated to worshiping God with written words."

Station 3: God is... "This wall of paper is for worshiping God through drawing. God has gifted many of you with amazing creativity. You can worship God with your God-given creativity by drawing images of who God is. Perhaps you'll want to draw a cross or something else that symbolizes God."

Station 4: Place of Prayer. "Some of you are coming tonight with burdens you need to talk to God about, or you want to praise God through prayer. This quiet space on these area rugs and around the candles is for you to kneel in submission to God."

Station 5: Area for Intercession. "Intercession means 'to go on behalf of someone else.' Perhaps you're here tonight because you want someone to pray for you. I invite you to come and share a prayer request with one of our mentors or students at this station and allow someone else to lift you and your needs up to God in prayer."

Station 6: Cross. "The cross is so much more than a piece of gold jewelry. The cross represents love and redemption. Our salvation is a free gift from God. But please don't confuse free with cheap. Our salvation didn't come without a cost to God. Our salvation came at a tremendous price. Romans 5:8 says, 'But God demonstrated His love for us in this: while we were still sinners, Christ died for us.' Some of you may want to come, linger at the foot of the cross, and reflect on the tremendous price of your redemption. Some of you may be struggling with an area of sin in your life that you need to surrender to Christ. If so, I encourage you to write your sins out as an act of repentance while clinging to the truth of 1 John 1:9: 'If we confess our sins, he is faithful and just and will forgive us our sins and purify us from all unrighteousness.' There are some 3 x 5 cards, pens, nails, and hammers around the cross."

Station 7: Communion. "'The Lord Jesus, on the night he was betrayed, took bread, and when he had given thanks, he broke it and said, 'This is my body, which is for you; do this in remembrance of me.' In the same way, after supper he took the cup, saying, 'This cup is the new covenant in my blood; do this, whenever you drink it, in remembrance of me' (1 Corinthians 11:23-25). If you've placed your faith in Jesus Christ as your Lord and Savior, I invite you to come to this table in remembrance of Christ. First Corinthians 11 warns us of partaking of Communion in an unworthy manner. Therefore, before coming to this table, perhaps you need to spend some time in personal confession at the cross." (I later returned to this station and held a loaf of bread and a goblet of juice for students to dip their bread into.)

Station 8: Offering. "A final way you can worship God tonight is by cheerfully giving your money to God. God loves cheerful givers. Giving our money to God is an act of obedience and an act of worship. One hundred percent of the money collected tonight will be given to our inner-city partnership ministry."

I concluded the tour with these words: "In a moment you'll have an opportunity to experience God and express your worship through these various stations. Perhaps you'll rotate through all these stations, or you may want to linger at only one or two stations. You have 25 minutes to interact with and talk to God. This isn't a time to talk to others. Please be respectful of those who truly want to worship God. As the guitar starts playing, you may stand, move around the room, and express your worship to God."

Students have been so incredibly responsive each time we have had worship stations. Many ask, "When can we do this again?" To keep these times special and to create a healthy anticipation, we've chosen to not dedicate more than one night each calendar year or semester to worship stations.

Other ways abound to facilitate worship stations beyond these examples. Some other ideas include:

> *Bibles with highlights:* This station would include a group of tables with Bibles on them. Each Bible has sticky note tabs. These tabs indicate pages with preselected, highlighted passages to guide the students to certain verses to read—encouraging them to meditate on God's Word. The verses can emphasize one central theme or a variety of biblical truths.

> *Prayer exchange:* Place 3 x 5 cards and pens around a basket. Students are encouraged to write a prayer request on a card (with or without their name on the card). As each student places her prayer request in the basket, she should take a card out, pause, and intercede for someone else. The card can be taken home as a reminder to continue to pray for the request.

> *Newspaper clippings:* Cut out news articles and pictures from current magazines and newspapers and glue them to pieces of posterboard. Students are encouraged to linger and pray for needs within the city, the country, and around the world. This is a wonderful way to keep our students aware of the needs around the globe. And it can train them to read the news not just for information, but for prayer topics.

> *Global prayer:* Using a global wall map and thumbtacks, highlight areas around the world where missionaries are serving God. Missionaries can be identified by their pictures and some prayer requests. If you have missionary prayer cards, encourage students to take one to place in their Bibles for future reference. Or use the global wall map to highlight global prayer needs in areas dealing with war, natural disaster, national tragedy, etc. Or highlight a few stories of people being persecuted for their Christian faith (see www.persecution.com).

> *Shredding sin:* Students are encouraged to write on pieces of paper areas of sin with which they've been struggling. Then have them write "1 John 1:9" or "Psalm 103:12" in big letters across their paper. After this act of repentance, students run their sheets through a paper shredder. Or if you don't have a paper shredder, have students seal their papers in envelopes and place the envelopes in the center of the stage or on the altar.

> *Worship art:* This station encourages students to use their creative abilities, beyond merely drawing, to worship God. The station can contain one art form or many art forms, including clay, paint, drawing instruments, or an assortment of craft supplies. In addition to tables, you may want to set up some easels and an area for students to display their worship art.

As you plan worship stations, keep a few things in mind. First, choose an appropriate number of stations for the size of your group and meeting area. If you have too many stations, students may feel overwhelmed or rushed or scattered. If you have too few stations, the congestion may become a distraction, or students might not spend as much time in this worship experience as you had desired.

Second, consider the placement of the stations. Should some stations be naturally placed near each other? Consider the flow around your area. Can students freely move around the area from one station to any other station? Seek to take advantage of your whole space.

Last, create a worshipful ambience. The physical atmosphere is important. Dim your house lights, utilize candles, play music softly in the background (or encourage silence), and use accent lighting to emphasize stations as ways to create a worshipful ambience.

Worshiping God in Silence

The following screen shot shows some of the text we used at Harvest to help our students worship God in silence while reflecting on God's Word. From a laptop on stage, I typed the text live during the program. We projected the computer's desktop directly on the screen through the video projector. Rather than listening to my spoken words, students read the words as they were typed word by word. It was as if students were reading an instant message. It was a powerful way to give students a time of silence while guiding them in a meaningful way. The worship band followed this time with some worship music.

moving forward > by looking back

> Noise is all around us. Sometimes it's hard to get away from noise...even in church. So tonight we want to give you a gift of a few minutes in silence.

> Some people routinely pray, "God, please be with me as I take this test...or go on this trip...or try out for this team..." Did you ever stop to think that we don't need to ask God to be present? God is omnipresent. God is everywhere...whether we ask God to be or not. What we should pray is, "God, please help me to sense your presence as I take this test..."

> Here's something to pray in silence: "God, please help me to sense your presence here tonight."

> Can you sense God's presence here? God is saying to you, "Here I am!"

> God is here.

While live typing can feel authentic because it's happening in the moment, it can be distracting because of typos. Another form to serve this same function would be pretyped words in a presentation, perhaps using PowerPoint, allowing the words to scroll across the screen.

A Dozen (a)doration Ideas for Small(er) Groups

Don't feel defeated if you don't have instruments or technology. Perhaps you meet in a home and don't have a stage. That's okay. You can still engage students with God. Here are a dozen ideas for smaller groups— or even for larger groups but while meeting in small groups. Even if you have a larger group, these ideas may keep your worship times fresh. Even if you have musical resources, it's healthy to model other forms to help students understand worship is more than music. Also, as you consider some of the following ideas, think about letting some of your leadership students facilitate some of these adoration exercises:

1. *God is...God has...* Hang two pieces of posterboard on the wall in your group setting. In the middle of the first posterboard write, "God is..." in large letters. In the middle of the second poster- board write, "God has..." Then allow students to get up and write statements of praise for who God is and what he's done. If you're able to leave the posters up for a few weeks, do so. Keep encour- aging students to add to them periodically. This can also be done in the context of a large-group worship time. Have the poster- boards on the side walls and encourage students to write while the group is singing.

2. *Alphabet adoration.* Praise God in prayer by beginning with the letter "A" and encouraging students to respond with any adjective they can think of to describe God (e.g., almighty, awesome, amazing, etc.). Then proceed to "B" and on through the alphabet. Since it can take some time to go all the way through the alphabet while keeping the students focused, I suggest limiting the time to five minutes and stopping at "F." Then pick up the list at "G" the following week or even a month later. Also, pause periodically to discuss some of the attributes being shared. Make sure students connect these attributes to who God is and what that means in our lives and in our relationship with him.

3. *Read and reflect on worship lyrics.* Encourage students to bring to the group lyrics of a meaningful worship song. Share the personal significance of the song, then have the student read the lyrics as a prayer to God. It's easy to sing lyrics without pondering the words. Taking the time to read a song's lyrics often leads to better comprehension and deeper meaning for students.

4. *Attributes of God.* Choose one attribute of God to reflect on and discuss together. Encourage students to brainstorm a definition, but have a definition ready to clarify.

Almighty	True	Forgiving
Compassionate	Holy	Merciful
Gracious	Good	Wise
Majestic	Infinite	Omnipotent
Sovereign	Omnipresent	
Omniscient	Perfect	
Transcendent	Patient	

Encourage students to look up specific verses or Bible stories which discuss the chosen attribute of God. If students don't know where to look, prompt them by suggesting certain passages. Then allow students to share how they've experienced this attribute recently. Avoid the temptation to discuss multiple attributes. Rather use your time to focus on one characteristic of God.

moving forward > by looking back

5. *Pray through a psalm.* Pick a psalm rich with God's attributes and use it to introduce your students to praying through Bible verses. Encourage them to personalize the Scripture back to God in a prayer. See chapter 1.3 for more instruction.

6. *Sticky Note Praise*—hand out several large sticky note sheets to each student and encourage them to write an attribute of God, a short letter, or a Scripture on their sheets. Then have the students stick them on the walls around the room.

7. *Journal prayers.* Give each student a piece of paper and a pen to write a letter to God. Have students start the letter with "Dear Father," and end the letter with "Love, your son (or daughter)." You can play a worship CD while students are writing if that helps create a more worshipful environment. When done, allow willing students to read their letters as prayers for the group. Close by discussing the benefit of writing out prayers. Here's another idea: Instead of the traditional morning devotional time on a retreat, give students paper to journal prayers to God.

8. *Popcorn praise.* Spend some time in one-thought sentence prayers: "God, I praise you because _____." Let students know they can "pop" in and pray several times if they wish. This can also be done in a large-group setting.

9. *Crayon worship.* Using a set of multicolored crayons or markers, encourage students to draw pictures or symbols that express who God is or what God means to them. Then allow students to share about the personal significance behind what they drew.

10. *"Why do you worship?"* Select a question related to worship to discuss for five to 10 minutes as a group. After discussing, pray together as a group. Pick another question on another night. Some examples—

    > Why do you worship?

    > What things can hinder your ability to worship God?

    > What attribute of God has been most meaningful to you recently?

    > Psalm 46:10 says, "Be still, and know that I am God." Is it easy or hard for you to be still before God? Explain.

> What was the most meaningful worship time you ever had? Why?

> How can you develop as one who worships God throughout the day?

> Read Colossians 3:23. How can you worship God this week by doing things "for the Lord"?

11. *Collect an offering.* Giving our money to God is an act of worship. Your group can adopt a service project, sponsor a child through Compassion International, or support a missionary family. Providing students with an opportunity to give their money can help develop this pattern of worship. This can also give your students a ministry focus beyond your group.

12. *Communion.* Read the apostle Paul's instructions for partaking of Communion in 1 Corinthians 11:23-28. Discuss why Christ-followers should participate in Communion, what the bread and cup symbolize, and the words of caution in verses 27-28. Encourage students to use a time of silence for personal reflection on the condition of their lives and on the sacrifice of Christ on their behalf before they partake.

    Option 1: Pass a loaf of bread around the room and encourage students to break off a piece of bread. Follow by passing a goblet of grape juice and encourage students to dip their bread in the juice and then eat the bread.

    Option 2: Have bread (or broken crackers) and juice in the front or back of the room. Encourage students to stand and walk to the elements to partake in communion as they are ready. You may choose to sing during this time or have silent reflection.

Expository Worship

Worship and the Word go together like macaroni and cheese. The apostle Paul writes, "Let the word of Christ dwell in you richly as you teach and admonish one another with all wisdom, *and* as you sing psalms, hymns and spiritual songs with gratitude in your hearts to God" (Colossians 3:16, emphasis added). Word and worship. Rather than singing for 30 minutes and teaching for 30 minutes, why not weave God's Word *and* worship together? Expository worship is when a passage of Scripture shapes a combined time of worship and teaching. The following example uses Isaiah 6. But you can use other passages from the Psalms, the Epistles, or Revelation to guide a time of expository worship. During the planning process, select a passage, divide it into an outline, and plan songs to correspond to themes of the textual outline. During the worship time, read the text and make comments about the passage. Then respond to God's revealed Word through singing.

10 minutes: Message, part 1—God's holiness

"I saw the Lord seated on a throne, high and exalted, and the train of his robe filled the temple. Above him were seraphs...and they were calling to one another, 'Holy, holy, holy is the LORD Almighty; the whole earth is full of his glory'" (Isaiah 6:1-3).

10 minutes: Worship—songs of God's holiness

> _____

> _____

> _____

10 minutes: Message, part 2—our sin and need for repentance

"'Woe to me!' I cried. 'I am ruined! For I am a man of unclean lips, and I live among a people of unclean lips, and my eyes have seen the King, the LORD Almighty.' Then one of the seraphs flew to me with a live coal in his hand...with it he touched my mouth and said, 'See, this has touched your lips; your guilt is taken away and your sin atoned for'" (Isaiah 6:5-7).

10 minutes: Worship—songs and prayers of repentance

> _____

> _____

> _____

10 minutes: Message, part 3—yielding our lives to God

"Then I heard the voice of the Lord saying, 'Whom shall I send? And who will go for us?' And I said, 'Here am I. Send me!'" (Isaiah 6:8).

10 minutes: Worship—songs of surrender

> _____

> _____

> _____

End with wrap-up and prayer.

Psalms of Ascent

Psalms 120 through 134 are commonly referred to as the "Psalms of Ascent." I have a playlist on my iPod with certain songs for when I'm jogging. These are my songs for the road. In a similar way, the Psalms of Ascent were songs for the road. The Jewish people sang them, possibly in sequential order, as they journeyed to Jerusalem for three annual worship festivals—the Feast of Passover in the spring, the Feast of Pentecost in early summer, and the Feast of Tabernacles in the fall. Since Jerusalem had the highest elevation of any city in Palestine, the Jews were *ascending* as they journeyed. Further, this collection of psalms helped their spirits ascend in worship as they prepared to meet with God.

Before entering into a night of worship, we recently encouraged students to prepare their hearts by guiding them through some of the Psalms of Ascent. Luke, our worship leader, shared:

> Worship now is very easy for us to engage in. We walk into a room at a preordained time, and—*boom*—we're worshiping. We talk about how the blood of Christ allows us to enter freely into the presence of God, but sometimes don't you feel kind of rushed into worship and unable to really engage with what's happening because of a sort of sensory overload? In the Old Testament it was difficult to

moving forward > by looking back

worship God. Worship only occurred at the temple in Jerusalem (a journey of several hundred miles for some of the people of Israel) and only at certain times of the year. All the worship-leading was done by priests who had to be born into a certain tribe and in a particular birth order. The high priest was allowed only once a year to approach the literal place where God lived, and when he did, he wore robes with bells embroidered into them so others could know he was still up and walking around in the Holy of Holies. When the Israelites were on the move, God and some of the nation's precious possessions were carried in a big box called the Ark of the Covenant—that was the thing Harrison Ford was trying to find, remember? When the people of God came to Jerusalem to worship, they would sing Psalms of Ascent on their journey as a way of preparation. Tonight before we worship in song, we're going to do some things to prepare ourselves. We're going to purify ourselves before we come to meet the living God.

We dismissed the students to walk silently through some candlelit hallways. During their *"ascent to worship,"* students paused momentarily to read and reflect on a series of posters:

> Hallway 1—ascent
Poster 1:

Meditate on the following Psalms of Ascent. Allow them to lift your heart toward the Savior.

(Assorted posters showed Psalms 120 through 134.)

> Hallway 2—remembrance
Poster 2:

This fountain was made for us to remember the great things God has done in our church. (We have an actual fountain in our lobby with stones of remembrance that signify God's work in our church. Consider ways to incorporate the unique features of your church when planning a worship journey in your context.)

Poster 3:

True worship comes from a heart of gratitude to God for showering us with undeserved favor. Spend some time thanking God for the things he's done in your life. Move when you're ready.

> Hallway 3—confession

Poster 4:

As our hearts are prepared for authentic worship, we quickly realize how far we are from who God's law requires us to be.

Poster 5:

Here at the foot of the cross true repentance is found. Take a card, write down the sins you're choosing now to renounce, and move toward the Savior.

Poster 6:

Real repentance doesn't come quickly. Take the time you need to allow your sorrow to realize the depths of God's grace.

> Hallway 4—preparation

Poster 7:

Holy ground is anywhere God dwells. Remove your shoes and leave them outside the room. This is holy ground.

Poster 8:

Psalm 24:3-4

Who may ascend the hill of the LORD?

Who may stand in his holy place?

He who has clean hands and a pure heart.

moving forward > by looking back

Poster 9:

Allow one of the leaders to wash your hands, then enter. It's time to worship God.

The walk concluded with students entering our worship center to engage with God through singing and Communion.

A Sample Program Outline for a Worship Night

Dedicating an entire ministry night to worship may prove to be your most meaningful night all school year. I'm always amazed (but no longer surprised) at how students eagerly desire to engage in worship through various forms beyond just singing—even rambunctious middle school students! There's certainly a place for dodgeball, gross games, and goofy skits in middle school ministry. But worship also needs its place. The following outline is from a recent Harvest Students middle school program. We called the evening "One" as we gathered on one campus to lift up one voice to one God.

4 p.m. Night begins.

> Gather students in a hallway outside the worship center. Worship center lights off except for the screen and stage lights.

> Students must take off their shoes (standing on holy ground, entering holy area). Mentors take students to designated areas in the church (their home-group breakout areas) to leave their shoes there.

> Return to the entrance of the worship center.

4:10 p.m. Students enter.

4:12 p.m. Welcome and explanation 1—"The One who saves"

> Welcome students and get them excited about being there and explain the focus of the night.

> Explain the importance of why we are here and how Christ made it possible—transition into students writing out the date or the

year of their salvation on slips of paper. Then have each student put the paper in a balloon and blow the balloon up to toss around during the first song in the celebration. (Have students stand now.)

4:19 p.m. Worship set 1
> Song 1: "Your Everlasting Love" (with movement and motions)
> Transition: Have students toss balloons to the side.
> Song 2: "Waves of Mercy"

4:27 p.m. Explanation 2—"The One we worship"
> Vertical—us to God. Explain how our understanding of God and who God is impacts our worship.
> Talk about what it means to worship God with awe, fear, and adoration.
> Scripture: Revelation, Job

4:31 p.m. Worship set 2
> Song 3: "Unchanging"
> Song 4: "Holy Is the Lord"
> Scripture: Isaiah 6 (have mentor read)
> Song 5: "Wholly Yours" (This recommunicates to worship not just in awe, but with faces in the dirt.) (Have the students sit and the band leave.)

4:46 p.m. Explanation 3—"The One who forgives"
> Start with someone carrying in the cross (as a symbol and reminder) from the back of the worship center up to the stage while explaining—
  - First: What the cross did (dealt with our sin issue)
  - Second: Sin is still an issue. (We need to draw close to God and be aware of our sin.)
  - Third: Finding forgiveness (Christ longs to forgive us; we must come before him to continue in worship of a holy God.)
> Explain the confession stations.

moving forward > by looking back

4:50 p.m. Confession stations

> Mentors stationed on both sides of the worship center pass out paper and pencils for students to write down what has been hindering them in their relationship with Christ.

(Have band return.)

> Band plays the first song of the next set over them (instrumental). (Have students sit or kneel for worship.)

4:55 p.m. Worship set 3

> Song 6: "Wonderful Cross"

> Song 7: "Light of the World"

5:03 p.m. Explanation 4—"The One we live for"

> Tie in the whole night up till now and then look forward to the "Now what?" question.

> Reference Romans 6:12-14 and what it's all about.

> Recognize this isn't just a once-a-year, monthly, or even weekly thing but every day.

> DVD: We videotaped mentors sharing ways they worship God daily to help expand students' understanding of worship.

[Have students stand.]

> Students declare a statement together. We had our students stand and declare: "You are the One. You are the One we live for. You are the One."

5:07 p.m. Worship set 4

> Song 8: "Marvelous Light" (This song starts with a verse from the Old Testament about what God truly desires in worship.)

> Song 9: "One Way"

> Transition: Start the song by saying, "Before we break into our home [or small] groups, let's use this as a declaration of the sacrifice we want to make to God. We're going to worship God with our lives!" (Be excited!)

> Song 10: "Take It All"

5:15 p.m. Small group breakout (Students gather in groups to reflect on the night and pray together.)

5:45 p.m. Hang out. Games and food available

6:00 p.m. Go home.

Since there's more to worship than students standing and singing five songs, how can you expand the practice of adoration in your ministry?

As you consider various adoration forms, let me offer a few words of caution:

> Remember—we worship God (period). Make sure students are not worshiping the creative expression. The expression must always be a means to worship God.

> The success of a creative worship expression in engaging students with God is usually directly connected to how the expression is introduced. Carefully consider the words you use to cast the vision for worshiping God beyond what students are accustomed to.

> High creativity doesn't always equal high impact. Sometimes simplicity is more profound than overdoing it in the creativity category.

The goal of this chapter isn't to give you an exhaustive list of creative adoration ideas. Rather, I hope you're now thinking about ways to worship beyond singing. My prayer is that your practice of worship will expand to include many more ways to engage your students with God beyond the ideas in this chapter.

moving forward > questions

Questions for personal reflection and team discussion:

1. What are some of the challenges you face in engaging students with God through worship?

2. Why must we model other expressions of worship beyond singing?

3. How can you avoid worshiping the creative expression rather than worshiping God?

4. How can your small groups grow as worshiping communities?

5. In what ways do you see worship and the Word belonging together as macaroni and cheese do?

6. What are some specific ways you can expand the practice of worship in your group?

7. What aspects of this chapter do you want to discuss with others on your leadership team?

I have grown in my understanding of worship since becoming a youth pastor.

I started in student ministry in the early '90s. I thought our youth group was pretty sweet when we sang karaoke style from the Amy Grant cassette *Songs from the Loft*. The words appeared on a tripod screen from a handwritten transparency on the overhead projector. And we didn't *just* sing. Our group knew all kinds of crazy arm and body motions choreographed to the song "Where Do I Go?"

I remember the year we graduated from cassette tracks to "live" worship with a college guy leading singing from a Yamaha DX-7 keyboard. Students affectionately referred to our volunteer worship leader as "the butcher" because of the way he played the keyboard. It was rough, but at least we had cool synthesizer sounds. The keys brought a change to our music style. Silly songs were out, and Maranatha! praise band songs were in.

We also graduated from the overhead projector to a slide projector for the song lyrics. Although this gave us a more professional look, we had one issue or another every night. Often the slides would jam, or they would appear backward—or the projector would just go berserk and shuffle through the slides without any warning.

After a couple of years of synth-led singing, we replaced the DX-7 with an acoustic guitar. The next year we added a full band with acoustic, electric, and bass guitars and drums. The band rocked. We inherited a soundboard following an upgrade in the sanctuary, and we didn't know what to do with all the channels. We hung a rack of lights with colored gels. This was the era when "The Happy Song" by Delirious? was popular, Sonic Flood was hot, and the Passion movement was emerging. Microsoft released PowerPoint, and we invested in a computer and a video projector.

It wasn't long before we had *the* youth group program in the area. Our student band began to travel to other youth groups and even led worship in the morning sessions at a national conference in Chicago. It felt as if we'd arrived. We had a great band, a great sound and lighting system, and a great reputation.

But things weren't really great. To be honest, our music was more concert than worship. It took me a few more years to understand that truly worshiping is more than having a rock band.

I'm continuing to grow in my understanding of the depths of worship—including what students can offer and knowing we need to allow them opportunities to shape our worship times.

Rather than being a ministry *to* students or *with* students or *for* students, Harvest Students strives to be a ministry *of* students. We believe God loves young people. Furthermore, God loves to use young people to do incredible things. All we have to do is thumb through the Bible to observe this truth:

> Josiah was eight years old when he became king of Israel. By the time he was a teenager, he'd taken an irreligious nation and turned it around to following God.

> When Samuel was sent to Jesse's home to anoint the next king of Israel, Jesse lined up his oldest and strongest and wisest and best-looking sons. He paraded them before Samuel as the bachelors on *The Bachelorette* TV show are paraded before the bach-

elorette. But Samuel wasn't impressed. He asked, "Isn't there someone else?" Jesse replied sheepishly, "Well, yeah. There's the shepherd boy David out in the fields."

> God used young Queen Esther to save the Hebrew people.

> When God called Jeremiah to become a prophet, he was probably in his late teens or early 20s.

> God used Daniel and his three teenage friends in captivity in Babylon.

> When God came to Planet Earth, he did so through Mary, a teenager.

> When Jesus realized he needed to create a movement that would far outlast his physical presence on earth, he gathered around him a dozen knuckleheads. They were young guys—probably in their late teens or early 20s. (I like to think of Jesus as being the world's first youth pastor.)

> Timothy was entrusted with the leadership of an entire church at a young age. Paul charged Timothy with these words: "Don't let anyone look down on you because you are young, but set an example for believers in speech, in life, in love, in faith and in purity" (1 Timothy 4:12). In verses 13 and 14, Paul encouraged Timothy to not neglect his gift but to give himself to the teaching of the Word.

God loves young people, *and* God loves to use young people to do incredible things. How does all this relate to worship? Stick with me.

My goal in my first decade of student ministry was to get students to participate in worship. I wasn't content with students just attending youth group. I wasn't content with students standing as spectators in the bleachers. I wasn't content with students just going through the motions. No. My goal was to move students beyond observing worship to participating in worship. But this is no longer my goal.

As I said, I've grown in my understanding of the youth leader's role in worship. I've also grown in my conviction that God longs to use students in ministry. Part of being a ministry *of* students is to move students from participating in worship to contributing to worship.

More than getting students to follow the prompting of the worship leader by standing, clapping, and singing, we want our students to contribute to the worship experience. We want our students to enter into worship by having opportunities to guide the worship gathering. When planning regular student programs, we intentionally plan elements to allow our students to *contribute* as worshipers. I hope this chapter will help you rethink the role of students in worship by offering ways to move students beyond being spectators and participants in worship to being contributors to your worship times.

Students Contribute to Worship

CONTRIBUTE THROUGH PUBLIC READING OF SCRIPTURE

Immediately after charging Timothy not to let anyone look down on him for his youthfulness, Paul continued with these words: "Devote yourself to the public reading of Scripture" (1 Timothy 4:13). A few years ago I pondered the implications of these words: What does it mean to be devoted to the public reading of Scripture in student ministry today? As a result we periodically invite students to come to an open mic to publicly read God's Word. I preface the time by telling the students this isn't a time for them to introduce themselves nor share personal comments about why the Scriptures are meaningful to them. Instead we want God alone to speak through the public reading of the Bible.

At first I was nervous. How would students respond? What if no one came forward? What if they didn't heed my instructions? Despite some uncertainty, I tried it. And it was amazing. Students searched their Bibles and slowly formed two lines on the sides of the room. Now when we do this, we usually have to cut off the line of students due to time. It's powerful to hear God's Word read by students. And it's powerful to have students guide the worship gathering in this significant way. These times have become some of my favorite moments in youth ministry.

In some faith traditions the following words are audibly repeated after Scripture is read: "This is the Word of the Lord. Thanks be to

God." This can be a way for all students to respond after each reading or at the end when all the readings are complete.

CONTRIBUTE THROUGH AN ART FORM

Some students are gifted artists. Does your ministry allow these students to contribute their talents as offerings of worship? Encourage a student to bring in a work of art as an expression of worship and interview her about the piece. Or scan students' paintings or sketches and use them as PowerPoint backgrounds. Or dedicate a wall for students to hang pieces of art for a worship gallery on a predetermined night. The gallery could have a theme, for example compassion, the passion of Jesus, God's love, the creativity of God.

Or create a mosaic together as a ministry using broken tiles and ceramic adhesive. Construct a four-foot square of plywood with a one-inch frame border. Then outline a master mosaic on the surface of the plywood using a permanent marker. Then allow students to participate by choosing pieces of broken tile and gluing them to the plywood.

CONTRIBUTE BY SUGGESTING SONGS

If you have an experienced worship band, you can put the titles of 20 songs on the screen and allow students to vote on which six songs they want to sing on a given night. During the announcement time the band and tech team can scramble to put the selected songs in an orderly worship set. Our students love it when we do this about once a year. By allowing students to choose the songs, we allow students to shape and guide the worship.

CONTRIBUTE THROUGH AN IMPROMPTU DRUM SECTION

Invite students to volunteer to bang on an assortment of objects in an impromptu drum section. Some objects to consider using include a 15-gallon plastic drum, a five-gallon bucket, some plastic paint pails, a cowbell, and lots of wooden spoons. If you're looking for a fun way to get students contributing, try this one. Perhaps you'll only want to use your extra drummers for the first couple of songs.

moving forward > by looking back

CONTRIBUTE THROUGH SUPPLEMENTS TO YOUR WORSHIP BAND

Do you have any students who play on the drumlines at their schools? If so, invite one or two students to bring their drumline tom drums on a certain week to play with the regular band by adding a new drum sound to worship. Or perhaps you have students who play other instruments in their schools' bands or orchestras. Why not include additional instruments periodically? Not only can having the fresh sound of a saxophone, violin, or trumpet aid in the worship, but it also gives more students a new opportunity to be a part of the worship team.

CONTRIBUTE THROUGH SIGN LANGUAGE OR CHOREOGRAPHY

Do you have a student who knows sign language? Signing can be beautiful and add a visual dimension to worship. Or pick a couple of students who could choreograph a worship song without being a distraction.

CONTRIBUTE THROUGH AN IMPROMPTU STUDENT CHOIR

Allow students to contribute vocally by setting up some choir risers on your stage and invite students to come and join your worship team for the evening. Having extra voices fills the room and provides more energy to your worship gathering. For special worship nights, invite some students to come a few hours early to form a choir and rehearse with the band.

CONTRIBUTE THROUGH TESTIMONY TIMES

These times can be scheduled with a student coming prepared to share a testimony related to the theme of the night. Or you can have an open mic for students to share spontaneously what God's doing in their lives. This has become a routine element in our high school ministry. It's amazing how students encourage and inspire one another to live for Christ.

CONTRIBUTE BY READING ASSIGNED SCRIPTURE

As students are walking in, hand out 3 x 5 cards with verses printed on them. Students read their verses aloud at prompted times. Or students can read a passage of Scripture from the sound booth in the back of the room as a planned transition during the worship set.

CONTRIBUTE THROUGH PRAYER

Rather than having an adult open or close in prayer, allow a student to volunteer spontaneously to pray. If you have a large group, take a mic to the student in his seat. Or schedule a student in advance to pray during the worship gathering. Or have students huddle into groups of three for prayer throughout the room. Or encourage students to pray aloud and all at one time.

CONTRIBUTE THROUGH SPECIAL MUSIC

Your group may have students with musical talents who aren't on your worship team. You can periodically schedule a time of special music for students to contribute to the worship time with instruments not typically used in worship band. This is especially meaningful to students who are affirmed in the school band or by a piano teacher but rarely feel their talents are valued in the church nor worthy of offering to God as worship.

Austin was a shy freshman boy. Hardly anyone knew this kid. I learned from his mom he was an accomplished pianist. Austin was embarrassed when I called and invited him to play for our worship gathering. Yet he reluctantly accepted my invitation. Before playing his piano solo, he shared about the song's personal meaning in his life. His words were so genuine. Then he began to play the song masterfully. I was so proud of him. God was glorified by his humble offering of talent as worship. And it impacted our group in an unexpected way. As Austin returned to his seat, he received a standing ovation. He didn't play for the applause of people, but this worship offering obviously had a deep connection with our students. We soon discovered Austin wasn't as shy as he seemed. He went on to become an active and respected student leader in our ministry.

CONTRIBUTE AS WORSHIP GUIDES

Choose a couple of students to guide other students in your worship gathering. These students don't need to be musical. In fact, it's best if they aren't routinely up front. These students (rather than other adults) can be in front to share a dramatic reading, guide students in prayer groups throughout the room, or provide verbal transitions. Perhaps you'll want to write out a script for what they should say and rehearse with them a few times.

CONTRIBUTE BY SERVING ON THE PLANNING TEAM

Hopefully, you have some faithful and godly students helping you plan your worship gatherings. Your leadership students know what connects with students and what doesn't. As I've grown as a listener, I've learned students do give helpful feedback. Because I value their perspective, I'm okay if our student planning team vetoes some of my ideas. Many students have great ideas for worship elements if we take the time to listen. And if you want to get lots of different students involved, dedicate one gathering a year for each grade to plan using representatives from each class.

CONTRIBUTE BY SERVING BEHIND THE SCENES

Students can contribute as worship leaders even if they aren't recognized by most as worship leaders. Use students to help set up and decorate your space for worship. Recruit students to serve on your audio team. Or have students format and run the video screen. Allow students to shoot and edit video footage. Encourage a grass-roots student prayer team. These are all ways for students to gain ownership and feel as though they're offering talents to the worship experience— especially if you reinforce what they're doing *as* acts of worship.

CONTRIBUTE THROUGH BEING IN THE WORSHIP BAND

I used to think that only students in the worship team were the ones who could contribute to worship. Obviously, my perspective has changed. Hopefully, you're discovering other ways to engage with God, too.

Although I encourage you to expand your forms of worship, I *do* recommend worship through music. Music is a great way to engage students with God. Form a student worship band if you have the resources. Over the years student worship bands have been a source of both great joy and tremendous tension in my ministry. I've learned some tough lessons through my leadership failures with student bands. My experiences have taught me to avoid three common dangers.

Danger 1: Using only students

I've learned it's best to have a nonstudent leader of the band. A college student or adult usually has the maturity to best fulfill this important role. Because he carries some leadership authority, he's able to call the shots. A worship leader needs to be responsible to oversee the setup, rehearsal, and teardown—including opening and locking up your church building when necessary. Adults can better keep practices on task. Students usually respond better to an adult's musical critique than a peer's. And hopefully, your band leader is a spiritual authority in the students' lives in a way another student can't be. Your worship leader needs to be above reproach and model a consistent Christian lifestyle.

All of this being said, you want to make sure you have a mentor and not a drill sergeant. You need someone who will command attention and shepherd the students. You need someone to lead students musically and spiritually. A good worship leader not only plans worshipful sets but also trains the band members in the elements of a good worship set. As students are trained, you want a worship leader who is willing to share the planning process with students.

When conflict comes (and I intentionally chose "when," not "if"), you'll be glad you have an adult leader to help you navigate through the tensions and seek resolution. And if discipline needs to take place

moving forward > by looking back

because of a breach of the team covenant or due to divisive spirit, an adult leader is able to act decisively in a way a student can't.

And although I say band leader, maybe band coordinator is a better title. It's not as if the whole student band needs to revolve around one adult who monopolizes all the singing, talking, and leading. You want someone who's strong enough to lead but humble enough to share opportunities with students.

Danger 2: Using any student

To protect the integrity of your leadership and your ministry, you must protect your selection process for choosing students to be in the student band. Here are some qualities we look for in students:

> *Personal spiritual growth.* Each student must be a believer and display genuine fruit of a personal walk with Christ.

> *Heart for biblical worship.* Each student must desire to be a worshiper before being a worship leader.

> *Teachability.* Each student must be humble enough to receive instruction.

> *Respected by other students.* Each student must be respected by other students, because they won't follow someone they don't respect.

> *Commitment to the ministry.* Each student must be committed to the ministry before being committed to a band.

> *Musical ability.* This is important, but it's last on this list.

Give me students with these six qualities, and we'll have a great experience together. Give me students who are missing only one of the qualities each, and it'll be a miserable experience. All six are absolutely essential.

You should audition and interview each student. The audition doesn't have to feel like a talent show. Instead invite students to an evening jam session. Part of the night is spent learning a song together. Then substitute students in and out of the band. This approach allows you to observe musical talent, team dynamics, and the teachability factor in a more relaxed and casual environment for all.

If students pass the audition stage, then personally interview the students. Remember, you're not looking for *any* student. Be clear about expectations and responsibilities.

After these steps, contact students and place them when appropriate. If students don't make the band, encourage them to keep practicing and try out again the following year. Or consider recommending some students to serve on your children's worship team first to gain more experience while serving children. If they're unwilling to lead children in worship, given the opportunity, that should tell you right away their hearts may not be in exactly the right place regarding being part of a worship band.

Danger 3: Using too many students

In your zeal to involve students, avoid the temptation to involve too many students. I've been down the path of three to four worship bands, with each band only leading once a month. Bad idea. My intentions were right, but the result was disaster for all. Too many students can also mean including too many instrumentalists, vocalists, or backup members in one band.

The larger your team, the harder it truly is to develop students as musicians and to give musical feedback. And it's harder to be involved at a personal level in their lives.

I've discovered it's best to have one band with one adult worship leader, four student instrumentalists and/or vocalists, and a couple of student techs. In addition to this core group, some students are on an on-call list. As students are faithful and available on an on-call basis, we begin to transition them into more regular roles. This reduces students' workload while creating a healthy dynamic that no single person is "the whole show."

Moving Beyond Participation

I hope this chapter has expanded your thinking about the role of students with worship. When planning our weekly programs, we intentionally incorporate one creative worship element allowing students

moving forward > by looking back

to contribute to worship. Although we seek to avoid the trap of one-upping the week before, we never want to have a gathering that's the same week after week. As we seek to keep our programs fresh, students really feel as though they're missing something if they aren't there.

As you plan your next ministry gathering, why not pick an idea from this chapter to incorporate? If you have a monthly or semester schedule, perhaps you'll want to pencil in some ideas for future weeks so you can plan accordingly. Once you create a rhythm of creative worship elements, it will become more and more natural to you and your students.

Let's move our students beyond being spectators or even participants in worship to being contributors to worship.

moving forward > questions

Questions for personal reflection and team discussion:

1. How has this chapter expanded your understanding of the role of students and worship?

2. What do we teach our students when the only students who contribute to worship are the ones in the band?

3. Worship is about God. How can you keep this in mind while encouraging students to contribute?

4. How can you reinforce that the efforts of students who contribute behind the scenes qualify as worship?

5. This chapter talks about some dangers in regard to forming worship teams—what are some you can think of in your own ministry?

6. What are some ways beyond the author's suggestions that students can contribute to worship in your group or setting?

7. What aspects of this chapter do you want to discuss with others on your leadership team?

"When students finish high school and leave your youth ministry, what do they believe about prayer, and how do they practice prayer?"[1]

I was thumbing through some books in the youth ministry section at a local Christian bookstore when this question captured my attention. The question was actually buried in the middle of page 88, halfway through chapter 7. It wasn't the focus of the book, but it quickly became the focus of my thoughts. I've pondered this question now for several years. I've discussed it with our staff team. It has been the subject of conversations over coffee with other youth pastors. I now challenge you to consider this two-part question and its implications for your life and ministry:

> *When students graduate from your ministry, what do you want them to believe about prayer?*

> *When students graduate from your ministry, what do you hope will be their practices of prayer?*

Make a note of this: Your students' beliefs and practices of prayer will be formed through what is taught and modeled to them.

Prayer must be a priority in your student ministry and in your personal life. The transformations we long to see in students' lives can only happen as supernatural works of God. We are called to serve God with faithfulness, but only he can grant fruitfulness. Jesus reminds us, "Apart from me you can do nothing" (John 15:5). Sometimes it takes ministry leaders a while to realize *nothing* means nothing. Not *some* things. But *no thing*. What we long to see happen in students' lives is beyond our personal abilities. We need to acknowledge our insufficiencies for leading students. We need to cease striving to produce fruit based on our charisma, creativity, and clever strategies. Down with being self-sufficient and up with being God-dependent through prayer. Before we focus on what we want our students to believe about prayer and how we want them to practice prayer, let's first take a look in the mirror at ourselves and our prayer lives.

Taking Responsibility for Yourself

Before you will have a ministry that prays, you need to be a minister who prays. Before prayer will become a priority in your ministry, it must first be a priority in your life. And when prayer is truly a priority in the personal life of you as a minister, it will naturally become a priority in your ministry.

My life is busy. I'm a husband and dad of three young children. I have carpool duties for school, karate lessons, and Little League games. I have additional family time commitments and a weekly date night with my wife, Camille. I'm a homeowner with plenty of projects to do inside and out. I'm a pastor with lots of ministry demands. I have ministry commitments extending beyond my church responsibilities. I'm in a small group. I'm training for a marathon. My life is busy. But there's a difference between being busy and being rushed. Being rushed is failing to maintain a healthy, balanced life—and then blaming it on busyness.

Student ministry is busy. Always has been—always will be. It's how we handle that busyness that counts.

The first five verses of Galatians 6 have helped me gain a biblical perspective on the loads we each carry. Verse 2 begins with, "Carry each other's burdens." And verse 5 reads, "For each one should carry his own load." These statements seem paradoxical. But are they?

What are ways we need to carry one another's burdens? Certainly, we all have times of crisis in health, relationships, and finances. We have moments when the demands of life are far greater than normal. In instances like these, we need to rally around our brothers and sisters in Christ and carry each other's burdens. We need to pray for one another, listen to one another, and go the extra mile in loving and caring for one another.

What, then, are the loads each must carry? More than likely things such as job responsibilities, family time, physical exercise, time management, and your personal relationship with God. You can't blame the church if your marriage is suffering because you aren't giving attention to your spouse. You can't blame your senior pastor if you're not properly managing your time. And you certainly can't blame the busyness of ministry for your lack of a prayer life. These are all loads you must carry. We must avoid the temptation to blame others for any lack of discipline in our own lives.

Jesus was busy but not rushed. Jesus had a healthy life rhythm. The first chapter of Mark records a typically busy day in Jesus' life. In the morning he was teaching in the synagogue. His working lunch involved healing Simon's mother-in-law. At sunset the whole town gathered at the door, including all the sick and demon-possessed.

A night of student ministry—leading, teaching, counseling, discipling, and playing "knock out" on the basketball court—can be physically and emotionally exhausting. Imagine adding the pressure of casting out demons and healing people one after another. No doubt Jesus was exhausted when he finally fell asleep. The text doesn't specify how much sleep Jesus got, but it's clear Jesus didn't "sleep in" the next day. Instead, "Very early in the morning, while it was still dark, Jesus got up, left the house and went off to a solitary place, where he prayed" (Mark 1:35). In the midst of the busyness of ministry, Jesus maintained his priority of communing with his Father in prayer. Jesus was busy but not rushed.

After a major ministry event we often read in the Gospels that Jesus withdrew for a personal retreat (see Mark 6:31-32 and 45-46; Luke

moving forward > by looking back

4:42 and 5:16). Sadly, for many in ministry a private failure rather than a personal retreat sometimes comes after a public success. No doubt someone's name was on your mind as you read the previous sentence. Jesus' pattern of personal renewal needs to be a call for all in ministry leadership.

When was the last time you had a personal retreat for your spiritual renewal? Personal renewal retreats can involve getting away for an overnight to spend with God in prayer, in God's Word, and journaling. But it doesn't have to be an overnight. It can be a day set aside for these purposes. You can go to a camp, a pastoral retreat center, a park, or even another church in your area. If you're honestly seeking to spend time with God, don't take books to read about ministry, your calendar for planning, or your laptop for sending emails. Instead devote the time to God.

Although getting away for a day or more is extremely valuable, a personal retreat can also simply be retreating from the distractions of people, activity, and noise for 20 minutes each morning before you start your day. Let's not neglect our daily disciplines in favor of a seasonal extended retreat.

I have to admit I've been a Christian for 30 years, and I still find prayer to be an enormous challenge. It doesn't come naturally to me, never has, and for all I know, never will. Prayer is hard work for me. I've discovered it takes a lot of perseverance. As a runner I can understand this.

Several years ago I was really out of shape. I looked like the Michelin man. So I started running. And I could hardly run for 10 minutes. My muscles were weak. It was so painful. It was miserable. And it was tremendously discouraging. But I kept going after it. Soon I was able to run for 20 minutes, then 30 minutes. Now I'm able to run for several hours. I know it sounds crazy, but I find pleasure in running now. Even though I'm running much longer distances than at the start, it's not nearly as painful because I've developed endurance. The same is true with prayer. Many of us have weak prayer muscles. It can be pretty discouraging when you're struggling to pray for even a few minutes. But with a bit of discipline, your prayer life can become a delight.

Are you more concerned with the spiritual condition of students' hearts than the condition of your own heart? In the midst of your busy life, are you too rushed to pray? When was the last time you pushed the pause button on your life to spend extended time with your God? Do you hurry in and out of the throne room of the Almighty, or do you linger in God's presence? Do you pray more generically for your ministry or in specific ways for your students? Do you tend to make audacious ministry plans and then in desperation pray, "Oh, God, you better show up!"? Or do you pray, *then* plan? Do you passionately pursue the presence of God?

As I write these questions, the Spirit is moving in my heart and convicting me to renew my own commitment to some things related to prayer. Perhaps now is a good time to put this book down and seek God in prayer.

Belief about Prayer

What do you want your students to believe about prayer?

As spiritual leaders in young lives, we need to take time to listen to students and their questions. Our ministries need to be places where students feel safe—otherwise they won't ask their questions. As I've listened to students' questions about prayer, all the questions seem to be variations of four general questions:

> Why pray?

> Does God answer prayer?

> Does prayer really work?

> How can I deepen my prayer life?

No doubt you've heard these questions before. As we move forward with prayer in our ministries, it's important to address these sincere questions. Jeremiah 33:2-3 is a brief yet amazing passage about prayer: "This is what the LORD says, he who made the earth, the LORD who formed it and established it—the LORD is his name: 'Call to me and I will answer you and tell you great and unsearchable things you do not know.'"

I routinely find myself pointing students back to this key Old Testament passage, because it answers many questions about prayer. Let's consider some of the things we can learn about prayer from this passage.

1. GOD INVITES US TO PRAY.

"Why pray?" The God of the universe invites us to commune with him in prayer. Marvel in the wonder of this for a moment. Let this reality sink in. This is why we pray. We pray because our Creator loves us so deeply he created us to live in fellowship with him. The same God who with the breath of his mouth spoke and caused millions of galaxies to come into existence—that same God extends the same invitation to us he extended to Jeremiah: "Call to me." This is absolutely incredible!

I love to receive invitations, especially to parties, sporting events, or anything that involves free food. An invitation makes me feel valued. It makes me feel wanted. It makes me feel loved. So it's incredible to me that our transcendent Creator, who formed and established the earth, invites *me* to call out to him in prayer.

And it's significant that God refers to himself in this passage using the more personal name *Adonai* ("the Lord"), rather than using the title *Elohim* or *Yahweh*. God uses this personal name to reinforce his genuine desire for us to experience an intimate fellowship with him. God longs for us to draw near to and commune with him through prayer. I pray regularly for our students to get beyond the *duty* of prayer (feeling obligated to pray) to experience *delight* in prayer (understanding the immense privilege of communing with God).

2. GOD ANSWERS PRAYER.

"Does God really answer prayer? I've asked God for things, but he doesn't seem to answer." Does this sound like a genuine question from one of your students? Notice the five-word promise in Jeremiah 33:3: "And I will answer you." God promises to answer prayer. And God does answer prayer. However, God doesn't always answer in the same way or with the timeline we request. We need to help our students understand the three kinds of answers to prayer:

> No—the request is wrong.

> Wait— the request is right, but the timing is wrong.

> Yes—the timing is right, and the request is right.

The apostle John writes, "This is the confidence we have in approaching God: that if we ask anything according to his will, he hears us. And if we know that he hears us—whatever we ask—we know that we have what we asked of him" (1 John 5:14-15). As we grow in our faith, we stop asking for dumb stuff and begin praying for things God gladly answers. However, in God's sovereignty, some requests— perhaps about a health concern, for a hardship to end, or for a loved one to come to Christ—God wants us to keep waiting on and trusting him. And as we wait and trust, we can be confident God's purpose will always prevail. Our ministries need to be communities where students can not only share prayer requests, but also be places where students can celebrate answers to prayer and encourage each other to keep persistent in prayer.

3. THERE'S POWER IN PRAYER.

Does prayer really work? If God has already determined [or planned or seen] what's going happen, why bother? Does prayer change anything? The Bible does teach that God is sovereign. "Oops, I didn't know that was going to happen" isn't part of God's vocabulary. But at the same time, the Bible teaches that God responds to the prayers of God's people.

Because we pray, God works through us in ways he otherwise wouldn't. God has made certain things dependent upon prayer, things God may not do unless we pray. But God has determined to use our prayers to accomplish his purposes on this earth. When we don't pray, we limit what God might do in our lives. James writes, "You do not have because you do not ask God" (4:2).

As an introduction to the Lord's Prayer, Jesus said to his disciples, "And when you pray, do not keep on babbling like pagans, for they think they will be heard because of their many words. Do not be like them, for your Father knows what you need before you ask him. This,

moving forward > by looking back

then, is how you should pray" (Matthew 6:7-9). Even Jesus acknowledges that in the Father's sovereignty God knows what you need before asking, but that shouldn't prevent us from praying.

God invites us to pray ("Call to me") and promises to answer prayer ("and I will answer you"). Next God says, "And tell you great and unsearchable things that you do not know" (Jeremiah 33:3). There's tremendous power in prayer. Not only does God love to answer prayer, but he also loves to answer our prayers in ways "immeasurably more than all we ask or imagine, according to his power that is at work within us" (Ephesians 3:20).

God does incredible things when we call out to him. In recent days I've seen God answer prayers about seemingly impossible situations: After a long bureaucratic battle our compassion ministry received favorable government permits, a prodigal student returned to Christ, and a marriage that was moving rapidly toward divorce is reconciling. Prayer taps into power that can change circumstances.

Sometimes our prayers don't change our circumstances. Instead prayer changes *us*. The apostles in Acts are great examples of this. God didn't always change their circumstances, but God gave them the grace they needed each day. Even in the garden of Gethsemane before his crucifixion, Jesus called out, "Father, if you are willing, take this cup from me; yet not my will, but yours be done" (Luke 22:42). In this prayer Jesus recognized that his Father was able to answer by taking the cup from him, yet he deferred to God the Father's will. God chose not to take the cup away from Jesus, but God gave him the grace he needed to face the cross. Jesus went from anxiousness—"his sweat was like drops of blood" (v. 44)—to being confident in his Father and his circumstances.

Sometimes the miracle isn't what happens on the outside. Rather the miracle is what happens inside us. Prayer has the power to change us.

4. PRAYER HAS MANY FACETS.

How can I develop a deeper prayer life beyond asking God for help on a test or to bless a meal? Sadly, most students associate prayer with asking God for stuff. For many students prayer is nothing more than telling God what to do: Give me a good day, help me pass a test, heal Grandma's infected wart, give me a date for homecoming, and help me make the team. We need to help our students understand God isn't a wish-granting genie and move beyond this elementary, one-dimensional prayer life.

Like a diamond, prayer has many facets. When God says, "Call to me," we need to understand the many ways to call out to God. One of the ways to develop a more meaningful prayer life is to experience various facets of prayer, including praising, interceding, listening, confessing, meditating, lamenting, etc.

The next few pages give examples of the many facets of prayer, but the bottom line is this: Developing a meaningful prayer life will only come through praying. I have dozens of books about prayer on my bookshelf, but each has had little value in my prayer life. Almost everything I've learned about prayer hasn't come from a book or a seminar. Rather it has come from calling out to God personally and praying with others who are more mature in their prayer lives. As with most things in life, prayer is developed through practice.

One of my favorite summer pastimes is going to the friendly confines of Wrigley Field. But just watching a lot of professional baseball doesn't mean I can play professional baseball. Even a child can play baseball, but it's another thing to make it to the big leagues. In a similar way, even the youngest child or newest Christian can pray, but having a big-league prayer life will only come through times of discipline and perseverance on your knees.

When your students leave your ministry, what will they believe about prayer? Will they believe God invites them to pray, God answers prayer, there's power in prayer, and prayer has many facets?

Practices of Prayer

Beliefs about prayer aren't always formed through being taught about prayer. Instead students' beliefs about prayer are more often developed through their personal experiences. If we want our students to practice prayer in their personal lives, we need to model prayer in our ministry—and more than just having a prayer at the start of a gathering to settle students down. The rest of this chapter offers ideas for engaging students with God through expanding our practices of prayer—both individually and as a community in our ministries.

PRAYING SCRIPTURE

Many students desire a deeper, more meaningful prayer life, but they don't know how to develop one. Training students to pray Bible verses may be one of the most rewarding things we can do in ministry. It is truly awesome when students pray the Word of God.

Ways to pray Scripture abound. You can repeat one of the prayers in the Bible word for word. The Lord's Prayer is an obvious example. But you can also pray a psalm or one of the prayers of Paul—try one from these passages: Ephesians 1:15-23 and 3:14-21, Philippians 1:9-11, Colossians 1:9-14, or 2 Thessalonians 1:11-12 or 2:13-17.

Another way to pray Bible verses is to take a passage and personalize it in a prayer to God. This happens by reading a line of Scripture and then reflecting the concepts in first-person language back to God in written or spoken form. This method of prayer isn't limited to prayer passages. Instead most passages can be personalized in prayer. Dr. Kenneth Boa has written two books dedicated to offering examples of praying the Scriptures in personal, first-person language. Below is a verse from the New International Version followed by an example of a prayer based on the same verse:

> "And you, my son Solomon, acknowledge the God of your father, and serve him with wholehearted devotion and with a willing mind, for the LORD searches every heart and understands every motive behind the thoughts" (1 Chronicles 28:9).

> "I want to know you, O God, and serve you with a whole heart and with a willing mind; for you search my heart and understand every motive behind my thoughts."[2]

Praying personalized Bible verses can be very effective in communities with small groups or with your student leadership team. At a previous church I had a young married couple whose primary volunteer role was to rotate to home groups to lead evenings of varied prayer—including training students to pray Scripture. Perhaps someone in your church could serve as a prayer guide in your ministry.

HISTORICAL PRAYERS

We can gain value in freestyle praying. But we also benefit from incorporating historical prayers in our ministries. As previously noted, the reference to prayer in Acts 2:42 is most accurately translated "the prayers." The definite article and plural form in the Greek indicates the early church had common prayers composed by certain people and repeated by others. This biblical practice needs to be rediscovered. Our Christian heritage is full of written prayers rich with depth of content and passion. Sadly, many students are ignorant of their heritage. A great way to connect our students' faith with the faith of those who have gone before us is to pray historical prayers.

Many Puritan ministers encouraged their congregants to put private prayer thoughts on paper and vocalize them. The Puritan tradition has preserved many written prayers and meditations that are readily available, including *The Valley of Vision: A Collection of Puritan Prayers and Devotions,* a book that has enhanced my prayer life. An historical prayer can be read by a worship leader or a student as a call to worship or within a longer prayer. It can appear on the video screen to encourage students to read aloud in unison. Or the prayer can be printed on cards and distributed to students for quiet reflection and to store in their Bibles. Exposing students to historical prayers can also encourage them to expand their personal prayer language.

PRAYING THE NAMES OF GOD

Many names for God appear throughout the pages of the Bible. Each title is significant in describing who God is. And each title can expand our prayer life and serve as a guide for praising God for these specific descriptions:

moving forward > by looking back

Hebrew names for God	Meaning
Jehovah Shalom	The Lord our peace
Jehovah Shammah	The Lord is present
Jehovah Rophe	The Lord heals
Jehovah Jireh	The Lord provides
Jehovah Nissi	The Lord my banner/victory
Jehovah Rohi	The Lord my shepherd
Jehovah M'Kaddesh	The Lord who sanctifies

His name shall be called...Jesus, Lord, Emmanuel (God with us), Redeemer, the Promised One, the Way, the Truth, the Life, King of Kings and Lord of Lords, the Good Shepherd, the Author and Finisher of our Faith, the Holy One of God, my Lord and my God, our Ransom, the Alpha and Omega, the Only Begotten Son of God, a Friend of Sinners, Messiah, the Righteous Judge, the Light of Life, a Lamb without Blemish or Spot, the Rock of Ages, Redeemer, Mediator, our Advocate, our Peace, Lord and Savior, Master, Teacher, the King Eternal, the Resurrection and the Life.

POSTURES OF PRAYER

Another dimension of prayer involves the physical positioning of our bodies. In his book about guiding students into spiritual formation, Mike King summarizes some of the biblical prayer postures with Bible references:

> *Kneeling*—expresses humble respect and reverence toward God (Daniel 6:10; 1 Kings 8:54; Luke 22:41; Acts 20:36)

> *Standing*—is a gesture of respect (Nehemiah 9:1-5; Mark 11:25)

> *Prostration* (falling on our faces)—is associated with repentance and sometimes despair (Numbers 16:4; Joshua 7:6-7; 1 Chronicles 21:16; Matthew 26:38-39; Revelation 7:11)

> *Bowing our heads*—shows respect and submission (Genesis 24:26-27; Exodus 34:8-9)

> *Positioning the hands*—including folded, spread out to heaven (1 Kings 8:22), raised hands (Nehemiah 8:6), covering face, palms up, and palm to palm[4]

Incorporating various prayer postures in your ministry gatherings helps to keep prayer times fresh. Students generally seem to be more engaged when incorporating body posture variety compared with the traditional pose of heads bowed as one person prays from the front. As students experience these postures, they're more prone to use them in their personal times of prayer. When encouraging various postures we need to remind students, though, God is most concerned with the posture of our *hearts*, not the posture of our bodies.

RHYTHMIC PRAYER

I've taught our students a rhythmic prayer. After breathing in, we breathe out five words: "God, speak to me today." It can be prayed getting out of bed and throughout the day. It's a reminder that God is continually speaking through creation, the Holy Spirit (in prayers and in our conscience), God's people, and the Bible. Other one-sentence prayers could include "Lord, give me grace" or "God, increase my love" or many others you can probably create yourself!

STYLES OF PRAYER

Many varied styles of prayer keep prayer times fresh in your student ministry. Below are some of the ones we use most routinely:

> *All at once*—everyone praying audibly, all at the same time

> *Laying on of hands*—placing hands on someone while interceding in prayer—one on one, one on many, many on one

> *Looking into eyes*—praying for someone else with your eyes open and looking directly at the person you're praying for

> *Popcorn praise*—praying one-sentence prayers (e.g., "God, I praise you because...")

> *Praying through an outline*—following the ACTS (Adoration, Confession, Thanksgiving, Supplication) or PRAY (Praise, Repent, Ask, Yield) pattern for prayer

moving forward > by looking back

> *Praying antiphonally*—whole group praying back and forth a section of Scripture, or a couple of students placed in each of the four corners of the room can pray after one another

> *Shouting prayers*—call, "What do you want God to do in your heart this semester?" Then encourage students to shout out a word or a phrase of description as a prayer to God.

CONCERT OF PRAYER

A concert of prayer involves combining elements of music and various forms of prayer. I developed the following outline using the PRAY acrostic for a concert of prayer at the start of a school year.

Praise: Worship God for Who God Is and What God Has Done
> Worship songs

> Popcorn prayers of praise: "God, I praise you because..."

> Worship songs

Repent: Confess Our Sins to God
> Read about confession and God's forgiveness

> Write out sins on sheets of paper, then put the paper in a paper shredder

> Worship songs

Ask: Present Our Prayer Requests to God
> Prayer walk around the church building

> Stand facing the direction of your school and pray (all at once) for your school or spiritually lost friends

> Prayer in small groups

Yield: Surrender Ourselves to God
> Kneel in prayer and commit in prayer to live for Jesus this school year

> Trace your hand on the paper wall and write your name in your hand as a symbol of yielding yourself

> Closing song

PRAYER WALK

Students who can walk and chew gum at the same time can walk and pray at the same time, too. The next time you gather your students for extended prayer, why not encourage them to move around rather than just sit? You have multiple ways to facilitate prayer walks.

In my early years of ministry I met students each Friday morning at our local high school to do a "Jericho Walk" around the perimeter of the campus before the start of classes. Each week a different student supplied handwritten 3 x 5 cards to guide the prayer time as we walked in groups of two or three. Students prayed aloud as we walked.

Another form of a prayer walk is to set up prayer areas throughout the inside of your church building. A prayer map can show the locations and prayer requests—auditorium (pray for worship services), offices (pray for the church staff), missionary wall map (pray for missionaries), front doors (pray for visitors), nursery (pray for children and families), etc. Or the prayer wall can focus primarily on spaces and needs in your student ministry.

Or the prayer walk can be around the outside of the church building. The following guide is an example of a script for a prayer walk around the perimeter of a church building.

Instructions to students: Get into groups of four to six and walk around the outside of the church building. As you leave, you may choose to go left or right. As you round a corner of the building, focus your prayers on the next topic listed on the sheet. Pray out loud and keep a prayerful focus while walking and when you return inside. Use this next list to guide your prayer times. Pray for a topic until you turn a corner, then move to the next topic.

Start:
> Pray for the ministry of the church and our pastor(s).
> Pray for weekend worship services.
> Pray for lives of people in our city transformed through various ministries.
> Pray for our pastors to demonstrate godly leadership.

> Pray for the pastors' families.

Turn a corner:
> Pray for our high school ministry leadership.
> Thank God for our pastoral staff, our ministry assistants, and our many volunteer mentors.
> Pray for wisdom in leadership for the staff.
> Pray for their personal lives and walks with Jesus.

Turn a corner:
> Pray for our high school ministry.
> Thank God for a fabulous summer and our summer camps and mission trip.
> Pray for our ministry to be a place for students to connect and grow spiritually.
> Pray for our program to be a time for students to worship and learn from God's Word.
> Pray for our ministry to be a welcoming and friendly ministry.

Turn the final corner:
> Pray for other high school students.
> Thank God for our many freshmen and pray for them to feel welcomed and to get connected soon.
> Pray for our students to live for Jesus on their high school campuses.
> Pray for students to have victory in areas of temptation.
> Pray for students to grow and apply the Word of God in their lives.
> Pray for students to reach out to their non-Christian friends with the hope of Jesus.

Another form of a prayer walk is to have various stations for reflection and prayer. I spoke at a camp recently where one of the afternoon electives was an outdoor prayer walk. Using some of the sayings of

Jesus from the cross, the youth pastor created four stations, each with a written explanation and some 8 x 10 laminated pictures depicting the station. Some had 3 x 5 cards and pens for journaling prayers. Students were encouraged to spend about 10 minutes at each station before moving to the next station. It was inspiring to see students gladly expressing their faith and hearing students share the impact the walk had on them.

BENEDICTIONS

Some church traditions and student ministries include a benediction when the group is concluding its gathered time together. The word *benediction* simply means "blessing." Closing with a benediction is a way to bless your students by raising your right hand with your palm toward the students while reading God's Word. Some common benedictions include—

> "May the God of hope fill you with all joy and peace as you trust in him, so that you may overflow with hope by the power of the Holy Spirit" (Romans 15:13).

> "May the God of peace, who through the blood of the eternal covenant brought back from the dead our Lord Jesus, that great Shepherd of the sheep, equip you with everything good for doing his will, and may he work in us what is pleasing to him, through Jesus Christ, to whom be glory for ever and ever. Amen" (Hebrews 13:20-21).

> "Mercy, peace and love be yours in abundance" (Jude 2).

> "To him who is able to keep you from falling and to present you before his glorious presence without fault and with great joy—to the only God our Savior be glory, majesty, power and authority, through Jesus Christ our Lord, before all ages, now and forevermore! Amen" (Jude 24-25).

moving forward > by looking back

SMALL GROUP PRAYER

Small group leaders should avoid closing in prayer the same way week after week. We encourage our mentors to keep their prayer times fresh by varying their practice of prayer. They can choose from the following list of ideas:

> A student closes in prayer.

> Pray throughout the small group time as a need surfaces.

> Have students write prayer requests on 3 x 5 cards. Then have them exchange with someone else in the group or give all the cards to you. (Bonus idea: Place the cards in plastic baggies so they can naturally stick to the wall of a shower as daily reminders to pray for friends in the small group. Yes, this works.)

> Students pray for different requests. Students can volunteer before the prayer time to pray for a specific request or spontaneously pray during the prayer time.

> Review prayer requests from previous weeks by referring to your small group prayer journal and asking students to share updates.

> Set a theme to guide the prayer request time: "Let's limit our prayer requests tonight to _____ as an application to the main theme of the night."

> Encourage each student to pray for the person on her left going around the circle clockwise. Be sure the students in your group feel comfortable praying in your small group setting first.

> Divide students into pairs to pray for each other.

> Popcorn prayers: The mentor can open with a short prayer, and students who want to pray can just "pop" in at an available pause. The mentor can close.

> Encourage students to pray in a variety of postures: Standing, kneeling, holding hands, palms up, walking, etc.

> Follow a pattern for prayer such as CHAT (Confess, Honor, Ask, Thank) or ACTS (Adoration, Confession, Thanksgiving, Supplication).

> Each student can pray audibly at the same time.

> Everyone who wants to pray takes a turn. Not everyone needs to pray.

> Split the group in half and pray together in two smaller groups.

> Pray silently. Have one person close the silent prayer time after a period of time with "Amen."

> You or another student prays aloud for each person in the group.

A Final Thought...

When students leave your ministry, what do you want them to believe about prayer, and what do you hope their practices of prayer are like? What will students learn about prayer by watching your life and listening to you? What will students learn about prayer through the teaching and practices of prayer in your student ministry?

May God help us grow as ministers and ministries who pray.

moving forward > questions

Questions for personal reflection and team discussion:

1. When students finish high school and leave your youth ministry, what do you want them to believe about prayer, and how do you want them to practice prayer?

2. What are some of the challenges you face in creating a prayer culture in your ministry?

3. Name one or two specific ways you need to grow as a minister who prays.

4. How can you help expand your students' understanding of the many facets of prayer? Of the various practices of prayer, which are some you want to implement in your ministry?

5. What are some practical things you can do to increase the prayer temperature of your group?

6. How can your small group's prayer life grow?

7. What aspects of this chapter do you want to discuss with others on your leadership team?

1. Alvin L. Reid, *Raising the Bar* (Grand Rapids, MI: Kregel, 2004), 88.

2. Kenneth Boa, *Face to Face, Volume 2* (Grand Rapids, MI: Zondervan, 1997), 42.

3. Mike King, *Presence-Centered Youth Ministry* (Downers Grove, IL: InterVarsity Press, 2006), 126-29.

(c)ommunity
engaging students with
God's people

Most Christians—students and adults alike—settle for friendships and never truly experience fellowship.

Christian friendship isn't necessarily the same as fellowship. When Christian students go shopping or to the movies together, that's friendship—not necessarily fellowship. When kids play video games together or in garage bands with Christian pals, that's friendship—not necessarily fellowship. Even when students hang out together at youth group or in small group Bible studies, they can do so without ever truly experiencing fellowship. Fellowship happens when there's a horizontal *and* vertical dimension to interaction.

The apostle John writes this about community: "We proclaim to you what we have seen and heard, so that you also may have fellowship with us. And our fellowship is with the Father and with his Son, Jesus Christ" (1 John 1:3). Community always has two dimensions—fellowship with others and fellowship with God. And fellowship with God is always a prerequisite for fellowship with others. Two nonbelievers can't experience fellowship. A believer can't experience fellowship with a nonbeliever. But often the relationship between two believers is more friendship than fellowship. Fellowship with others only occurs when fellowship with God is a part of your life.

FAMILIAR   FRIENDSHIP   FELLOWSHIP

The first set of circles represents people who are acquaintances. The second set shows two people in a friendship with each other. The third set of circles is fellowship—when a person's relationship with God overlaps with his relationship with another person. The sweet spot of fellowship is when the three circles intersect.

My son is playing his first season of Little League. I'm having a blast these days in the backyard, coaching him to catch, throw, and hit a baseball. I explained to him that he doesn't want to hit the ball off the top part of the bat or down by his hands. Instead he wants to make contact with the ball in the sweet spot—the area of the barrel with the Louisville Slugger logo.

The sweet spot of fellowship is when God is central in one's life—and in one's relationship with others. Recently at camp I walked into a cabin at 11:30 p.m. to find a dozen junior guys in their boxers huddled with their arms around each other's shoulders and praying for one another. These guys were going beyond the typical late-night farting and wrestling (or, more accurately, farting *while* wrestling), and experiencing the sweet spot of fellowship.

When students discuss God's Word, or share what they're learning through their devotional time, or talk about a message from youth group or church, they experience the sweet spot. When students are transparent about hardships and struggles, they enter the sweet spot. As students listen to one another's faith stories, they enter the sweet spot. As a student enters into an accountability relationship with another student, she's in the sweet spot. And as students are in community and living the "one another" passages of the New Testament (see the sidebar), they experience the sweet spot. You can program small groups, but you can't program fellowship. And this frustrates guys like me who want to control outcomes. Fellowship is a by-product of a relational and spiritual connection.

Community encourages the sweet spot of fellowship—not just Christian friendships. And since fellowship doesn't automatically happen when Christian friends get together, we need to model fellowship in our interactions with students. We need to take the initiative. When was the last time you initiated a spontaneous prayer huddle with students? Are you quick to spur students on by sharing what God is teaching you through your personal Bible study time? Would students be more broken if they saw brokenness in you? As students experience genuine fellowship with us, it can encourage them to pursue it with their peers.

We need to teach these fellowship principles to students and train our adult volunteers to model them and teach them as well. In a message about living in community, I used three student volunteers to each hold a hula hoop to illustrate the circle diagram of familiar, friendship, and fellowship. The concept clicked with our students when I shared this object lesson along with several examples to illustrate the point. I can't remember a message where I received more positive feedback from students. Students long for genuine community. Sometimes all we need to do is to model and encourage them.

Our ministries need to be communities that move friendships toward experiencing the fellowship that marked the early believers in the book of Acts.

(c)ommunity in Acts

"The Acts of the Apostles" is the actual name of the book of Acts. The formal title is fitting because it's an historical book about what the apostles *did* after Jesus' ascension. The book describes how the apostles lived out their mission given to them by their Master—including applying both sides of the Great Commandment coin—loving God and loving your neighbors. The adoration chapters of the book you're reading address the priority of *loving God* with all your heart, soul, strength, and mind. But loving God is incomplete without loving others. The chapters in this second section focus on the community part of the Great Commandment—*loving your neighbors.*

The believers in Acts were devoted to doing life together. Their commitment to each other is seen in the frequency and depth of their fellowship. Start circling "together" every time you see it in the book of Acts, and you'll run out of ink pretty quickly. The believers were together day after day. They were together in the temple. They were together in their homes. They ate together. They shared together. They praised together. They prayed together. They cared together. They lived in *koinonia* (i.e., fellowship) together—experiencing all the blessings of genuine fellowship with the body of Christ.

They had incredible depth to their community.

But much of what is considered fellowship today is a poor substitute for New Testament fellowship. The Acts fellowship was more than hanging out, playing games, and eating pizza in the "Fellowship Hall." Their fellowship was a natural by-product of their devotion to each other and to their mission. Community for the early believers was a relational and a spiritual connection. And they didn't have a "come-to-an-event-for-fellowship" mentality. Community was organic. The believers experienced it inside and outside the walls of the church as an everyday reality.

> Those first Christians of Acts 2 were not devoting themselves to social activities but to a relationship—a relationship that consisted of sharing together the very life of God through the indwelling of the Holy Spirit. They understood that they had entered this relationship by faith in Jesus Christ, not by joining an organization. And they realized that their fellowship with God logically brought them into fellowship with one another. Through their union with Christ they were formed into a spiritual organic community.[1]

Their commitment to each other can only be explained by God's transformational work in their hearts and lives. Five things strike me about the Acts 2:44-47 community:

> All the believers were together and had everything in common. Selling their possessions and goods, they gave to anyone as he had need. Every day they continued to meet together in the temple courts. They broke bread in their homes and ate together with glad and sincere hearts, praising God and enjoying the favor of all the people. And the Lord added to their number daily those who were being saved.

THEY WERE REMARKABLY UNIFIED.

The Acts believers were on the same page together. They were united in spirit and purpose. They didn't have some things in common—or most things in common. They had *everything* in common (v. 44). This is an incredible statement. This doesn't mean they were identical.

There's a difference between unity and uniformity. Most likely, you have a diverse student ministry as I do. We have students from different schools and different kinds of schools, and all the different grades are represented. Students have a diversity of family situations: Some students live with both parents, some come from divorced homes, some are adopted, and some have lost parents. Some live in luxury homes and others in efficiency apartments. The kids have a diversity of interests: We have athletes, musicians, artists, cheerleaders, and computer geeks. Some are Cubs fans, some are White Sox fans, and some couldn't care less. We have diversity of race and ethnicity: We have Caucasians, African Americans, Asians, Latinos, Poles, and students from other heritages. And these are just a few examples of diversity. Diversity makes student ministry challenging yet exciting. How boring it would be if everyone were alike!

God doesn't desire uniformity but longs for unity. How awesome is it when our unity in Christ transcends barriers, and students who might not normally hang out together do so within the church? This presents a testimony to a watching world. A mark of a healthy community is when everyone is included—when no one feels left out.

THEY WERE SACRIFICIALLY GENEROUS.

Generosity begins with compassionate awareness. As the Acts believers were aware of needs, they were eager to make generous sacrifices. A practical barometer of a person's devotion to Christ is in his sacrifice. The early Christians had a "what-is-mine-is-yours" mentality. Talk about being sacrificially generous. They didn't just drop a few bucks in the offering plate. They were willing to make personal sacrifices—including selling valued possessions and property to reach out to and care for others in need (v. 45). This giving and receiving wasn't compulsory as in communism. Instead they voluntarily gave of their resources to minister to the poor and needy among them. John would later write, "If anyone has material possessions and sees his brother in need but has no pity on him, how can the love of God be in him?" (1 John 3:17).

This generation of students wants to make a difference in this world. I'm inspired by their compassion and eagerness to take action on behalf of those in need. Many are willing to roll up their sleeves and dig deep into their pockets. A sign of a transformational student community is its willingness to care for others in need within the body. Paul writes, "Let us do good to all people" and then adds, "especially to those who belong to the family of believers" (Galatians 6:10). The early church embodied this by being so actively generous that by the time we get to Acts 4, no one among them was needy (verse 34).

THEY WERE RELATIONALLY CONNECTED.

The relationships of the early believers extended beyond gathering in the temple and included being together and breaking bread in homes. *Breaking bread* can refer to Communion or a fellowship meal or both. Most scholars believe the reference in Acts 2:42 is to Communion and that 2:46 refers to a fellowship meal. So the believers were both sharing meals together and remembering their God in Communion.

Sharing a meal with someone has been an expression of relationship in all times and all cultures—including their first-century context and our 21st-century context. Going out for a burger is a sign of friendship. But having someone in your home for a meal is a whole different level of relational connection. The early believers' relationships didn't just happen at church or at a comfortable distance. They ate meals together in their homes as a symbol of sharing life together. A mark of a student ministry that's been transformed by God is when students like to be together—inside and outside the church.

THEY WERE GRATEFULLY GLAD.

Their fellowship was more than being relationally connected; it included a vertical dimension as well. Praising God was vital to their fellowship with each other. The whole passage (Acts 2:42-47) seems to suggest that an atmosphere of praise and gladness permeated the early church. The church went beyond having a worship service and was part of the daily fabric of doing community together.

The believers are described as having glad and sincere hearts (v. 46). Gladness isn't something that can be mustered up. It's something that overflows from a joyous heart. How's the gladness temperature in your student ministry? Gladness disappears when gratitude is absent. And gratitude disappears when people feel as if things in life are rights, not privileges. The Acts believers saw food, fellowship, gathering in the church, and worship as precious gifts from a gracious God. These were privileges to them, not entitlements. They had a genuine appreciation for life—whether life was good or bad at any given moment. Like the church in Acts, we need to help our students to not take community for granted by continually reminding them that every good gift comes from God.

THEY WERE EXPONENTIALLY GROWING.

The early church grew from the inside out—not the outside in, as many student ministries seek to do today. As the believers lived out biblical community, others were attracted to them and their God. Their community was so compelling to the watching world, they enjoyed the "favor of all the people." As a result, "the Lord added to their number daily those who were being saved" (v. 47). This statement is very significant.

First, *the Lord added to their number.* Their growth wasn't based on some clever seeker-driven strategic formula. God simply used their Spirit-filled worship (adoration), genuine love (community), faithful proclamation of the Word (truth), and generous caring (service).

Second, *God added to their number daily.* Their growth wasn't occasional or sporadic. It was a common reality.

Finally, *God added to their number daily those who were being saved.* Their growth was more than filling seats. Any youth worker can add numbers to a youth group by offering activities or giveaways to attract a crowd. But only God can redeem people. Only God can transform lives. As the early believers were faithful to the kind of ministry God empowered, they became firsthand eyewitnesses to lives transformed by God.

Community was part of the lifeblood of the early church. A defining characteristic of a student ministry that's been transformed by God is its commitment to community—engaging students with God's people.

A Biblical Theology of (c)ommunity

I have more than a dozen different volumes of theology textbooks on the shelf directly below my yellow foam Green Bay Packer cheese head and an 8 x 10 photo of my first Colorado whitewater rafting expedition. Each book contains dozens of theological topics, including bibliology, Christology, soteriology, ecclesiology, eschatology, and more. Most are more than a thousand pages long and thicker than my Webster's dictionary. Despite the comprehensive nature of these books, none addresses the subject of community. Not one. Nevertheless, it is possible to identify a biblical theology of community through a careful study of the Old and New Testaments. And a biblical theology for community must begin with God.

GOD IS COMMUNITY.

Community is rooted in the very essence of God. God is a plurality of persons—Father, Son, and Holy Spirit—in oneness of being. God is three in one. God is triune, and God is unity. God is tri-unity. Over the years this concept has been illustrated by various objects—egg (white, yoke, and shell), apple (seed, meat, and skin), and the different states of H_2O (water, ice, and steam). Although none fully explains the incredible mystery of God, each does represent three in one.

In speaking of the communal nature of God, Andy Stanley and Bill Willits write, "Throughout the Scriptures, the Trinity is seen expressing a unique, affirming kind of relationship toward one another. They are seen enjoying one another (Genesis 1:26), encouraging one another (Matthew 3:17), supporting one another (John 14:23-26), loving one another (Mark 9:7), deferring to one another (John 14:10), and glorifying one another (John 17:1)."[2] It's not enough to say God desires community. God *is* community.

God is a plurality of persons in oneness of being, but this doesn't mean God is human. God isn't an elevated being at the top of the food chain. God is deity. To truly understand the nature of God, we must embrace the communal nature of his deity—plurality and person. Julie Gorman writes—

> Because God is a person, he is capable of having relationships. He is not an inanimate object, a force, a principle, or an impersonal dynamic. God is a person enjoying and pursuing relationships...The entire account of Scripture is a record of his commitment to developing relationships with others. Think of how different your perspective would be if God were a power or machine and not a person.[3]

GOD CREATED US FOR COMMUNITY.

"In the beginning God" (Genesis 1:1). The creation narrative begins with these four profound words. Then God spoke: "Let there be light" (Genesis 1:3). And God got what he asked for. And God saw that it was good. The sequence continued the next day. God spoke and the sky was formed. And it was good. He created the land with

moving forward > by looking back

vegetation and gathered the waters. And it was good. He hung the sun, moon, and stars in their places. It was good. And God filled the seas with an assortment of cool creatures and filled the sky with some amazing winged birds. It was all good on the fifth day.

Finally, God said, "Let us make man in our image, in our likeness" (Genesis 1:26). This statement is significant for two reasons. First, God reveals himself as plurality—let *us* make man in *our* image, in *our* likeness. Second, God reveals that humans are made in God's image. All of creation reflects God, but only humans are made in God's likeness. What an incredible reality!

The creation story in Genesis 1 closes with these words: "God saw all that he had made, and it was *very good.* And there was evening, and there was morning—the sixth day" (Genesis 1:31, emphasis added). All God had previously made was very good, yet God reserved *this* affirmation for immediately after creating humankind.

What comes next may come as a surprise. In Genesis 2:18 God says, "It is *not* good" (emphasis added). What? Not good? What's not good? After affirming all aspects of creation, God makes this observation about the pinnacle of creation. "It is *not* good," God continues, "for the man to be alone."

The context for this statement is significant. Stuart Briscoe once told me, "If you take the text out of the context, you're left with a con." It's a memorable statement that has stuck with me. Sin entered the picture with the fall in Genesis 3. But God made this statement in Genesis 2. Therefore, our need for community isn't a result of sinful depravity. Neither is it a result of broken fellowship with God. It's a purposeful quality modeled and created by God. Make a note of this: Even though it wasn't good for man to be alone, God's creation of humankind was very good.

God created us in his likeness. We're created as relational beings to be in relationship with our Creator *and* in relationship with others. We're created to be in community.

Some Christians proclaim, "God is all you need." I disagree. Before you close the book and label me a heretic, please read on. God did create us with a spiritual need. But God also created us with physical needs. We need air, right? Which of us would be alive if we didn't have oxygen in our lungs? We need water. We need food. We need sleep. In a similar way, we're created as relational beings with relational needs by a relational God. Community isn't optional. Community is essential. It's a created necessity in our lives.

Adam lived in a perfect, intimate relationship with his Creator. He literally walked and talked with God. Yet God still said, "It is not good for man to be alone." God created us with horizontal relational needs God alone doesn't satisfy in our vertical relationship with him. We desperately need a relationship with God, but we also need relationships with others.

JESUS MODELED COMMUNITY.

Since God is community and since God created us for community, it shouldn't surprise us that Jesus showed us real community while on earth. Jesus modeled community in his incarnation and ministry.

The gospel of John opens with words that parallel the creation story. "In the beginning was the Word, and the Word was with God, and the Word was God. He was with God in the beginning. Through him all things were made; without him nothing was made that has been made" (John 1:1-3). In stating that Jesus was God in the beginning, John affirms that God is community. Most consider only the Father as the Creator, but Jesus was present at and shared in the creation of all things (see also Colossians 1:15-17). Then we read these remarkable words about the incarnation: "The Word became flesh and made his dwelling among us" (John 1:14). The Creator became flesh to live among the creation. Jesus is *Emmanuel*, "God with us." This title embodies community.

Jesus' ministry was more than a preaching ministry. He didn't come as royalty to reveal only a calculated public persona. He came to hang out ("dwell") with humans. Jesus got close to humans, and humans got close to him.

Jesus' public ministry began when he called his initial followers with relational words such as, "Come, and you will see" and "Follow me" (see John 1:39, 43). Philip quickly understood the relational aspect of Jesus' call. After responding to Jesus, he found Nathanael.

When Nathanael questioned the legitimacy of Jesus' credentials, Philip said, "Come and see" (John 1:46). Mark uses communal terms to describe Jesus' calling of his disciples: "He appointed twelve—designating them apostles—that they might *be with him*" (Mark 3:14, emphasis added). Jesus called a group of guys to be with him and as a part of a community transformed by God.

Jesus' ministry was marked more by spending time with people than by speaking to large audiences. Jesus had time for many individuals—including Nicodemus and the Samaritan woman. He invited himself over to Zacchaeus' home to spend time with him. Lazarus and his sisters were close friends of Jesus. His critics ridiculed Jesus for hanging out with tax collectors and sinners. After most of his large ministry events, Jesus often withdrew with his disciples to spend focused time with them.

Jesus didn't spend most of his public ministry in public ministry. Rather Jesus did life in community with his 12 disciples.

I hope you haven't missed some of the obvious ministry implications for us today. Do you hang out with students, or is your ministry only a public ministry to an audience of students? Do you get close to students and let students get close to you? Do you make time in your schedule for individuals? Are you going to where students are—rather than always having students come to you? Do you seek to balance time between Christian and non-Christian students? Is there a smaller group of students you're intentionally discipling?

Relational ministry is a challenge. I love students, but I'll be honest and admit this has been a personal struggle for me. The urgency of teaching preparation, event planning, parent letters, and church staff meetings can often monopolize my time. I've set an expectation for our staff team to spend at least 10 percent to 20 percent of our time in relational ministry with students outside of ministry programs. This has forced us to work more efficiently. We've learned we'll never *find time* for relational ministry. Instead we need to *make time.* And making time for relational ministry can be a challenge some weeks, but it's always worth it. We feel that if community was important to Jesus, it should be important to us, too.

Community was so important to Jesus it was on his heart within hours of his betrayal. John records these words: "My prayer is not for them alone. I pray also for those who will believe in me through their message, that all of them be one, Father, just as you are in me and I am in you. May they also be in us so that the world may believe that you have sent me" (John 17:20-21).

Our community is important to God. Think about all the things Jesus could've prayed for his followers. He could've prayed for perseverance to the call to follow him. Or protection from persecution. Or boldness in the proclamation of the gospel. Yet his primary concern was with the depth of relationship among his followers. Why? Because our unity is extremely important. And take note: The standard for unity is the relationship between the Father and Son. Just as the Father and Son are one, we're to be one in spirit and mission. And when we're one, we glorify God.

Our community points people to God. This prayer has missiological implications. It reflects a statement Jesus made in John 13: "As I have loved you, so you must love one another. By this all men will know that you are my disciples, if you love one another" (vv. 34-35). When will we wake up to the reality that the best way to point people to God isn't by wearing "A Bread Crumb & a Fish" T-shirts, carrying our Bibles in public, or displaying "No Jesus. No Peace. Know Jesus. Know Peace." bumper stickers? Our unity and love for one another will draw people to God. It's easy to wear a T-shirt, carry a Bible, or slap on a bumper sticker. It takes a lot more work to live in unity. It's hard work to forgive one another, to support one another, to carry each other's burdens, and just to get along with one another. But this is what our world is searching for. Francis Schaeffer writes, "Our relationship with each other is the criterion the world uses to judge whether our message is truthful. Christian community is the final apologetic."[4]

Imagine If...

Imagine if we were truly devoted to community. Imagine if our students pursued the sweet spot of fellowship rather than settling for

Christian friendships. Imagine if our students were committed to unity in the midst of diversity. Imagine if there was an increased awareness of needs within our groups, and students were eager to generously give and sacrificially serve. Imagine if our ministries were unified in spirit and mission. Imagine if everyone embraced community as absolutely essential rather than optional. Imagine if we devoted more time to relationships with students and not just to ministry to an audience of students. Imagine if we were more intentional about getting close to students and students getting close to us.

Would our ministries be any different? Might we see God transforming lives? Might we experience exponential growth?

---

moving forward > questions

Questions for personal reflection and team discussion:

1. How would you describe the community temperature in your group now?

2. How would you describe the difference between having Christian friends and experiencing biblical fellowship?

3. How can you model the sweet spot of fellowship in your group?

4. How does Jesus' model of community inspire you?

5. What are some of the challenges of devoting 10 percent to 20 percent of your time to relational ministry?

6. Would your ministry be any different if you were to renew your commitment to the priority of community? If so, in what ways?

7. What aspects of this chapter do you want to discuss with others on your leadership team?

---

1   Jerry Bridges, *True Fellowship* (Colorado Springs, CO: NavPress, 1985), 16.

2.   Andy Stanley and Bill Willits, *Creating Community* (Colorado Springs, CO: Multnomah, 2004), 41.

3.   Julie Gorman, *Community That Is Christian* (Grand Rapids, MI: Baker, 2002), 24.

4   Francis Schaeffer, *The Mark of a Christian* (Downers Grove, IL: InterVarsity Press, 1970), 14-15.

Starbucks is in the business of selling more than grande one-pump hazelnut extra-hot skim lattes. Perhaps you've seen this table tepee at your local Starbucks: "Create Community. Make a Difference in Someone's Day." Flip the card around, and the back reads, "When you work at Starbucks, you can make a difference in someone's day by creating an environment where neighbors and friends can get together and reconnect while enjoying a great coffee experience."

Starbucks is in the business of creating relational community. And they're definitely succeeding in this goal. They have me hooked. Starbucks is my second office and the place I most often go to connect relationally. And I'm not alone. My local Starbucks is packed with people from 5 a.m. to 11 p.m. The large comfy chairs, stone fireplace, and soft lighting are all part of creating an ambience to welcome people into relational community. Not only have businessmen and soccer moms discovered this, but our students are also increasingly flocking to Starbucks.

In addition to coffee shops, students can experience relational community at school, at the mall, in a friend's basement, on a sports team, in the yearbook club, in jazz band, or at the movies. Students can even experience community through Facebook and text messaging. Students have endless social outlets.

Although our ministries need to create environments for relational connection, we shouldn't be satisfied with simply generating relational community.

If students can get relational community in lots of ways outside of the church, what does the church have to offer? More than providing relational community, a transformational student ministry provides students with spiritual community. We have more to offer than simply relational community. But relational community is where it starts.

The ABCs of (c)ommunity

Stephanie had moved from out of state and was hoping to make friends in her new church. I encouraged her to get involved in the high school ministry. I saw her in our church lobby a few weeks later and inquired about her experience. "Students were friendly," she said. I smiled as I took personal satisfaction in her positive assessment. After a brief pause she continued, "But it's hard to make friends." This is an insightful statement from a 16-year-old student. Unfortunately, her statement is acutely true. We'd worked hard to be a friendly group. We had student greeters, magic-marker nametags, ministry team students looking for new students, and a fun and inviting atmosphere. But students aren't just looking for a friendly group: They're looking for friends.

Community begins as students join in genuine friendship with each other. Students long to have a place of safety and trust where they can share their highs and lows in life with others who truly care. Relational community has three essential building blocks—affirmation, belonging, and care.

(A)FFIRMATION > TO CELEBRATE AND BE CELEBRATED

Rejoice with those who rejoice; mourn with those who mourn.
(Romans 12:15)

Why is it that we often have a dyslexic understanding of Romans 12:15? The apostle Paul doesn't say to mourn with those who rejoice and rejoice with those who mourn. But isn't that often our instinctual thought? Rather than rejoicing when a Christian brother is rejoicing, we can weep inwardly because of jealous envy, wishing we were the one rejoicing, right? And if a sister is weeping, rather than entering into her sorrow, we secretly rejoice we aren't the ones going through her trial. We need to create environments to encourage our students to live out this verse in tangible ways.

Part of being effective in youth ministry is remembering what it feels like to be a student. Think about all the significant moments and special days our teenagers are experiencing when we need to be genuinely enthused and celebrate with them. Obviously, birthdays come to mind, but they have many other special moments. Remember when you were 16 and got your driver's license? Do you remember how excited you were and how you couldn't wait to show others? What are other special moments? Going to the homecoming dance. Scoring a goal in the game. Making first chair in the flute section. Getting braces off teeth. Completing an art project. Being baptized. Getting a part-time job. Making the honor roll or getting inducted into the National Honor Society. Part of forming community is celebrating these significant moments with our students.

moving forward > by looking back

I confess I used to be one of those youth pastors who viewed our local schools as opponents in a competition for student involvement. I was agitated when students missed youth group because of a sporting event, a choir concert, or even an awards night. How about you? As I've matured with experience, I've realized perhaps the best place for some of our students isn't always *inside* the church, but making an impact *outside* the church. Now I find myself eager to affirm and celebrate student accomplishments outside the church.

Rejoicing with our students is an important way to build a connection with them and for them to feel loved by others. As we affirm students, we help them feel accepted and secure. Our lips should be filled with encouraging statements such as: "I'm so happy for you!" "That's awesome!" "You're awesome!" "I'm so proud of you!" "You did a fantastic job!" "I'm a big-time Tyler fan!" And we should be quick to praise students in front of other students and leaders.

Few things are more meaningful to students than when their youth leaders show up at their games, plays, concerts, or part-time jobs. I still remember feeling loved by Kevin, my youth pastor, when I saw him in the stands at one of my soccer games. He knew soccer was important to me. Therefore, he made going to one of my games an important priority in his busy schedule.

Not only do we need to rejoice with those who are rejoicing, but Romans also exhorts us "to weep with those who weep." Some of the most significant times of community are born during times of hardship. We need to guard against being so busy we miss opportunities to be there for a student who's grieving the loss of a loved one, care for a student whose parents are splitting up, listen to a student who feels picked on by others, comfort a student who recently broke up with her boyfriend, or show sympathy for a student who didn't make the team or get accepted to a certain college or get hired for a job. These are prime-time moments. You can be there for students 99 other times, but you can't miss the prime-time moments of hardship.

Our students long to be affirmed in the ups and downs of life. They long to be celebrated for who they are and what they do. Affirmation is an essential building block of relational community.

(B)ELONGING > TO KNOW AND BE KNOWN

Therefore, as we have opportunity, let us do good to all people, espe-cially to those who belong to the family of believers. (Galatians 6:10)

Do you remember the famous line from the Cheers theme song? Try your memory with this quick multiple-choice quiz:

a) "Sometimes you want to go where everybody is having fun."

b) "Sometimes you want to go where everybody is part of a large crowd."

c) "Sometimes you want to go where everybody is entertained."

d) "Sometimes you want to go where everybody knows your name."

Cliff and Frazier were regulars in the cozy basement pub in Boston being served by their favorite bartenders, Sam and Woody. As the front door swung open, they enthusiastically greeted their big beer-loving friend with, "Norm!" Everyone wants to go where everybody knows your name.

Students want to go where they feel as if they belong. Dale Car-negie once said, "The sweetest word in the English language is your own name." There's something special about hearing your own name. Recently, I had lunch with our middle school pastor at Panera. We fin-ished our meals and were talking about the upcoming Michigan–Ohio State football game (a lively conversation as he is from Ohio, and I have roots in Michigan). The ambient noise level was high because of all the chatter. But above the noise I heard, "Craig!" An employee was calling out the name of another patron. He'd been calling out names throughout our lunch, but I hadn't heard any names—until Craig. Have you ever noticed how your ears perk up when you hear your name called out?

Yesterday my mind was wandering during an all-staff meeting, but someone mentioned my name from the front, and immediately I was mentally engaged.

Hearing your name mentioned creates a powerful connection. And when someone addresses you personally by name, that indicates a re-

moving forward > by looking back

lationship. Students constantly play the "Do you remember my name?" game with me. But it's not really a game. They're serious about it. Our students long to belong to a group where they can know others and be known by others—including their leaders. This is definitely an area of growth for me. How about you?

I was enlightened by a comment a mom shared with me after a winter retreat. She'd approached me in the church lobby to thank me for the work I put into the retreat the weekend before. Turns out that on the drive home from the church after the retreat pickup, the mom asked her sophomore daughter, "How was the winter retreat?"

"It was great, Mom," Allie said without hesitation. "What I wanted to have happen happened."

"And what was that?"

"I wanted Craig to talk to me and get to know my name. And he did both."

How sad is that? She'd been a part of our ministry for 18 months, and she longed for me to know her name. Believe me, I haven't forgotten her name since.

Proverbs 27:23 says, "Be sure you know the condition of your flocks, give careful attention to your herds." It's impossible truly to know the condition of our sheep if we don't know students' names. But knowing names is only the beginning of really knowing students.

Students long for when others truly know them as they really are. Students often share at the surface level, leaving us wondering if we're making any difference. Most students don't immediately disclose their hurts and hopes. But as we create a relationship of acceptance and trust, students are more than willing to share these things and so much more. Students do want to share how they're really feeling inside—but not until they sense real caring from you and others.

Students long to belong. They long to be known. They long to be noticed. They long to be noticed when they're at youth group and when they aren't. They long to be personally connected. Students will not stick around a ministry very long if they don't feel a sense of belonging.

Make a note of this: Students' longing to belong is universal—and it includes students who don't yet believe in Jesus. In previous generations students would belong to a group only after expressing belief in Christ. However, recent observations show that through belonging to a Christian community first, many students later express a faith in Christ. *Belonging* frequently precedes *believing*.

The deeper we know each other, the greater our ability to truly care for and love each other.

(C)ARE > TO LOVE AND BE LOVED

Dear children, let us not love with words or tongue but with actions and in truth. (1 John 3:18)

You don't have to be a totally cool or an amazing teacher to be a great youth leader—but you do need to love students. Do you? I suspect you wouldn't be in student ministry or reading this book if you didn't love students. So a better question might be: Do your students *know* you love them? It might not seem so, but there's a huge difference between these two questions.

My first year after college I traveled alone to Romania to partner in ministry with a friend. My flight on Romanian Airlines was a nerve-racking experience—primarily because from the moment I boarded the plane in Chicago, everything was foreign to me: The food, the TV entertainment, the literature, and the spoken language from the flight attendants and the passengers all around me. My transcontinental flight ended in Timisajuara. The airport was converted from a former communist military base just a few years prior to my trip. We deplaned using the portable steps brought to the plane parked on the tarmac. Military personnel armed with semiautomatic weapons escorted us to a small building housing the baggage claim and customs. I was very tense as I fumbled through the pile of luggage while the other passengers were speaking in their native tongue with each other. Above all the noisy chatter I heard some distinct words, "Hey, Larry! I found your luggage!" These words, spoken in English, brought great comfort to me. It wasn't as if no one had spoken during the 10-hour flight, but no one was speaking in a language meaningful to me.

Author and counselor Gary Chapman has identified five love languages. These love languages apply to the context of married couples as well as to our relationships with students (and for that matter, friends, siblings, parents, etc.).

1. Words of Affirmation—*speaking words of encouragement to someone.* James 3 teaches us how powerful the tongue can be. Even though it's small, it can cause tremendous damage or inspire people to greatness. When you catch a student doing something good, commend her. Use phrases such as: "I'm proud of you." "I appreciate _____ about you." "I care about you." And "Thank you for _____ ."

2. Quality Time—*giving focused attention to someone, spending time with him doing something he enjoys.* Many students spell love T-I-M-E. And quantity time doesn't guarantee quality time. Quality time involves being quick to listen and slow to speak (James 1:19). It involves seeking to understand what's going on in the life of the other person and responding in a genuine way. Christ's priority wasn't programs, but people. We must avoid the all-too-common tendency to be too busy with ministering to spend time listening to and being with students. Ever been there? When we make ourselves available to students, we communicate their importance.

3. Acts of Service—*doing a kind thing for someone without expecting anything in return.* 1 John 3:18 commands us to love with actions and in truth. More than saying we love students, we need to show it. Actions do speak louder than words. This could involve going to a sporting event or concert, offering to help with a project, allowing students to go before you in the cafeteria line on your winter retreat, and more.

4. Receiving Gifts—*offering tangible things to people to show you were thinking of them, and you care about them.* (Yep, the language is receiving gifts, which means you offer gifts to these folks.) This could be as simple as mailing a card of encouragement, sharing a stick of gum, giving away a gift certificate, buying a cola, sending a birthday card, etc. And gift receivers don't care about the price; they just love knowing others were thinking about them this way.

5. Physical Touch—*extending appropriate physical contact to people*. God created all human beings with the need for human affection. Although many physical gestures are inappropriate from adults to teenagers, some are very healthy touches. These include handshakes, pats on the back, high fives, "the pound," side arm hugs, squeezing an arm, etc. Expressing affection to students through touch communicates to students that they're worth loving. Students need healthy physical touches from adults since many aren't receiving healthy physical touches from their parents. And studies have revealed if adolescents don't receive healthy touches from caring adults, then they become more vulnerable to seeking unhealthy touching and sexual activity. But because different people set different boundaries for appropriate physical touch, make sure you first consult with your church leadership before setting policy—and then make sure your leadership team knows what are and what aren't appropriate forms of physical touch.

Which of these five languages are most meaningful to you? Go ahead and circle the top two ways you feel cared for. In other words, without which two expressions of love would you truly feel unloved or lacking love?

Words of Affirmation

Quality Time

Acts of Service

Receiving Gifts

Physical Touch

Chapman contends that we tend to express love to others in the same way we feel loved. However, we need to seek to understand our students' love languages and express our love in a balanced way.[1]

moving forward > by looking back

A girl in your small group may have quality time as her love language. Even though you serve her faithfully each week, hand out candy, and hug her whenever you see her, it's possible she doesn't feel loved by you. Your relationship becomes awkward. You truly love her. You're confused by her apparent emotional distance, so you give her even more candy and hugs. In the end both of you are frustrated with each other. The problem is, you're speaking in Romanian, and she needs you to speak in English. She doesn't need ongoing candy and hugs—she needs you to pause each week after your small group time simply to listen and give her focused attention.

Our love must be sincere.

From Youth Group toward Spiritual Community

My curly-haired little girl jumped into my arms as I walked in the door tonight. Her face was beaming with excitement because she'd learned her ABCs. Together we danced in our family room as she sang with her sweet little toddler voice about the foundations of our language. And while of course there's more to language than ABCs, you can't have language without the ABCs.

"What should I focus on first?" This question came from a soon-to-be youth pastor while I was sipping on an iced venti Americano at Starbucks. Matt had just accepted a position at a church, and he wanted some advice on establishing his ministry foundation. I encouraged Matt to write this quotation from my friend, Bill Alison, on his napkin: "No relationship = no ministry. Know relationship = know ministry." I then shared with him about the building blocks of affirmation, belonging, and care.

The ABCs of community are where ministry begins. These are foundational building blocks for relationships with students. And just as with language, there's more to community than the ABCs—but you can't have relational community without the ABCs. This is where it begins; it's where it has to start.

But being a youth group with relational community isn't our ultimate goal. To get to our goal of being a spiritual community, we need to have a foundation of relationships. (I say "toward" a spiritual community in the section title because it's a process. It's a journey. We can do things to promote relational connection, but we can't create a spiritual community.)

We can get students to sit in a circle in a small group to talk about God. But just because students are in a small group doesn't mean they're experiencing spiritual community, right? We can prioritize certain elements and point our students to God, but being a spiritual community is a supernatural gift from God.

As you read these words, your spirit may be yearning to move your youth group toward becoming a spiritual community, but perhaps you're unsure of what it looks like. Let's consider six indications of a healthy spiritual community.

1. PRAYING TOGETHER

...pray for each other (James 5:16b)

When I was a rookie in student ministry, Mark, one of my mentors, modeled to me the value of a simple question: "How can I pray for you?" I can't have a conversation with Mark without his asking me this question. Inevitably, the question leads to both of us sharing with each other and praying together—even if it's as simple as praying for 30 seconds with each other. Just asking this question moves relational connection to spiritual community.

I've seen the profound impact of this question on students. Some students are surprised by the question and don't know quite how to respond. I tell them my interest is genuine...and guess what? More times than not, students really open up and share what's on their hearts. This question has a way of causing students to think about things they may not otherwise. The value isn't just in hearing their hearts, but stopping and praying together.

Group prayer is another way to grow as a spiritual community. An incredible bond develops as students pray together and for each other. Acts 20 records Paul's emotional farewell to the church in Ephesus. After reminiscing about his ministry, "he knelt down with all of them and prayed. They all wept as they embraced him and kissed him" (Acts 20:36-37). Prayer has a way of knitting people together in love.

2. REACHING OUT TOGETHER

...honor one another above yourselves (Romans 12:10)

...serve one another in love (Galatians 5:13)

John F. Kennedy inspired a nation when he said, "Ask not what your country can do for you; ask what you can do for your country." A healthy sign of spiritual community is when students ask not what others can do for them but what they can do for others—including caring for relational, physical, and spiritual needs.

Relational. It's easy for our students who feel loved to be ignorant that some students do not feel loved and welcomed. I know a youth pastor who asked one of his volunteers to videotape the interaction time during one of his regular ministry nights. This "hidden camera" captured a lonely high school guy wander in and out of the youth room packed with dozens of students. For more than 10 minutes this guy paced back and forth and back and forth hoping to connect with someone. He slowed as he walked past several groups of students caught up only with themselves. He lingered at several game tables. But no one noticed. The youth pastor showed this videotape to his leadership students at the next ministry team meeting. The following week the lonely guy was the most loved kid in the entire group.

Physical. I was very proud of some Harvest Students who were aware of a physical need of a student in their small group. Joel's dad had been laid off from his job for several months. Although Joel rarely talked about it, the students were perceptive enough to realize his family had real financial need. The other students in the group pooled their money and bought the family a grocery store gift card. The family was very grateful for the thoughtfulness and generosity. What a tangible act of living as a spiritual community!

Spiritual. One of the greatest signs of spiritual health is how students relate with each other outside the walls of the church. I'm aware of students who meet together early once a week before school to pray. Others have their own Bible study time with students from multiple churches in their schools. Others meet for accountability. A sign of spiritual health is when the spiritual community transcends the organized ministry programs and is a part of students' day-to-day lives.

The apostle Paul writes, "Do nothing out of selfish ambition or vain conceit, but in humility consider others better than yourselves. Each of you should look not only to your own interests, but also to the interests of others. Your attitude should be the same as that of Christ Jesus" (Philippians 2:3-5). A youth group moves toward being a spiritual community when it's concerned with caring for others' needs.

3. DISCUSSING GOD'S TRUTH TOGETHER

Let the Word of Christ dwell in you richly as you teach and admonish one another with all wisdom (Colossians 3:16)

A group moves beyond simply being a relational community to becoming a spiritual community when it's engaged in the study and discussion of God's Word. The Bible should be studied not only personally, but also within the context of community. A healthy sign of spiritual community is not only when the Word is talked about in small groups, but also when conversations naturally include the truth of God's Word.

4. WORSHIPING TOGETHER

...speak to one another with psalms, hymns, and spiritual songs (Ephesians 5:19)

Perhaps nothing is more personally inspiring than to see students worshiping God with passion. It's powerfully contagious. It makes others want to join in and experience the joy of their salvation. Although we worship God for who God is and not for how it makes us feel, worshiping God together can create some incredible moments as a spiritual community. Some of my most memorable ones have come during impromptu times of worship on ministry trips where we stood together with our arms around each other, singing from our hearts.

5. SHARING JOYS AND STRUGGLES TOGETHER

Encourage one another and build each other up (1 Thessalonians 5:11)

I long for our students' relationships to go beyond a superficial connection. A friend posted these words on his blog recently:

I want our student ministry to be a place where students can present their wounded selves and still be loved. I want to stop with the superficial, shallow greetings and move to deep conversations that bridge today with eternity. I want our students to dream with me and our leaders about what it means to be fully alive in community. When they graduate, I want them to remember they didn't have to be perfect to be a part of our community. The ground at the foot of the cross is level.

What a visionary statement! These words fire me up.

But students aren't going to get beyond the shallow greetings to deeper conversations if they don't feel secure in an environment of trust. Trust is developed through sincere interest in students and active listening. We need to listen to more than students' words—we need to listen to their hearts. We need to listen to feelings, not just facts. I have to admit, listening isn't one of my strong suits. I can easily get distracted by other things rather than giving full attention to a student speaking to me. How about you? I also tend to interrupt. I can comment about my own opinions or experiences instead of just listening. As I've been intentional with seeking to grow in this area, I've found students are more willing to share not only about joys, but also struggles. Basics such as focused attention and eye contact are important. But the biggest thing that's helped me is asking the "next" question—an open-ended question like "What do you mean?" or "How did that make you feel?" I wonder how many opportunities for meaningful ministry I've missed because I failed to ask the "next" question.

As youth leaders we need to be quick to share joys and struggles, too. Our students need to see us as real—not as posers. We need to share exciting things in our lives and be vulnerable enough to admit areas God is growing us. Students need to know the Holy Spirit convicts us when our attitudes and actions don't line up with who God wants us to be. As we're authentic with our students, our students will more likely be authentic with us and others.

6. BEING ACCOUNTABLE TOGETHER

...confess your sins to each other and pray for each other (James 5:16)

...spur one another on toward love and good deeds (Hebrews 10:24)

Accountability is a sign of students growing beyond superficial relationships and embracing spiritual community. We need to encourage our students to have godly friends—not just good friends. Godly friends are ones who care more about your relationship with God than your relationship with each other. I've heard my pastor say, "Godly friends are there to hold you up when you're hurting, and they hold you down when you're straying." How true. We need friends who'll encourage us, but we also need friends who'll hold us accountable.

Although accountability can happen in small groups, the most effective accountability is when students choose to meet one-on-one outside our ministry programs.   Although we can encourage accountability relationships, we can never force them. However, the more mature and committed a student is to the ministry, the more he should be expected to be in an accountability relationship—especially if he has expressed interest in leadership roles such as the student ministry team, missions team, or volunteering in the middle school ministry. With increased involvement and leadership, you can leverage a student to be in an accountability relationship.

I believe each adult leader needs to be in an accountability relationship, too—but with another adult. Are you in an accountability relationship now? Most students don't want to be accountable to an adult, and it's unhealthy for an adult to be in an accountability relationship with a student. I'm not saying we can't have some accountability in a small group between an adult and some students. And I'm not saying we can't be grace in the face and speak the truth in love to our students. But it's unhealthy for a student and an adult to be in an ongoing accountability relationship with mutual vulnerability. We should never be in a dependent relationship, needing a student to minister to us and help us through sin areas.

We were created to live in community. We need to move beyond being youth groups to being spiritual communities where students are

moving forward > by looking back

experiencing the "one another" passages of Scripture. Our ministries need to be places where students can engage with God's people—building meaningful relationships with both peers and caring adults.

moving forward > questions

Questions for personal reflection and team discussion:

1. How would you assess your group's love for each other?

2. How do you celebrate students in your ministry?

3. Students long to belong. They won't stick around a ministry very long if they don't feel a sense of belonging. Do you agree or disagree? Why?

4. How would you describe the difference between loving your students and your students knowing you love them?

5. What are some ways you want to see your group grow as a spiritual community?

6. What are three practical things you can do to help your group more toward becoming a spiritual community?

7. What aspects of this chapter do you want to discuss with others on your leadership team?

1. *The Five Love Languages* (Chicago: Northfield Publishing, 1992, 1995).

2.2 MOVING FORWARD
(c)ommunity as a ministry culture

Do you consider yourself an environmentalist?

Every student ministry leader should be an environmentalist. We should be concerned not only about things such as room setup, but also the community environment. Our student ministries should be more than places to play games, sing songs, and hear Bible lessons. I hope you caught the vision for moving beyond being a youth group toward being a spiritual community. But it's one thing to have a vision; it's a whole different matter to turn that vision into reality.

When the topic of community surfaces in most youth ministry books and seminars, the focus shifts exclusively to small groups. It's as if the solution to the need for community is: Provide small groups. And if small groups are offered, then students will experience community. This assumption is understandable. Small groups can allow for community. But let's not fool ourselves into thinking that because we have small groups, we have community or that community is limited to small groups.

We need to wake up to the reality that a culture of community is essential in *all* our ministry environments. If our whole-group times are lacking community, then they'll be stale regardless of how dynamic the teaching, energetic the worship, or fun the activity.

This chapter begins to merge our desire to be a biblical community with our ministry programs. It'll focus on practical ideas for creating a culture of community in three distinct yet equally important ministry environments: Small groups, whole-group gatherings, and ministry trips.

Creating Community > Small Groups

The Acts church gathered regularly in two contexts—in the temple and in their homes. Small group ministry isn't just a temporary fad—it's biblical. We need to follow the model of the early church and gather corporately and in small groups.

Even a small youth group needs small groups. Our church has planted dozens of churches. I routinely meet with pastors and lay leaders about getting student ministry started in their settings. One of the most asked questions is: "When should we start small groups?" My response is always, "As soon as you can. If you have a ministry with more than 15 students, you *need* small groups. It's hard to care effectively for the needs of 15 guys and girls. Think about the model of Jesus. He limited his primary ministry to 12 guys."

You can use four general models to structure small groups within your ministry. And one particular way isn't the correct way. As you consider these four approaches, consider your own ministry setting, size, and circumstances.

MODEL 1: BRIEF SMALL GROUPS AFTER A LONGER WHOLE-GROUP TEACHING TIME

Students and adults participate together in a whole-group setting— usually with elements like games, worship, and teaching. Then at the end of the program they break into groups to discuss the message and seek life applications together. This is an effective model for ministries that value personal connection during a whole-group night.

MODEL 2: EXTENDED SMALL GROUPS AFTER A SHORTER WHOLE-GROUP TIME

This model is a variation of the previous one. However, instead of small groups supplementing a program, they're the central part of the gathering. Some ministries gather all the students together in a room only for announcements or a time of worship. Then students and adults are dismissed to areas throughout the church building for extended time in small group Bible study. This is an effective model for ministries that emphasize extended small group time but value a corporate connection on the same night.

MODEL 3: SMALL GROUPS MEETING INDEPENDENTLY

Unlike the first two models, this one doesn't have a whole-group component—at least not connected to the small groups. This approach allows small groups to meet at various times throughout the week. Or all the small groups could meet at the same time on the same night, but they meet independently of each other. These small groups may gather in the church building or scatter to homes, schools, coffee shops, etc. This is an effective model if the ministry puts a premium on small groups having varied and flexible meeting times.

MODEL 4: MEDIUM-SIZED CLUSTER GROUPS MEETING TOGETHER AND DIVIDING INTO SMALL GROUPS

This model is when a larger group is divided into medium-sized cluster groups, often by region or school. Within these medium-size coed groups are multiple small groups (guys with guys, girls with girls). The evening includes time together as a cluster group and time in small groups. This is an effective model if the ministry values decentralization according to communities where students live.

Small Group Formats

Just as four general models for small groups exist, there are four general formats for small groups.

FORMAT 1: DISCUSS A MESSAGE.

This format is mostly associated with model 1. The goal of the small group is to discuss a message presented during the whole-group time to encourage understanding and life applications. Accountability can also play a part in this format.

FORMAT 2: PRAYER AND SHARE

This format encourages students to get together primarily for prayer, to share about their daily lives, and to provide accountability. Minimal emphasis, if any, is put on a Bible study or lesson. This group exists for mutual ministry—encouraging fellowship among students.

FORMAT 3: FREE TO CHOOSE

This format gives each small group freedom to choose what they want to study and discuss together. The small groups should be given several options (a Bible study, a book study, a discipleship workbook, etc.). Within this format some ministries allow students to choose their small groups based on content (as an elective). Other student ministries establish the groups first, then allow the students and leaders to determine the content piece.

FORMAT 4: UNIFIED SERIES

Regardless of when and where small groups meet, each is encouraged to follow a unified series the other small groups are using as well. The series can be a Bible study, a book study, or a discipleship workbook, but each small group is committed to doing the same series. Because the groups use a unified study plan and vary in age, gender, and spiritual interest, the leader is encouraged to adapt the lesson plan more than accomplish it by getting through all the questions.

I've been in student ministry since the early '90s and have served in several churches over these years. The truth is, I've used all four models and all four formats at one point or another. Each has pros and cons. One isn't better than another. And certainly no one model or format is the correct way to facilitate small groups. Each ministry setting is different. You may be in a setting where your small groups can meet on nights other than your normal whole-group time. Some groups may be limited to combining both on the same night. You need to consult with your church leadership and decide which approach is best for your ministry setting. And if you have small groups going in your ministry, I recommend you periodically evaluate the effectiveness of your small groups.

Group Covenant

Once your small group has formed, I encourage you to develop a group covenant as a group project and bonding experience. Rather than having students sign a generic covenant (either from a book or a statement of your personal expectations), involve your students in the process of crafting the covenant. And because you may have multiple small groups in your ministry, each covenant should be unique to each group. Hopefully, the covenants will be similar to each other yet embody the personality of each group.

Begin by asking your students, "What do you want to see happen in this small group and in your lives?" If, after a time of brainstorming, students are still missing some essentials, just say, "What about...?" Follow up with, "How will these things happen?" Brainstorm some goals for the group. After dialoguing together, jot some of these things down on paper and have the students sign it. The small group leader can guide the process, but make sure the students own the direction of the covenant—otherwise it won't mean anything to them.

A covenant may look something like this:

> It's our hearts' cry to experience fellowship as together we grow in a love relationship with God and live out our faith in a way that genuinely impacts others.
>
> Therefore, we commit to:
>
> > faithful attendance and participation
>
> > studying and discussing God's truth
>
> > authenticity

Personalized Discipleship Plan

Spiritual formation is about growth and change. Are your students more like Christ today than they were three months ago? Do you want to help them take the next steps in their discipleship journeys? If so, encourage students to identify one area for personal growth in each of the three categories of Spiritual Discipline, Character, and Relationship. At the beginning of your small group season, have students write the three areas for personal growth on two 3x5 cards – one to keep and one to give to you. This provides focus for the students, focus for your prayers, and focus for your follow up. It also helps personalize discipleship. Review the areas routinely during the 90 days, then identify three new areas for the next 90 days. Best of all, this plan works regardless of the model or format of your small group.

Spiritual Discipline

> Personal Bible study—hunger for God's Word, regular time of reading, studying, and meditating on the Word

> Prayer life—praise, confession, intercession for others, journaling, and listening

> Scripture memory—systematically memorizing and reviewing Scripture

> Giving—cheerfully giving a biblical portion to God's work

> Corporate worship—engaging with God through consistent participation in weekend worship services

> Accountability—connected in a relationship for the purpose of transparency and personal growth

> Serving—actively involved in shouldering weekly kingdom responsibility

> Fasting—routinely fasting (from food, media, activity) to seek God through prayer and dependence

> Sabbath rest

> Other:_____

Character

> Boldness—not being afraid to share who Jesus is with confident assurance; being gentle, kind, and loving

> Compassion—empathy for others' circumstances and acting on their behalf

> Contentment—being at peace; not given to anxiety, jealousy, or envy

> Even Tempered—not given to sinful anger and temper

> Faith—confidence in God and his promises for you regardless of circumstances

> Forgiveness—releasing someone of a wrong done to you

> Honesty—being truthful and above reproach in all things; not deceptive nor hypocritical

> Kindness—acting in love and grace by helping others

> Patience—a spirit of longsuffering

> Peace—sense of fulfillment from being rightly related to God and others

> Purity—thinking and acting in godly ways; not given to lust and sexual immorality

> Self-controlled—bringing thoughts, emotions, and actions under the control of the Holy Spirit rather than flesh

> Selfless—considering the needs of others above yourself

> Truth in Love—willingness to speak truth in a spirit of grace; not passive (love without truth), not harsh (truth without love)

> Wholesome speech—quick to encourage and build others up; not given to vulgarity, gossip, slander

> Other:_____

Relationship

> Dad

> Mom

> Brother

> Sister

> Friend

> Classmate

> Coworker

> Witness with non-believer

> Other:_____

> loving each other in words and actions

> accountability and prayer

> reaching out

As you train your small group leaders, you may choose to give them a sample covenant to help them catch the vision, but encourage them to allow the students to feel ownership. The greater the students' ownership, the more meaningful the covenant will be for the group.

As you consider how to structure small groups, you need to consider your setting, size, and ministry objectives. And remember: Just because you have small groups doesn't mean you've created community. Any six to eight students can get together to become a small group, but it takes something special to create biblical community. Similarly, don't fool yourself into thinking community is limited to small groups.

Creating (c)ommunity > Whole-Group Times

Creating a culture of community in your whole-group times is essential. It doesn't matter if your whole-group time involves 20 students, 60 students, or hundreds of students. However, the larger your group, the greater the challenge in creating community.

A great time for community is before and after the program. I know a student ministry that offers "hoops, homework, and hangout" after school and before their midweek gathering. Little needs to be done to facilitate this time, but providing it allows students to connect socially with each other.

Students usually prefer to hang out after the program instead of before it. It's a healthy sign when students want to hang out rather than bolting out the door when the program is done. But hanging out won't happen automatically. You need to provide an inviting and relaxing environment...and food.

Food has a way of creating healthy times of interaction—but please don't think you need a student café to facilitate fellowship. While you do need something more than a white-walled church classroom with round tables and folding chairs, your youth room shouldn't feel like a school classroom! Perhaps your church will allow you to claim a space where you could have some sofas, paint the walls, hang up posters and pennants from local schools (or other memorabilia), put in a soda machine, and set up a game table or two.

Don't limit your thinking about community to students hanging out before and after the program. Thinking intentionally about how to create community the program is also very important.

HERE ARE SOME IDEAS TO GET YOU THINKING ABOUT INCORPORATING TIMES OF COMMUNITY INTO YOUR LARGE GROUP GATHERINGS.

Mixer activities

Beyond the typical youth group games that are gross or only involve four participants in the front, think about getting all your students interacting with each other so they aren't just sitting around the same friends or in the same seats each week. Mixer activities get students out of their seats and interacting with other students. Mixers don't need to be silly, but they should be intentional.

Couch chats

We periodically do "couch chats" by inviting three students to gather on a comfy sofa with a pastor sitting among them. Through this informal and interactive interview time students share about their personal lives and what God is teaching them. The couch chat is more casual than the traditional stand-in-front-of-a-mic or the boring let's-have-three-students-sit-on-stools-and-share-down-the-line. This time creates community as students get to hear what's going on in the lives of other students and models the benefits of sharing their personal lives with others.

Testimony times

These can be spontaneous or planned. You can have students spontaneously share what God's doing in their lives. If you do this, it's always best to give some clear guidelines, such as—keep your sharing to how God has been growing your faith in the past couple of weeks. (If your group is big enough to necessitate microphones, it's best for you to hold the microphone; that way you have better control over what's shared and for how long.) Another way to have testimonies is to schedule a student in advance and have her come prepared to share three minutes related to the theme of the program. Few people are inspired by the I-want-to-tell-you-about-how-I-trusted-Jesus-when-I-was-five-years-old story. We had to reculture our students so they understood sharing a testimony doesn't equal sharing a salvation story. God's writing their story day by day, and our testimonies should be more about what God's doing in our lives presently than about what he did in the past. For students to understand this, it needs to be modeled to them over and over again.

Community prayer

You have various choices for practices of prayer in large group settings. You can pray. You can spontaneously invite a student to pray. You can preselect a student to pray. You can encourage students to pray out loud all at once. You can encourage students to get into groups of three to pray. And while students are in these smaller groups, you can guide multiple topics for prayer time. When you get students into smaller prayer groups, you can encourage them to stand together, kneel together, put their arms around each other, or join hands. Each of these physical postures can build a sense of community.

Perhaps the most meaningful expression is laying hands on students in prayer. Recently, we encouraged students to stand if they were going through a tough period. As students stood, the other students gathered around those who were standing to lay their hands on them in prayer. Then a student volunteered to pray for those dealing with a tough situation. Next I asked students to stand if they felt lonely. What an amazing time of ministry and affirmation of these students as we took time to lay our hands on and pray for them. Obviously, you could use many other categories for prayer for students—students who feel spiritually dry, defeated by an area of sin, discouraged, and more. These can be powerful times of prayer and meaningful times of community.

Recap videos

A fun way to create community and celebrate what God is doing is to show highlight videos or slide shows from a ministry trip or event. And besides, most students love to see themselves and their friends on the screen. It's a great reminder of the spiritual growth and community shared by the entire group. With the development of technology, videos and slide shows are easier than ever. And don't feel as if you need to be the one to put it all together. Why not ask a student or adult volunteer to do it? It will give him a sense of joy and significance after contributing his talent and time.

Announcements

Even your announcement time can create community if done correctly. We strive to have our announcements reflect our commitment to doing life together as a ministry, so rather than simply telling students what events are coming up, we promote it as an opportunity for us to do something together. And the more you can incorporate students and humor in the announcements, the better.

Use students during the program

Few things stifle community more than students watching adults monopolize all the up-front time. Be sure to use students in the planning process, as greeters at the door, for announcements, in skits, emceeing various aspects of the program, in the worship team, and leading in prayer. In addition to up-front responsibilities, seek to share behind-the-scenes responsibilities such as audiovisual, office help, and stage setup. These are all ways to help students feel a greater sense of community in their ministry. Being a ministry of students builds community.

Worship

Perhaps one of the greatest ways to be a spiritual community is through worshiping God. As students unite their voices together in singing, a bond takes place. And you don't need to have a band and sound system to worship God. The first section of this book describes dozens of ways to worship God in community without singing.

Interactive teaching

Community can be created or stifled based on the style of teaching. Chapter 3.2 is dedicated to getting students interacting with their Bibles, with you (the speaker), and with other students. The chapter unpacks some basic principles and practical ideas to help you speak with students—rather than to students or at students.

Response times

Why do we have our students bow their heads and close their eyes during a response time? Why do we say, "Okay, since no one else is looking around, please put up your hand quietly if you need prayer or if you want to surrender your life to Christ"? I know some of the common answers, but I don't see them in the Bible. In facilitating these private forms of response, we rob our groups of a time of being in community. We also prevent the students' responses from being supported by their communities. Recently, one of our high school pastors literally built a cross during his message. At the close he invited all the students who wanted to surrender their lives to Christ for the first time to come forward and lay hands on the cross. Dozens of students poured onto the stage. Then he invited other students to come forward to renew their commitments to deny self, take up their cross, and follow Christ. And all this was done with students' eyes wide open. It was a powerful time of community and a memory I won't soon forget.

Cast vision for community.

This is more than students verbally repeating a mission statement for your ministry. We regularly need to affirm our love for our students and dream with them about being a group of students who get beyond superficial greetings to experience the depth of community. We should be quick to talk about being authentic, loving each other, and being a group where everyone belongs. We should be talking about living in community each time we gather together—whether it's part of our welcoming at the beginning, in a comment during the worship time, as an illustration within the messages, in our prayers, or as we close our programs.

Room setup encourages or stifles community.

The more crowded a room, the greater the feel of community. You want your students sitting as closely together as possible. But don't set up lots of extra chairs—or rope off sections if you need to. If the kids have a lot of seat space between them, then they won't be as connected with other students nor as engaged with the teaching, worship, etc. If you have flexibility in your room setup, I encourage you to rearrange your room periodically. Turn the chairs to face the middle of the room instead of the front of the room. Eliminate the chairs and have students sit on the floor. Have students sit at round tables. Varying the room setup helps break up the norm and creates community.

YOU HAVE LOTS OF WAYS TO SPEND TIME TOGETHER AS A WHOLE GROUP.

Beyond the regular whole-group program, make sure you're building community through informal activities such as a summer day at an amusement park, a weekend camping trip, an overnight lock-in, a turkey bowl football game, a pool party, tailgating and games in the parking lot, spring training Wiffle ball (or kickball) tournament, popcorn and a movie night, PlayStation challenge, a ski day, paintball, fifth-quarter open house after a school's basketball game, three-on-three basketball tournaments, white-water rafting, bowling, and more. The key isn't the activity, but the intentionality of spending time together in relationship with one another.

I was taught only to do an activity if it had a purpose and if the purpose fulfilled our ministry's purpose. This is great advice. But sometimes I think we can overthink this—and avoid having fun times by adding a Bible lesson or having evangelistic expectations. Sometimes our purpose needs simply to be being together. And in being together, you're building community that's essential for your greater purpose.

You have literally thousands of ways to build community in your wholegroup. Perhaps you can adapt some of these ideas for your ministry. Or better yet, I hope these ideas have inspired you to think of other ways to create community in your ministry context.

Creating (c)ommunity > Ministry Trips

Creating community takes time. And lots of it. There's no better way to get quantity and quality time with students than on a weekend or weeklong trip. A MasterCard commercial could be made to describe the value of a ministry trip with students:

> Bus = $25
> Camp and food = $65
> T-shirt = $10
> Retreat = priceless

Think about all the ministry time you get with students on a retreat or weeklong trip. You can get an entire year of ministry time with students in a weeklong trip. The relational time is priceless.

HERE ARE SOME PRACTICAL IDEAS FOR CREATING COMMUNITY ON MINISTRY TRIPS:

On the road

Make the travel time fun. Nothing stifles community more than movies and iPods. Take the initiative to start conversations with students. Or start a game. A sure winner is playing Battle of the Sexes. Or read Would You Rather...? Tell jokes. Do tongue twisters. Play MadLibs. Bottom line: Make your travel time fun.

Mix up room placements

Did you know you can intentionally place students in rooms for retreats, camps, conferences, and ministry trips? I'm a frequent speaker at youth retreats. As I've observed other student ministries, I've often wondered if the leaders understand this universal fact. Most groups pull into the camp, and students stampede to the cabins the moment the van doors open. When students preregister for trips, it is well worth the time to place them in cabins. You can think through which students are good together and which students need to be separated for their own good and the good of the group. You can also think through which students you would like to see get to know each other better on the trip.

Hang-out time

Try not to program every minute of the day for your students. Ministry times can happen when students have free time to hang out with each other. It's good to give high school students plenty of free time, but it can be detrimental to give middle school students too much free time.

Team competitions

Few things unify a group of students better than giving them a chance to compete in some fun games together. Assign students a team color and give them the freedom to choose their team name. Give teams a piece of cloth to create a team flag or cardboard to create a team poster. Award points for team victories as well as spirit points for team cheering, participation, and enthusiasm. Make sure your games are fun and don't always highlight athletic ability. Play games that incorporate teamwork—such as relays and team challenges—more than sports events.

Cabin conversations

Never plan a ministry trip without scheduling small group time for students to share how God is at work in their lives. Don't prolong these times. Usually, 20 minutes is sufficient but necessary for helping students verbally process the trip and receive spiritual guidance in the context of community. At the end of our retreats and camps we ask our cabin leaders to turn in a form giving brief feedback on each student in their cabin. This form is helpful for two reasons. It helps our mentors reflect on each student in their cabins. And it's helpful for our pastors to have a better pulse as we seek to intentionally shepherd individual students.

Walks and talks

We periodically send students out of the meeting room in pairs for 10-minute walks. We encourage students to walk in one direction for five minutes then turn around and walk back. As they're walking out, one student is to share with the other what God is teaching them during the trip. On the walk back the other student shares. Some students blow off this time, but more than half really do what we ask them to.

It's worth doing for those who do take advantage of it. Or rather than sitting in folding chairs in a room, we encourage small groups to go for a 20-minute walk—they can keep walking or stop somewhere in the woods to talk.

Mealtimes

If you take the time to be intentional, you have many ways to create community during your mealtimes: Simple things such as categories for creating an order for getting in line, random seating assignments, topical sharing at the tables, guys serving the girls their meals, and more. All these things can help make the mealtime fun while getting students interacting with each other.

Beyond "Kumbayah"

You can unite your group as a spiritual community by providing a time of spontaneous sharing and singing. The natural inclination is to do this around a bonfire. Certainly campfires can be good settings, but there are other contexts, too. We've had our final session at our summer camp on the beach with the sun setting in the background. You can encourage a time of sharing in a candlelit meeting room. You can sit in a big circle on a field or on the side of a hill. Some of the most memorable times of spiritual community are when students have a chance to share verbally their commitments to Christ.

We have a small vegetable garden in our backyard. I cannot make our tomatoes grow. But I can provide an environment so that the combination of soil, water, air, and sunlight can help the vegetables grow. Similarly, while you cannot make students grow spiritually, you can provide environments that nurture growth. And supporting your ministry environment with community is essential for nurturing their spiritual growth. Students won't stick around long if they don't feel a sense of community.

moving forward > questions

Questions for personal reflection and team discussion:

1. What are some of your fondest moments of community with your group? What made those times so special?

2. What are some of the challenges you're facing in experiencing community in your ministry programs?

3. How effective are your model and format for small groups in your ministry setting? Describe.

4. How can you be more intentional with community in your whole-group times?

5. What are some ways you can cast the vision for community to your group?

6. What are three practical things you can do to be more effective in creating community in your ministry?

7. What aspects of this chapter do you want to discuss with others on your leadership team?

Jesus' life was about connecting the disconnected.

God the Son came to Planet Earth so he could connect us with his Father after we were disconnected as a result of our disobedience. His mission was clear. The Son came to seek and save the lost. In other words, Jesus came to connect the disconnected.

Jesus modeled the importance of caring for the disconnected. Think of the people Jesus chose to hang around. He didn't hang out just with the popular, the outgoing, and the wealthy. Jesus didn't hang out just with those who were natural leaders with the most potential to make his ministry better. The Gospels tell story after story of Jesus hanging out with the disenfranchised and those rejected by society. Jesus was intentional about connecting with the lepers, widows, tax collectors, adulterers, prostitutes, and sinners. Jesus sought out the misfits, the distant, the proud, and the downcast. No doubt some of these individuals gave Jesus attitude and made it hard for him to love them. Yet Jesus pursued them. He didn't wait for them to open up to him. Instead Jesus went after them because he genuinely cared for them. Can you think of any students in your church who seem to be misfits or distant or proud or downcast?

Probably one of the most well-known examples of this is found in Luke 19. The crowds flocked to Jesus as he passed through Jericho. Yet Jesus noticed a wee little man who had climbed up to a balcony seat in a sycamore tree. Jesus didn't just give Zacchaeus a head nod and move on. Jesus stopped and talked to him. Jesus showed a genuine interest in him. Not only did Jesus speak with Zac, but Jesus also invited him down from the tree so they could hang out together. And Jesus chose to hang out on Zac's turf.

Jesus also told the parable of a shepherd with one lost sheep. Even though the shepherd had 99 sheep safe in the sheepfold, he was aware one of the sheep wasn't with the flock. And he wasn't content with this reality. In an act of compassion he left the herd momentarily to go after the one that wasn't with them.

These examples should cause us to pause. Are you content having students in your church who are disconnected from your student ministry? Have you even noticed these students? Or do you only see the 99 connected to your group? Are you guilty of only noticing the crowd of students who flock to you as their leader? Do you only hang with students already connected in your ministry and neglect the student who's up in the balcony, curiously wondering if you'll take an interest in him or questioning whether or not he'll find a place to belong in your group? Is your heart stirred with genuine compassion for students who are misfits or distant or proud or downcast? Or are you turned off by these kinds of students?

Jesus was about connecting the disconnected. And we should be about connecting the disconnected, too. Think about it this way: If you're not connecting the disconnected students, who will?

We have two of types of disconnected students *within* our church walls. Some are disconnected and want to be connected. Others are disconnected and like it that way. Regardless, we're called to faithfully care for and seek to connect the disconnected.

Welcoming New Students

Do you have a plan for welcoming and assimilating students who are new to your group?

I recently visited a church on a Sunday morning while vacationing out of state. The experience of being a visitor reminded me how it feels to enter an unknown place. Consider the anxiety many students feel as they come to your group for the first time. Students are thinking: Do I know where to go? Will I know anyone? Will anyone notice me? Will it be fun? But the number one thing students are thinking is—can you guess it? Will I be accepted?

We've identified seven points of connection for new students:

1. Students greeted (as they enter the building)—new students are identified and receive Frisbees. If a student is alone, we try to connect him with students from his school.

2. Up-front welcome—we think visitors rock! We don't always have visitors stand, but we always publicly greet them.

3. Small group—get students connected with a small group of students and collect contact information.

4. Mail handwritten note from pastor along with a series schedule and some candy. (It's easy to throw in a stick of gum, Airhead, or Twizzler into the envelope—and it's more exciting for the student than just a note.)

5. Small group mentor calls within 48 hours.

6. A student in the small group or on student ministry team calls within the week.

7. Do a Facebook or email follow-up after a week.

This is our plan. It's not rocket science. And we have many other ways to follow up with students. The key is to have a plan and be faithful to it.

Have you identified your plan? If so:

- can your adult volunteers articulate the plan?
- do your leadership students know the plan?

- do you follow through with the plan...or is its application inconsistent?

Assimilating Weekend Worship Service Students

Another group of disconnected students are those who come to weekend worship services but aren't connected with the student ministry. And each church has plenty of these students. Some students are dragged to church by their parents when they don't want to come. But many are godly students who live a distance from the church, are naturally shy, or are just busy with other activities. Although we can't persuade all students to get involved, it's important not to ignore these students.

Call out of a service—we periodically "call out" students from the weekend worship service. Our senior pastor has all middle school and high school students stand after the worship time and before the beginning of his message. He verbally affirms the students and parents of our deep commitment as a church to help this young generation of students passionately follow Jesus. Then he releases them to designated rooms where our student leaders and adult mentors are ready to welcome them with doughnuts. It's a cool thing for the church body to see this young generation of students among them. This gives us 45 premium minutes with all our students—especially those whom we haven't met or seen in a while yet who attend a weekend worship service.

We utilize this time to get to know them, play a game together, take their pictures, collect information, share about upcoming ministry events, and get them interacting with other students. We usually choose to do the "call out" on a weekend in January because it is the start of the second semester and our winter retreats are in February—both great times for the disconnected to get connected.

Call using a phone—one of our priorities is to seek to call each of these students during the year just to make contact with them. Our intention isn't to lay a guilt trip on them. I've never found harassing a student into coming to our student ministry to work. So when we call, we simply want to express our caring. We talk about their interests and activities. And we listen. Then we say something such as, "Hey! Because we care about you, we want to let you know what's going on, and we miss you when you aren't around."

It takes time and effort to call students, but the payoff is huge when a student truly feels cared for regardless of whether she comes to our student ministry events. If we get voicemail, we'll leave a message. Many times parents call back thanking us for seeking to connect their teenagers. I know a student ministry pastor so committed to this form of personal contact that he calls every student in his ministry's database a few weeks before his annual winter retreat. Does it surprise you that many students sign up after receiving a personal phone call?

Pursuing MIA Students

Students long to belong. They long to be noticed—when they're present and when they're absent. Do you have a system for tracking students' participation? This is different from counting heads. I've noticed it's possible to have the same total attendance numbers, but 50 percent might be different from the week before. If we're going to be faithful in shepherding the flock God has entrusted to us, we need to pay attention to individual sheep.

We have small group attendance sheets we complete after each ministry gathering. Our small group mentors indicate three things weekly: Attendance, reason for not being there, and method of contact. Beyond just checking off whether a student was present, our mentors use the following codes:

Contact Codes
- FB: Facebook
- IP: In person
- E: Email
- T: Text
- HW: Handwritten
- P: Phone

Reasons for Missing
- HW: Homework
- OT: Out of town
- W: Work
- F: Family
- L: Lame
- S: Sports

moving forward > by looking back

Having this additional weekly data has helped us better care for individual students and has been a good accountability check with our mentors.

If a student is missing, write a quick note on a card as part of small group time. Each month these attendance sheets are analyzed, and students are followed up with accordingly. Along with the pastor or small group mentor, we mobilize our ministry team students to help pursue MIA students. We realize we can't get all the students involved, but we can fail trying.

Even though we don't want to neglect MIA students, we must remind ourselves not to be too focused on who's *not* there—and miss out on ministering to students who *are* there.

Transitioning Grades

Kevin Johnston, the middle school pastor at Saddleback, jests with his eighth-graders that when they transition to high school, they go from being "top dog on a silver platter to a booger on a paper plate." And he's got some point, right? It's critical for student ministries to build community while transitioning students from grade to grade—especially when entering middle school, high school, and college. Harvest Students is one ministry to three age groups—middle school, high school, college. Each age group meets separately, but we work hard at being a unified ministry—including cooperating together during those critical transition years. Rather than being possessive, we seek to keep what's best for students in mind.

We transition our students in all three of these ministries at the start of the summer. A June transition is important for students to build new relationships over the summer—especially at summer camp and on other ministry trips. But we also do several intentional things during the school year to help with the coming transition:

> Our pastors rotate to other age group ministries to teach periodically (e.g., the high school pastor will teach middle school).

> Our eighth-graders are invited to join the high school spring break work trip to begin building relationships before the official transition.

> Our college staff joins the senior trip team during spring break.

> We combine our middle school and high school ministries periodically during the school year.

In early June, we provide welcome parties (one for new sixth-graders and one for new freshmen) to give these students a connection with their new pastors and adult mentors. Student leaders are also there, gladly welcoming these new students into the ministry.

In late August we offer a sixth-grade and parent welcome night and ice cream party. And we do the same for our freshmen and their parents. The welcome parties happen on the same night but in different rooms within the church.

When I was serving at Elmbrook Church, we offered a freshman-only Colorado adventure trip at the beginning of August. The road trip and week of outdoor activities with each other provided an incredible bonding time. You may not be able to pull off a trip to Colorado with your freshmen, but maybe you could do a weeklong canoe trip, a weekend camping trip, or a sleepover at the church. Or host a "Freshmen Fall Fest" with outdoor games and a hot dog roast. There are many benefits of having an extended activity with a group of students coming into the ministry.

Some youth ministries offer a big brother-big sister type program where each freshman student is adopted by an upperclassman student. Some do a freshman initiation. For many years I recruited some adults and students to join me in kidnapping freshmen from their beds at 6 a.m. (all this with prior parental permission). Initiations can be tons of fun for all involved if they're carried out in the right spirit. You need to make sure it's fun for all involved and avoid poking fun at or humiliating students. Otherwise an event such as this can backfire big-time.

My experience has shown that if students aren't connected (yes, connected—not attending once or twice) by the end of October, we'll have a very difficult time ever getting them connected later.

Ministry to Seniors

Have you ever grown weary of the senior "been there–done that" attitude?

I used to get so ticked at students with this attitude. For years I blamed them for being prideful and having bad attitudes. One day the Spirit convicted me: Actually, I was prideful and had a bad attitude. Rather than blaming the seniors, I began to take responsibility for making it easy for seniors to feel this way. A dose of humility helped me see I was fostering a been there–done that mentality by not making the senior-year experience unique. Honestly, if I were a senior, and my fourth year in the ministry was the same as my first three years, I'd be bored, too. I still get weary of this attitude, but I'm committed to making a student's senior year unique. If we don't make changes and truly challenge seniors with greater responsibilities, it won't be long before they're disconnected from the ministry.

Our student ministries should provide seniors with special opportunities to keep them engaged in the high school ministry, such as—

> *Host a senior barbecue, pizza party, or breakfast.* I've discovered it's critical to gather seniors together at the start of the school year and periodically throughout the year. Providing some food and a time for casual interaction draws the seniors together. Then we challenge students to seize the school year for God—and not just live to be in college. I believe one of the main reasons seniors tune out in many areas of life during their senior years is because they fail to live for the days God still has for them in high school. We encourage our seniors to write themselves letters of commitment about their senior years and the legacies they want to leave, seal the letters in envelopes, and write their addresses on the envelopes. We mail these self-addressed letters to the seniors in early winter as accountability reminders of their commitments at the start of their senior year.

> *Offer a senior fall retreat.* Some ministries get their senior class together in the fall to unite them during a weekend at the church or away at a camp.

> *Allow the seniors to plan the theme and elements of your winter retreat.* A great tradition you can begin is to allow the seniors to plan many elements for your annual winter retreat. It's cool to see students rise to the challenge if you give them a bar to jump over. Think about the ownership seniors will feel if they can help choose the theme of the retreat, select T-shirt colors, create promotional videos, plan program elements, serve as emcees, provide special music at the retreat, and even teach elective workshops (if your retreat format allows for this element). Giving seniors some responsibilities with an event such as this will keep them engaged for many months. *Warning:* This can create tension among seniors who have conflicting ideas and personalities. But even the tension can create wonderful teachable moments in a protective environment. Most students don't learn how to handle conflict in healthy ways while in high school. We should be looking for opportunities to help students deal with conflict and work toward resolution in positive ways while they're still in high school.

> *Encourage mature seniors to assist in leading small groups.* One of our goals for students graduating from Harvest is to be able to lead a Bible study in their dorm starting their freshman year in college. If students are going to be able to do this when they get to college, they need to be trained and given some experience in this during their senior year in high school. If you don't have student-led small groups in your high school ministry, perhaps some seniors could become small group leaders in your middle school ministry.

> *Offer some seniors up-front time during programs.* Students should never have up-front responsibilities just because they're seniors, but it's healthy for the ministry and the seniors to allow some seniors to have up-front leadership with announcements, welcome times, praying, and sharing testimonies.

> *Provide a senior study.* If you have the time and resources, I recommend you offer a four- to six-week seniors-only gathering to solidify convictions before graduation. This can be offered in successive weeks in the fall or spring or once a month through-

moving forward > by looking back

out the duration of the school year on a Saturday night in the leader's home. Possible topics could include leaving a legacy, knowing God's will, friendship to fellowship, handling conflict, money management, reading the Bible contemplatively, sharing your faith with grace and truth, etc. These are some of the topics I really want our seniors to grasp before they graduate.

> *Provide a spring-break senior trip.* I believe the most significant event we offer is a spring break senior trip to Florida to celebrate the kids' years in high school and prepare them for life after high school. I heard this statistic once: Three out of four churched students walk away from their faith within 18 months of high school graduation. I don't want this to be true of the students I minister to. This trip encourages discovery-oriented learning, group presentations, times of solitude for reflection, small groups to process life, and tons of fun on the beach.

> *Seniors speak out.* Dedicate the last night of your ministry year to allowing seniors to share with the underclassmen about favorite memories and advice they want to leave with them.

> *Celebrate with seniors program.* We honor our graduating seniors with a special program in May. Parents of seniors and underclassmen are invited to attend. The program includes video highlights, a photo slide show (baby, childhood, and senior pictures of each graduate), special music by a senior, male and female senior addresses (à la valedictorian speech), and brief comments about each senior as he comes forward to receive a gift from his small group mentor. Of course, we offer graduation cake and ice cream afterward. I know a ministry that has a similar format on a Saturday morning with a catered brunch.

Finally, we believe it's critical to transition our seniors into our college summer break at Harvest program immediately after graduation in June—before they go away to college. This is an important value for us for a number of reasons. First, we want our college pastor and college leaders to make a connection with these students before they go away to college. It's hard to care for college freshmen who are at a campus out of town if they never made a personal connection over the summer. Second, we want our graduating seniors to have something to look forward to when they return home on breaks and in subsequent summers. It's much easier for away students to get connected with the home ministry if they made the connection before leaving for college. Last, we want our high school ministry to begin bonding as a ministry over the summer, giving younger students an opportunity to assume leadership roles vacated by the seniors before the start of the school year.

These are just some ideas. Obviously, you can't do them all. Perhaps picking a few you can do will help retain your seniors and better prepare them to live for Christ after high school—after all, isn't developing lifelong followers of Jesus Christ really what ministry is all about?

In *Field of Dreams*, a farmer becomes convinced by a mysterious voice that he's supposed to construct a baseball diamond in his Iowa cornfield. The voice whispers, "If you build it, he will come." The farmer goes to work on the baseball diamond despite the heckling townspeople. One day several deceased players from the 1919 Chicago White Stockings—including Shoeless Joe Jackson—show up at the diamond to play baseball.

If only student ministry were this easy.

Let's not be deceived by the mentality that if you...

...build a student center

...plan a cool program

...develop a student band

...or mail full-color brochures that they will come.

If you want to connect disconnected students, it requires the work of intentional contacting and pursuit. And not just by the adult leaders, but by connected students as well. Students don't run to where the action is, but they run to where the love is.

moving forward > by looking back

moving forward > questions

Questions for personal reflection and team discussion:

1. What kinds of students are disconnected in your church? Who are some students that come to your mind?

2. Do you have a plan for assimilating new students into your ministry? If so, is it working or are there ways for you to improve it?

3. How do you transition new classes of students into your middle school, high school, and college ministries? Do you see ways to improve these transitions?

4. What can you do to help your seniors not have a been there–done that mentality?

5. What are three practical things you can do to be more effective in connecting the disconnected?

6. What aspects of this chapter do you want to discuss with others on your leadership team?

(t)ruth

engaging students with
God's Word

3.0 LOOKING BACK
@ (t)ruth

Dan was weary as a youth pastor.

He had served faithfully at his church for more than six years and was well liked by the students, parents, and adult volunteers. Even his senior pastor and the elders appreciated his ministry at the church. The youth group had a solid 75 students and a good reputation at the local high school and in the community. However, Dan was questioning his effectiveness in ministry.

Dan was growing weary because he was sensing his weekly messages weren't making any difference in the lives of his students. Students were restless, and they seemed bored by it all. The students weren't bringing their Bibles to youth group, and they seemed to tune him out every time he said, "Turn in your Bibles to _____."

Feeling defeated as he drove home on a Wednesday, he sensed something needed to change. He thought, "If I can't beat them, I'll join them."

The following weeks Dan sought to teach biblical principles without letting the students know what he was doing. Holding a Bible in his hand seemed to be a barrier, so he began to teach only from his typed notes. He shared biblical stories without referencing the Bible. Sometimes he changed the details to create more modern-day stories. He taught the Bible but in a way so the students didn't feel as if they were being taught the Bible. Although students seemed to enjoy this new approach to teaching, Dan still felt as if his messages lacked power.

While shopping for some CDs at his local Christian store, Dan discovered a few books filled with funny stories and creative illustrations for student ministry talks. He began to incorporate these ideas into messages. This helped capture the students' attention, but only momentarily.

So rather than using the illustrations to supplement the messages, the next few weeks Dan tried to build a few messages around a gripping illustration, object lesson, or movie clip. Even though the students were paying attention a bit more, he still didn't sense the messages were impacting students.

Before their annual Christmas party Dan surveyed his students about which topics they wanted to go through during the second semester. The written survey was very helpful as it revealed two topics almost every student voted for: sex and the end times. No other topic got more than a handful of votes.

Dan started the second semester with a series on love, sex, and dating. However, he got a response from the students he wasn't expecting. The content for the series was solid, and the illustrations were creative. But it was as if they already knew what he was sharing with them. They already knew that sex outside of marriage is wrong, that the biblical standard is more than virginity—it's purity, and to respect yourself and your date. As the series ended, he wondered why they'd picked the topic if they'd heard it all before.

The latest *Mission: Impossible* movie was being released in theaters that spring. Because Dan was hesitant to teach on the end times to begin with, he thought, "I should capitalize on the popularity of this movie theme. The logo is cool. We can use the soundtrack. And we can do some *Mission: Impossible*-type activities around the church. I think this theme has a lot of potential and can really work. Surely, I can figure out a teaching series based on this theme. I should begin looking in my Bible to find some passages to use." The series had a sweet promotional campaign, including a video, banners, and a color mailer. It was the most creative and planned series he'd ever done with his students. The students responded well to the thematic elements and activities. Yet Dan didn't think the students were any more transformed by the teaching in this series than they had been in any of the earlier series.

The school year ended, and Dan had poured his life into the ministry throughout the school year—but where was the fruit? Dan had spent many hours each week preparing messages for the students, but they seemed to be empty. Something still seemed missing.

And Dan was still weary as a youth pastor.

Have you ever felt like Dan? If you were a friend of Dan's, and he asked you for advice, what would you share with him?

(t)ruth in Acts

The first characteristic mentioned in the description of the church in Acts 2:42 is their devotion to the apostles' teaching. A defining characteristic of a student ministry transformed by God is its commitment to truth—that is, engaging students with God's Word.

Obviously, the Bible as we know it didn't exist in the first century. Therefore, if the early church was devoted to the apostles' teaching, what were the apostles teaching?

For one thing, the apostles were teaching the Old Testament. In Peter's first sermon in Acts 2 he quoted the Old Testament over and over again. Acts ends with these words about Paul: "From morning till evening he explained and declared to them the kingdom of God and tried to convince them about Jesus from the Law of Moses and from the Prophets" (Acts 28:23). The apostles' teaching clearly included the Old Testament.

The apostles' teaching also included aspects of the Gospels—namely the gospel message itself. They were continually bearing witness to the life, death, and resurrection of Jesus. The apostles must've been teaching the things Jesus had taught them. Remember what Jesus commissioned them to do? He said, "Therefore, go and make disciples...teaching them to obey everything I have commanded you" (Matthew 28:19-20).

moving forward > by looking back

The apostles were the same guys who wrote the Gospels and some of the epistles. It stands to reason they were probably teaching at least some of the same stuff that became part of the New Testament. So when we put all this together—the Old Testament, the Gospels, and the epistles—what do we have? In essence...the Bible. That's what the apostles were teaching. The early church was devoted to God's Word. We, too, must be devoted to God's Word.

The hunger for truth was an everyday norm for the early church. "Day after day, in the temple courts and from house to house, they never stopped teaching and proclaiming the good news that Jesus is the Christ" (Acts 5:42). The Word was central in their personal lives and their gatherings both in the temple and in their homes. Understanding the context of this verse is crucial, too. This is the last verse in a chapter detailing the intense opposition against the believers. The Jewish religious leaders were so enraged, they rose up to kill the believers. But fearing that martyring them might actually advance their cause—or worse yet, find the Jewish leaders opposing God—they decided *only* to beat the apostles to bloody pulps and ordered them no longer to proclaim the truth of Christ. Then they let the apostles go.

So let me ask you a question: What would you do if the Supreme Court ordered you not to teach about Jesus?

The religious leaders may as well have ordered the sun not to shine when they ordered the apostles not to proclaim the truth of Christ—because neither was going to happen. The apostles left their time of beating "rejoicing because they had been counted worthy of suffering disgrace for the Name" (Acts 5:41). Even more unbelievable than being enthusiastic about their sufferings, they "never stopped teaching and proclaiming the good news that Jesus is the Messiah" every day in the temple and from house to house (v. 42). God's truth was so transforming, the apostles were deeply convicted they must teach the truth no matter the cost. It was part of their DNA. Furthermore, I think it's safe to assume they taught with passionate conviction. What about you? Do you have a conviction that you *must* teach God's Word? And if so, do you teach with passionate conviction?

Although this is the end of Acts 5, the story continues in chapter 6.

Their convictions about the centrality of teaching God's Word led the disciples to restructure their ministry. Overwhelmed with the ongoing demands of ministry, they had a leadership team meeting. One of the apostles spoke up: "It would not be right for us to neglect the ministry of the word of God in order to wait on tables" (v. 2). The demands of ministry were so great that the apostles realized they were neglecting to care for some of the needs of the whole group of believers—particularly the needs of the widows. They were at a critical crossroads as a team. If they cared for all the physical and relational needs of their growing community, they'd neglect the teaching of the Word. But if they continued to teach the Word, they'd be neglecting the needs of people.

Ever feel this way in student ministry? I know I've struggled with this tension for years—and continue to. If I care for all the students' needs and organizational responsibilities of the ministry, then my teaching ministry takes a backseat and suffers due to a lack of adequate preparation. But if I devote all my energies to preparing to teach and writing small group lesson plans, then I'll have to neglect many important student needs and organizational responsibilities. Can you identify? What do you do?

TEAMWORK IN ACTS

The disciples faced a dilemma that continues in most student ministries today. Because they truly cared for people, they enlisted others to help as part of their ministry team. They didn't just take anyone who volunteered, but they looked for those who were "known to be full of the Spirit and wisdom" (Acts 6:3).

The apostles realized they couldn't do it all, so they looked for God's provision. Adding more people to their ministry team enabled them to devote themselves primarily to "prayer and the ministry of the word" (Acts 6:4).

It isn't as if they didn't care for people. In fact, quite the opposite. Perhaps the most caring thing you can do is *not* care for the needs of every student in your ministry. Rather, the most caring thing you can do is raise up others to help care for the needs of students. It isn't healthy for you to meet the needs of everyone in your group—

moving forward > by looking back

Enlisting Volunteers

Not everyone who volunteers to serve in youth ministry should be a volunteer in youth ministry. Quite the opposite: Our volunteers should be subject to the same criteria the apostles had for selecting ministry partners. They went after ("chose") people they knew ("from among you who are known") who were godly ("full of the Spirit and wisdom"). The best way to enlist volunteers isn't through the bulletin or a platform announcement; instead you should choose people and invite them to serve. But regardless of how well you may know someone, I recommend having a paper application, a face-to-face interview, a background check, and a trial period to observe (this benefits both the potential volunteer and the ministry). Not only should our volunteers be energetic, dynamic, and fun, but it's imperative to select godly individuals who will live like Jesus, lead like Jesus, and love like Jesus. The people we choose as volunteers must be able to say the words of the apostle Paul to the teenagers they lead: "Follow my example, as I follow the example of Christ" (1 Corinthians 11:1).

regardless of whether your group is small or large. It's not good for you or the students if they're solely dependent on you. A student ministry transformed by God doesn't revolve around one leader—but the leader gladly shares significant ministry with others.

The disciples raised up others to care for the physical and relational needs of people so they could devote their attention to prayer and the teaching of the Word. If you're the youth pastor or youth leader, you're called to lead spiritually. The apostles didn't give away the primary teaching to others. And neither should you. Too many youth pastors just want to be cool, hang out, plan fun events, and perfect their video gaming skills. This isn't biblical.

You need to be devoted to the Word and develop as a teacher of God's Word. It's great if you can be cool, hang out with students, and plan great events, but never neglect the ministry of the Word of God. That said, you don't need to be the only one teaching the students, either. Too many youth pastors and lead youth workers monopolize all the speaking—each Sunday school lesson, every youth group night, all the outreach events, and every retreat. I'm amazed at how many of my volunteers are gifted teachers of God's Word when given the opportunity.

I've learned over the years I need to devote myself to building relationships with students, organizing the ministry, and teaching the

Word. But I can't do all three of these things equally well in the same season. Therefore, I'm willing to share teaching times so I have time and energy to focus on other things. If it's a more demanding teaching season, my volunteers and staff know my dependence on them to care for the students' and organizational needs.

The resolution to the apostles' dilemma reflects the power of multiplication and a direct application of their disciple-making mission. After listing the names of the rookie ministry partners, the text details the outcome of their critical decision: "So the word of God spread. The number of disciples in Jerusalem increased rapidly, and a large number of priests became obedient to the faith" (Acts 6:7). Amazing. They didn't compromise their commitment to the truth, and God transformed lives—the number of followers of Christ was growing. Even some from the in-charge group of Jewish priests most opposed to the believers embraced a genuine faith in Christ.

Make a note of this: As they were faithful to the Word, they were fruitful in ministry. Throughout the book of Acts we see this connection. Acts 12:24 says, "the word of God continued to increase and spread." This was the standard for church growth in the early church—more of the Word of God, more people impacted.

Could it be that in the midst of the busyness and the business of ministry we've neglected the ministry of the Word of God with students?

A Biblical Theology of (t)ruth

Ever get frustrated when someone finishes your sentences? I do. But I'm going to give you permission to finish my next sentence.

God loved us and gave us his _____.

How did you finish the sentence? You are probably in the company of the vast majority of readers if you said, "Son." This is true: God loved us and gave us his Son. But this is equally true: God loved us and gave us his Word. Unfortunately, most people think of God's love only being demonstrated in the giving of his Son, not his Word. God reveals himself through the Word (Jesus, the Son) and the Word (the Bible). The Bible is a letter of love to us and a gift of love for us.

Many student ministry leaders (especially volunteers) haven't had formal Bible college or seminary training. If you're among those who have, perhaps the next couple of pages will be a helpful review for you. Most theological studies begin with bibliology, the doctrine of the Bible. Let's consider this Bibliology 101 three-point outline:

I.   The Word of God is authoritative.

II. The Word of God is sufficient.

III. The Word of God is effective.

THE WORD OF GOD IS AUTHORITATIVE.

All Scripture is God-breathed and is useful for teaching, rebuking, correcting and training in righteousness. (2 Timothy 3:16)

The Word of God consists of the words of God. This is what we mean when we speak of the authority of Scripture.

All Scripture is God-breathed—or inspired by God. Therefore, the Bible is our ultimate authority and standard of truth. And because it's authoritative, we can proclaim truth without apology. It's not because we're arrogant but because God's truth is authoritative. I've learned to begin my messages by telling students: "I don't know much. However, I do know God speaks through his Word. So open your Bibles to..." The authority doesn't come because of my education or my position or title. The authority comes from God because the Scriptures are God's divinely inspired letter to humanity.

In John 17:17, Jesus prayed, "Sanctify them by the truth; your word is *truth*." Notice, Jesus didn't say, "Your word is true." Instead of using an adjective, Jesus used a noun form: "Your word is truth." God's Word isn't simply true but is truth itself. It's not true because it conforms to a higher standard of truth. The Bible itself is the final standard of truth.

This truth stands in contrast to postmodern culture, which embraces a pluralistic view: Everyone is entitled to have his own perspective of truth, and it's just as valid as everyone else's perspective. According to pluralism, we can't know absolute truth—we can only have our own perspective. This, of course, is contrary to biblical teaching and presents challenges in student ministry today.

Because the Bible is inspired by God and thus authoritative, it's profitable for at least four things—teaching, reproof, correction, and training. When I teach this passage to sixth-grade students, I liken the Word of God to being on a road. While moving both of my arms in unison up and down I create an invisible road. I tell students that the Word of God *teaches* you what the right road in life is, *warns* you when you veer off the right road, *corrects* you by getting you back on the right road, and *trains* you on how to stay on the right road. This is the meaning of teaching, reproof, correction, and training. It is amazing how memorable this illustration is for middle schoolers. I've had some students show me the motions while remembering the four benefits years after I first taught them.

THE WORD OF GOD IS SUFFICIENT.

All Scripture is God-breathed and is useful for teaching, rebuking, correcting and training in righteousness, so that the man of God may be thoroughly equipped for every good work. (2 Timothy 3:16-17)

The Word of God is sufficient for our spiritual growth, enabling us to be *fully* equipped for a life of godliness and goodness.

The Bible doesn't contain everything about God. Yet it sufficiently reveals God to us. Theologian Wayne Grudem writes, "The sufficiency of Scripture means that Scripture contained all the words of God he intended his people to have at each stage of redemptive history, and that it now contains everything we need God to tell us for salvation, for trusting him perfectly, and for obeying him perfectly."[1] The Word of God sufficiently communicates God's character, explains the gospel, teaches God's moral will, and equips us to live the Christian life.

When we speak of the Word of God being sufficient, we affirm that God didn't leave anything out he wanted us to know. It's not as if God's in heaven saying, "Oops! I forgot to add this or that." Therefore, we must not add to the Bible—including extra legalistic requirements for spirituality or additional prohibitions not addressed in the Bible. Further, we aren't to consider other writings as of equal value to the Scriptures. We need to be careful not to add to the Scriptures by considering other, modern best-selling books at Barnes & Noble as truth.

In writing to youth leaders about engaging the soul of the youth culture, Walt Mueller states—

> It's not surprising that similar books that redefine spiritual truth, God, and humanity—including books by Deepak Chopra and *The Da Vinci Code* to name a few—are all finding their way to the top of the bestseller lists and into the collective spiritually hungry heart and mind of our culture. With this type of thinking, believing, and living increasingly serving as the worldview foundation of the emerging generations, how can we steer them in the right direction? It starts with our commitment to live in that direction ourselves by being a student of the resurrected, living, reigning, and written Word."[2]

THE WORD OF GOD IS EFFECTIVE.

For the word of God is living and active. Sharper than any double-edged sword, it penetrates even to dividing soul and spirit, joints and marrow; it judges the thoughts and attitudes of the heart. (Hebrews 4:12)

Our God *is* living and active. Therefore, it shouldn't surprise us that God's Word is living and active. The Bible isn't an old, lifeless book. The Word is powerful and effective. The writer of Hebrews uses the same word for sword as found when speaking of our spiritual armor in Ephesians 6:17. Like a sword, it's able to penetrate even our minds and hearts. It has the power to convict and transform lives.

The Word of God *is* effective. Let's not fool ourselves into thinking we make the Word effective because of our clever illustrations, funny stories, movie clips, or creative outlines. The power isn't in our words. The power is in *the* Word. The Word of God has supernatural power. Therefore, we must keep the Word central in our teaching—including in our discipleship small groups and outreach events.

When we're committed to communicating God's Word, we allow

God's Spirit to speak to students. And as our living and active God speaks, lives are changed. As God's Word is proclaimed, God transforms lives.

I've never understood student ministries that are hesitant to teach God's Word. If we desire God's transforming work in student ministry, the Bible must be central in our teaching. The Word of God is effective—it's been effective and is still effective today. If you want to be fruitful in ministry, be faithful to the Word.

Do these biblical truths reflect your theological convictions? If so, do your theological convictions guide your leadership and your student ministry?

It's one thing to believe these truths in the classroom, but something else altogether to practice your theology in student ministry. It's one thing to read these points in this book and nod your head in agreement, but a whole other thing to allow these truths to shape your approach to teaching God's truth to students.

> *Do you believe the Bible is authoritative?* Or are you hesitant to proclaim truth because you think you're being arrogant?

> *Do you believe the Bible is sufficient?* Or do you feel like you need to adjust the Scriptures by changing or adding to them or cutting out certain parts?

> *Do you believe the Bible is effective?* Or do you feel your own insights or creative illustrations or movie clips or the latest discipleship curriculum is more effective in transforming students?

At Harvest Students we strive to teach God's truth clearly to students. We've discovered when we're faithful to communicate the Word, God is at work. God empowers the teaching. God transforms lives.

Imparting a Passion

I'm deeply concerned that the role of the Bible is being minimized in many student ministries. I like to think this isn't happening intentionally, but its reality is apparent. We need to return to the centrality and priority of God's Word in our ministries and in our teaching.

A friend of mine encouraged me to order a CD message John Piper delivered to a group of youth leaders. As I listened, I was gripped by Piper's conviction. His introduction to the message wasn't a humorous story to engage the audience. Rather he started with these sobering words:

> When your present generation of students graduates and leaves your group or when you leave the group you've been ministering to, will you be able to say what the apostle Paul says in Acts 20:26-27: "Therefore I testify to you this day that I am innocent of the blood of all of you, for I did not shrink from declaring to you the whole counsel of God"? (ESV)

He continued his passionate plea:

> Have you even set a tone where a statement like that could be heard with any seriousness? Would that sound so strange coming out of your mouth, that "I am innocent of your blood, young people"? Would that sound so strange to them given how you've ministered to them that you wouldn't even dare say such a thing because it would sound so screwy in their heads? Let alone be true because you've devoted yourself for three years or six years to delivering the whole counsel of God to them? So that's my challenge to you—that you would go home and develop a two-, three-, four-, six-year plan to impart to your students the whole counsel of God so that when they graduate and at the banquet of the send-off, you might say to them with all earnestness that "your blood is not on my hands."[3]

As student ministry leaders we have a responsibility to teach our students the whole counsel of God—not just feel-good, give-them-what-they-want-to-hear topics.

Some student ministry leaders advocate implementing a teaching strategy of repeating a small number of topical themes year after year. The themes are essential for students to know and embrace as they grow as followers of Jesus. And I understand the rationale of repetition for emphasis and retention. But I'm concerned with reducing the Scriptures to a half-dozen or so memorable phrases and principles. What about teaching students "the Word of God in its fullness" (Colossians 1:25)?

I'm convicted that if we're committed to teaching the whole of the Bible first and foremost, the repetition of major themes relevant to students and the teenage years will be a natural result. The Word of God is amazingly sufficient and effective. It has been for the past 2,000 years and continues to be today.

Our high school ministry recently completed a four-part series in Genesis based on the life of Joseph. Consider these topics addressed in our "Not Your Average Joe" series: Sibling rivalry, family relationships, why bad things happen to good people, temptation, purity, living for God (even when no one is looking), when others wrong you, bitterness, forgiveness, trusting God, and more. And these were the main themes. Most of the major themes for teenagers will naturally repeat themselves in many books of the Bible, too. We just need to have a conviction to let God speak for himself through the Bible.

Imagine If...

Imagine if we were to renew our commitments to devote ourselves to prayer and the ministry of the Word. Imagine if we were to renew our commitments to teach Jesus as the Christ with the conviction that Jesus is the Christ. Imagine if we were less dependent on the power of an illustration and more dependent on the power of God. Imagine if we were more concerned with telling our students what God wants to say than what our students want to hear. Imagine if we were committed to present the Word of God in its fullness instead of just the

moving forward > by looking back

appealing parts of the Bible. Imagine if our seniors upon graduating were truly grounded in the Word and had convictions about truth. Imagine if we were to share in the same conviction of the apostles and say, "It would not be right for us to neglect the ministry of the word of God" (Acts 6:2). Imagine if the Word of God were to increase in our lives and in our students' lives.

Would our ministries be any different? Might we see God transforming lives?

moving forward > questions

Questions for personal reflection and team discussion:

1. In what ways could you identify with Dan's experience in the introduction? What advice would you give Dan?

2. How would you describe the role of truth with the early believers in the book of Acts?

3. Have you ever felt the tension between responsibilities to teach the Bible, care for students, and organize the ministry? Describe.

4. What are the ministry implications of the Bible being authoritative, sufficient, and effective?

5. What are your thoughts about John Piper's passionate plea from Acts 20:26 to "declare the whole counsel of God" to students?

6. Would your ministry be any different if you were to renew your commitment to the ministry of the Word? If so, in what ways?

7. What aspects of this chapter do you want to discuss with others on your leadership team?

1. Wayne Grudem and Jeff Purswell, *Bible Doctrine* (Grand Rapids, MI: Zondervan, 1999), 58.
2. Walt Mueller, *Engaging the Soul of Youth Culture* (Downers Grove, IL: InterVarsity, 2006), 179.
3. John Piper, *Imparting a Passion* CD. Desiring God Ministries: DSYW.

3.1 MOVING FORWARD
a recipe for teaching

One of my fond memories growing up was when my parents invited guests over to the house for dinner. Combine the fact that my dad was a pastor and my mom definitely had the gift of hospitality, and you can guess we had a lot people over. I wasn't so interested in the guests, but I loved to eat.

Our family had three boys, so my mom soon realized keeping us fed was a necessary survival skill. Her meals were never fancy but always filling. Let's just say I never left the table hungry. But when guests came over for dinner, the meal my mom cooked rivaled Martha Stewart's. She started cooking in the morning, and the oven was still going strong when the guests came in the front door. I could hardly contain my chubby little body because of the smell of food throughout the day.

Teaching the Bible is a lot like serving a home-cooked meal.

When people came over to our home for a meal, my mom's job wasn't to force our guests to eat. Rather it was to present a dinner worth eating—tasty and nourishing. But she couldn't do this if she didn't spend the necessary time in the kitchen preparing it. And she couldn't prepare the meal if she didn't first purchase the right goods at the grocery store. And before she went shopping for the goods, she needed to determine what to serve for the meal.

Similarly, God's Word is referred to as *food* in both the Old and New Testaments. Jeremiah writes, "When your words came, I ate them; they were my joy and my heart's delight" (Jeremiah 15:16). The author of Hebrews calls the Word "solid food" (5:14), while Peter says it's "pure spiritual milk, so that by it you may grow up in your salvation" (1 Peter 2:2). As food is to the body, God's Word is to the soul. Jesus acknowledges that we don't "live on bread alone, but on every word that comes from the mouth of God" (Matthew 4:4). God's Word is the nourishment our souls need to grow as followers of Jesus.

And just as we can't force anybody to eat a dinner we serve, we're not to *make* our students digest God's truth, either. However, we do have the responsibility of serving students a tasty and nourishing meal from God's Word. But we can't do this if we don't spend the necessary time preparing our messages. And we can't prepare our messages if we don't spend the time studying the "goods" of God's Word. And before we can study God's Word, we need to decide what to study. So determining the meal (identifying the text or topic), shopping for groceries (studying the text), preparing the food (crafting the message), and serving the meal (delivering the message) are all essential to give us the best spread possible as we invite students to feed on the riches of God's truth.

Before we continue, I want you to know I'm not approaching this chapter as an expert—but as a fellow youth worker in the trenches weekly speaking to teenagers. I'm seeking to grow along with you in this journey. I'm so inadequate. Believe me. I have so many insecurities and struggles. But I take comfort in the fact that God once spoke through a donkey. And if he can speak through a donkey, maybe he can speak through me, too. The book of Acts details how God used some unschooled, ordinary guys who "turned the world upside down" (Acts 17:6 ESV). God is always eager to use our offering—even if we think our couple of fish and few loaves can't make a difference.

This chapter is designed to help you grow as a communicator of God's truth regardless of whether you're a youth pastor, a Young Life volunteer, a Sunday school teacher, or a small group leader. And while the main focus here is thinking through the steps needed to prepare messages from scratch, the principles are completely transferable for those weeks when you only have time to adapt an existing curriculum to suit your needs and context.

This chapter addresses the *what* of the message (content) while the next chapter focuses more on how to engage students with the message (delivery). Student ministry leaders refer to teaching students with a variety of terms: Talks, lessons, messages, sermons, devotionals, etc. This chapter will use the word *message* as a universal term for teaching students God's truth.

Determining the Meal: Identify the Text or Topic

"What do you want for dinner?"

"I don't know. What do you want?"

"Whatever."

"Let's look and see what's in the fridge for something easy to serve."

Although this might be a frequent pre-mealtime conversation in many homes, it's not a wise approach for teaching students the Bible. Unfortunately, it's all too common in many youth ministries.

Teaching students can be overwhelming. We need to be on our game week after week, month after month. Students expect us to bring something fresh every time. If you feel that pressure, know you're not alone. I feel it, too. Sometimes we can get so caught up in the prep-deliver-prep-deliver-prep-deliver cycle that we're unable to step back to think through where we're really going.

How do we determine the meal from God's Word that we'll serve our students? There are three general ways to approach teaching:

As it relates to teaching the Bible, Harvest Students is convicted about these things:

1. We take students through chunks of Scripture—instead of creating our own messages supplemented by a verse here and a verse there.

2. We study topics within the broader context of scriptural chunks—instead of building a series around a topic, we seek to address topics as they come up in the Bible passages we're teaching.

3. We relate God's Word to the everyday life of a teenager—instead of teaching God's Word for basic information or general application.

4. We use interactive teaching at three distinct levels: Students interacting with God's Word, students interacting with the speaker, and students interacting with other students.

5. We train students to study the Bible through consistent modeling of observation, interpretation, and application—instead of just teaching students *about* the Bible.

6. We use small discipleship groups to balance application and accountability—instead of only discussion groups.

Determine Text, then Topic and Theme

Determine Topic, then Text and Theme

Determine Theme, then Topic and Text

Although there are advantages and disadvantages to the first two approaches, I believe it's a fundamental mistake to determine a creative theme and then figure out what topic you'll teach. For example: "Survivor is popular, so let's do a series called 'Survivor.' Okay, now that we have a theme...what should we teach?"

God speaks through his Word. When we teach God's Word, God speaks. If we want to see God work in our student ministries as with the early church, we must be devoted to the Word as well. Therefore allow your theme to reflect what God wants said.

I'm not suggesting that every teaching series with our students needs expository preaching in an exegetical, verse-by-verse manner. But I am advocating "text messaging"—messages that are biblio-centric. It can be very effective to take students verse-by-verse through a section of Scripture, but sometimes a topical approach is best. Still, there should be a balance. And when doing a topical series, we should seek to land primarily in one, central passage rather than hop around to three, four, or more verses to support our clever outline.

Note: Your approach to teaching profoundly impacts students' perception of God's Word—probably more than you realize. So if all you do is jump around the Bible and pick verses out of their context, what do you think you're teaching your students? Don't you think they'll do the same in their quiet times? More than teaching a "How to Study the Bible" class, we should be training our students how to study the Bible by modeling how through our teaching.

Shopping for Groceries: Study the Text

Shopping for the perfect summertime watermelon requires a certain skill. Picking the watermelon on top of the bin usually turns up disappointing results. Trust me. It's taken me many trips to the grocery store to realize I need to look for certain signs when picking a good watermelon. First, because watermelons don't ripen until after they're picked, a glossy coating is a sign of immaturity, while a ripe one has a drab, slightly dull rind. Second, the color of the stripes should have little contrast. And last, you should hear a thump, not a hollow ring, when smacking the melon. Shopping for groceries can take some acquired skills—and so does studying the Bible.

Once you've identified your text or topic, it's time to figure out what you'll teach. This is critical because it will greatly affect—positively or negatively—the subsequent steps.

1. Begin with prayer by asking God to illuminate the Word, give you fresh insight, and allow the text to burn inside you. John Piper speaks of studying the text until it burns with passion in you. I find this truth challenging. Certainly, some weeks I'm just plain exhausted and don't want to teach. These weeks especially are when I need to beg God to allow his truth to burn inside me—otherwise it's not likely to burn inside my students.

2. Next I commend the discipline of reading and rereading the passage you plan to teach before you open a commentary or other study tool. Read it fast. Read it slow. Read it with a pen in hand. Jot down some initial thoughts. Read it some more. And in some ways the more familiar the passage, the more you need to reread the passage. Sometimes I need to read and reread a passage eight to 10 times. Allow God's Word to come alive in your heart.

3. After reading the text contemplatively, truly begin to study it— identify key principles, do word studies, and seek to understand the historical and textual context. Ever get frustrated when someone focuses on one sentence you said while ignoring what you said before or after that sentence? You end up misunderstood because what you said was taken out of context—or worse, you're misrepresented. I wonder how often we do the same with God with our propensity to lift verses from their context in an effort to teach *our* messages.

4. While studying the Bible, I suggest jotting down notes and observations on a piece of paper as well as circling or underlining words and phrases in your Bible. Cross-referencing can provide additional insights. Having a study Bible and a couple of good commentaries on hand can be very helpful at this stage of your study. In addition, several software programs and free online resources provide study helps. As it relates to commentaries, I prefer the ones written by pastors more than academic scholars because they're less complex and offer practical ideas for communicating truth. Remember—commentaries are comments *about* the Bible. The Bible is inspired; commentaries aren't.

5. Avoid the tendency to skip over difficult passages. If you're not helping students navigate through and understand confusing texts, they'll never know what to do with a passage they don't understand. If you skip difficult verses, your students will develop the habit of doing the same when studying the Bible on their own. I used to fear students would tune me out if I sought to explain an unclear portion of Scripture. However, I've discovered the opposite to be true. Students tune in more because they're truly interested in learning how to understand new insights into God's Word. And if you don't understand a passage even after studying it, let your students know you don't understand it. This will show your students they don't need to have all the answers, either, and you'll avoid deceiving your students into something that might not be true. (I'm thinking about starting a club for student ministry leaders who don't know it all. Do you want to join?)

Doug Fields and Duffy Robbins have written an excellent book called *Speaking to Teenagers*. I greatly appreciate this book and recommend it to all youth workers. The authors identify three important principles (which I totally agree with) for effective study of the Bible text:

A. Allow the text to speak for itself, untarnished by your assumptions and preconceptions.

B. Identify the timeless message God has for his people.

C. Consider what these timeless truths mean for your life and for the lives of your students.[1]

Students in general really want to be challenged and dig deeper into God's Word. They don't just want to be entertained—but they don't want to be bored, either. I never want to lose students when giving a message. But I'd rather lose students due to challenging them than lose them because the message is shallow.

6. After taking good personal notes and supplementing your study with other resources, it's time to take your groceries home to your kitchen where you can begin preparing your message.

moving forward > by looking back

Spending Time in the Kitchen: Crafting the Message

I'm culinarily challenged. Can any of you identify? But even though I have my cooking issues, waffles are one of a few things I can prepare in the kitchen. Waffle night has become a fun little family tradition in our home. In fact, two of our kids have requested waffles for their birthday parties. Our kids like waffle night because it's more than a meal; it's an event. All three kids want to participate, and as do actors in a play, each kid knows his or her role. I place the ingredients on the counter with some mixing bowls and the waffle iron. But just having the ingredients for waffles doesn't mean we *have* waffles yet. We have to combine the appropriate amount of flour, eggs, milk, cooking oil, and baking powder together to create the batter. Then, using a one-cup scoop, we pour the batter and start cooking the waffles.

In a similar way, even though you've studied the Bible, you aren't yet ready to teach. You must take your study notes and mix them together in a way to connect with students without compromising the truth of the text.

Many books talk about how to organize a message. Regardless of the various models, most include three general elements of a message: An engaging introduction, tasty and nourishing content, and a compelling conclusion.

AN ENGAGING INTRODUCTION

The three most critical minutes of your message are your first three. Why? Students will only give you a few minutes to convince them the message is worth listening to, and then decide whether it's relevant to their lives. Don't just assume students will be interested in what you have to say. You must first create interest for them.

You have many good ways to start a message. Some of the most effective are—

> a funny story
> a personal story about you
> a startling statement

> an engaging illustration

> an object lesson

> a current event

> a newspaper headline

> a moral dilemma

> a vision for your students

> a stimulating question

Whatever you do, your introduction needs to be captivating. And it needs to be brief. You'll begin to lose the very students you're trying to engage if your introduction is any more than five minutes—and a three-minute introduction is often better. Believe me, I've learned this reality the hard way.

Recently, I began a message by telling a story that included setting the context, reading three paragraphs from a newspaper, and explaining the significance. When it was all done, it took more than eight minutes. Even though students were captive at the start, I lost them about halfway through the second paragraph of the article. And I could feel it. I began to ramble and repeat things as I tried to recover. The rest of the message was a struggle because I failed to keep the students engaged at the beginning. I learned several things that day: Limit the background details to only the essentials, have a clear plan for getting in and out of a story, read only a few lines of a quotation (a paragraph at the most), and put a picture of the article on the video screen so students can read along, too.

You need to create introductions with the end in mind. Therefore, I recommend this actually be the last step of your drafting process. Since introductions should point to where you're going, it helps to know where you're going first. I usually jot down a variety of introduction ideas as I go and then decide on the introduction after everything else—including the conclusion—is done. (In fact, the introduction to this chapter was changed multiple times as the content of the chapter came into clearer focus.)

TASTY AND NOURISHING CONTENT

Keep these essential principles in mind:

Every message should have one central theme.

Students should be able to tell you immediately after your message (and even a few days later) what your message was about. Your message may have several supporting points, but plan your message with one central idea to reinforce repeatedly. Some call this "the big idea" or "the one thing." Another way to think about it is—"What's the one nail you want to pound during the message?" The central idea is the hub of a wheel with all the spokes connecting to the hub. Andy Stanley talks about the impact of a statement that sticks. He calls it a "sticky statement." I like that. The central theme needs to be a sticky statement if you want it to stick with your students. And when you can summarize your message in a single sentence, you not only help your students remember the message, but you'll also keep your message focused.

Know your students.

Your message shouldn't sound like a Sunday morning message for adults. As you organize your thoughts, think about to whom you're speaking. Are you speaking to middle school, high school, or college students? Are you speaking to a group comprised primarily of believers or non-Christians? What's going on in the lives of students? Has someone in the group recently experienced a hardship or difficulty? Is the group usually receptive to hearing God's truth or not? What are the common issues your teenagers are facing in everyday life? How is God's truth relevant to your students? You need to understand the Word and understand your audience.

And you should be able to answer each question in a short sentence *before* you speak.

Flavor the message with illustrations.

Illustrations are the spices for the meat of God's truth. You wouldn't eat a plate full of steak sauce with a few morsels of rib eye. When grilling, you start with a thick, juicy steak, then you flavor it with a few spices. The same is true with your message. Start with God's truth. Then sprinkle it with some stories and illustrations.

You can find illustrations in a lot of places. Your personal stories can be incredibly valuable because they create a human connection between you and your students—especially if you tell a funny story or one showing an authentic side of you. You have a unique set of personal experiences that makes you uniquely interesting. Most listeners appreciate speakers who share from their unique experiences. In addition to personal illustrations, look for ones in the newspaper or magazines, on Google, in regular books or kids' books, from your family, in funny photographs, and on YouTube.

Although there are many 101-illustration-type books available, I've found them to be little help in providing illustrations that connect with students. Illustrations are all around if you take the time to look. The key is to become an observer of life. And if you find an illustration, file it away on your computer hard drive, or as a hard copy, for future use. Then when you need an illustration later, you have it on file.

Don't complain about your students' short attention spans. Most often the problem isn't their attention spans, but their *interest spans.* And don't blame students for their interest spans. You can't blame a student for being bored if your message is boring. Television executives understand people's interest spans are short. Set your stopwatch the next time you watch your favorite prime-time sitcom, drama, or reality show. Every five minutes comes a short break from the regular program.

We need to understand this reality when speaking with students and add "commercials" to our messages. Meaning, if we aren't mixing up the tempo of our messages every five minutes or less, then we're losing students. I'm not suggesting showing a video advertisement. Commercials should feel natural and keep you moving in a positive direction while providing a change in tempo to your message. So let's do the math. If you need a commercial every five minutes, you need six of them for a 30-minute message (or four for a 20-minute message). Without these throughout your message, you'll struggle to keep the students' interest.

Use humor.
Everyone loves to laugh. And laughter can create a powerful connection with students. You don't have to be a stand-up comic to get stu-

moving forward > by looking back

ILLUSTRATION IDEAS

Illustrations

Use personal examples.

Quote a random statistic.

Watch a video clip.

Use an object.

Build something.

Show a picture.

Tell a story.

Use a sound clip.

Paint something.

Use props to tell a story.

Use anything involving a kid or a puppy.

Use word pictures or analogies.

Speak with colorful language.

Point out newspaper headlines.

Read a story from a book.

Participatory Illustrations

Have students read a passage with you.

Quote a quotation together.

Act out a passage.

Get a student to tell a story spontaneously.

Take something from a student in the audience.

Give something to a student in the audience.

Sit with the students in the audience.

Have students do a "neighbor nudge."

"Repeat after me."

"Finish my sentence."

"Write this down" or "Underline this."

"All in favor of..."

"Raise your hand if..."

"Turn to someone next to you and say..."

"Hey! Everyone look at me."

dents to laugh. Learn to see humor in life. And look for humor in the biblical text. Funny stuff abounds in the Bible if we take the time to put ourselves in the story. In *Speaking to Teenagers*, Doug and Duffy write about five categories of humor:

> Exaggeration—any kind of overstatement related to people, places, sizes, the way people feel or act, or personal experiences.

> Surprise—making use of unexpected or unusual feelings, events, or facts. Setup is crucial to maximize the element of surprise.

> Absurdity—using materials illogical in thinking or in language.

> Human problems—when a person appears foolish or is simply the victim of everyday life.

> Sarcasm—bringing attention to someone's faults can be very hurtful. But anytime you can make fun of yourself, you'll win your audience.[2]

Encourage students to see themselves in the story.

The Bible is full of great stories—and we can engage students in God's Word by becoming storytellers. This generation of students loves stories. The Bible has it all—action, drama, romance, tragedy, and even comedy. The Scriptures are based in real times and on real places. Really. Joseph, Esther, the paralytic who was lowered to Jesus through the roof—these were all real people. Even the nameless people in the Bible were *real* people with feelings and experiences. Make the story come to life by helping students feel how it would be if they'd been there. Say, "Imagine with me..." and then tell the story with as much vivid description as possible. Engage students in the story itself. Further, ask them, "Where do you see yourself in this story?" Encourage them to identify with one of the characters or put themselves into the biblical setting.

Use the metanarrative of the Bible.

Not only do we need to teach the stories of the Bible, we need to teach the entire story of the Bible. We need to go beyond telling the narratives and tell the metanarrative (or big story) of the Bible. I've discovered many students know Bible stories. They know about Noah and the ark, David and Goliath, Daniel in the lions' den, and Jesus feeding the 5,000. But most don't understand how the collection of the individual stories encompasses the big story.

Connect the text to the everyday life of your teenagers—often.

The teaching model I learned in college was hook, book, look, took. This isn't necessarily a great model. The problem is, if you speak for 20 to 25 minutes before you ever get to the "took" (application), you'll lose students along the way. My senior pastor seeks to include application to life every five minutes in his messages—and this is a goal I'm working on, too. We need to connect the text to the everyday life of our students throughout our messages.

Put your message on paper.

You can organize your thoughts on paper in three general ways: Outline, manuscript, or a combination of both. Outlines arrange concepts. Manuscripts arrange words. Some manuscripts are word for word while others generalize the wording. I manuscript most messages because it encourages me to filter what I say and helps me cut out unnecessary parts or parts time won't permit. Some speakers are aided more by outlines for their speaking notes. One method isn't better than another. Figure out what works for you and use it. Some speakers are proud of not writing down concepts or words because they want to go freestyle and be open to the Spirit's guidance. However, we shouldn't forget that the Spirit guides during the preparation process, too.

Even though I manuscript my messages, I never speak them word for word because I don't read the manuscript. Because I'm clumsy with full sheets of paper, I've learned to shrink my notes to a front and back half-page of paper. Then I'm able to tuck this note page into my Bible. I can refer to the notes as I need, but I'm also seeking to adjust as I feel prompted by the Spirit or sense I need to adapt based on the response from students.

By the way, did you catch that I said I tuck my notes in my Bible? What's up with a youth leader who teaches without a Bible? The Bible is our authority. And students must see us holding and using our Bibles. This will encourage them to do the same. But more important, it communicates to students that we aren't sharing just our words, but God's Word.

Format your message.
Some messages are naturally narrative in style. Others are better when structured by an outline. My natural tendency is to be an outline guy, but I seek to vary my style. We distribute message handout sheets (with printed announcements on the back) and encourage our students to take notes. It's encouraging how many students do take notes. I've learned a lot about outlining messages in recent years. Students don't engage with the dull biblical-observations-only outlines. Nor do they like gimmicky and cheesy outlines. Outlines should be memorable. Sometimes rhymes, alliteration, and acrostics work. Sometimes not. I lean more toward statements students can identify with and verbally repeat. Rather than using second- or third-person statements, I lean toward first-person statements whenever possible. My growth in this area didn't happen overnight. It has taken years to develop, but I usually find the time spent making outlines is well worth it. Bottom line: If you use outlines, keep them simple, clear, and relevant to your students.

A COMPELLING CONCLUSION

Never begin a message if you don't know how you're going to end the message. The Bible wasn't given for our information, but for our transformation. Our goal isn't simply to teach the Bible to students, but to teach students the Bible in a way they'll understand and apply it to their lives.

You need a compelling ending the same way you need an engaging introduction. There are two major conclusion no-nos: The I-don't-know-how-to-end-so-I'll-just-ramble-on-without-end ending and the I-don't-know-how-to-end-so-I'll-just-abruptly-shut-up ending.

Perhaps you join my company in admitting you've ended messages in these ways in the past. No doubt you've heard messages with these endings. These moments are awkward for everyone involved—awkward for the speaker. Awkward for the students. Awkward for the band or whoever is to follow.

Good conclusions are determined in advance and are clear and concise. A good conclusion should be five minutes or less and contain one or more of the following elements:

√ *Tell a story*—a personal story of application, an ending to your opening story, or a story of summary.

√ *Reiterate the central theme*—while avoiding being redundant by reviewing the entire message.

√ *Encourage life applications*—by suggesting some everyday examples. Avoid giving the impression your examples are the only ways to apply the message. Encourage listeners that the Spirit might be prompting them to apply God's Word to their lives in many ways. And here's a caution: Don't save all the applications to unload at the end of the message. Instead seek to spread them out during the message so the conclusion only needs to review action steps for emphasis.

√ *Allow time to reflect and respond*—avoid the tendency to hurry out of your message into something else. Plan for a few minutes for prayer or silent reflection or a time to write something down or _____. For this to happen, you can't go long with your message, or the students will be restless.

moving forward > by looking back

10 Mistakes

As I coach our college students who are emerging as youth communicators, I share this list of 10 mistakes related to delivery of their messages with them before they speak and review it with them after they speak:

- √ Avoid a monotone voice—communicate with passion in your voice; mix up the tone, speed, pitch, and volume.

- √ Avoid being stiff—don't just stand in one place or just with your arms at your side.

- √ Avoid being distracting—don't move too much by pacing or unnecessary gesturing.

- √ Avoid being long—know your time limit and don't go over.

- √ Avoid being someone else—don't try too hard to be funny or imitate another speaker.

- √ Avoid being dull—supplement your message with stories, illustrations, object lessons, etc.

- √ Avoid being aimless—keep your message focused.

- √ Avoid being silly—be fun but not immature.

- √ Avoid being redundant—don't say things over and over and over and over again; avoid being redundant.

- √ Avoid being wordy—choose your words carefully. Also stay away from "um," "you know," "like," etc.

- √ *Encourage students to get into groups of three or four*—to share their thoughts about applications of God's truth and one prayer request.

- √ *Challenge students to a verbal declaration*—as a united, verbal response, encourage students to declare an aspect of who God is or what they're committing to as individuals or a group.

- √ *Close with a song of worship*—select a song reflective of a testimony of the desired application from students.

My thinking about conclusions was expanded after reading about the "we" factor in a book by Andy Stanley. He suggests ending each message with an inspirational challenge casting the vision beyond personal application to community application. He writes, "In this closing moment you call upon your audience to imagine what the church, the community, families, maybe even the world would be like if Christians everywhere embraced your one idea...This is when you remind your audience that the Scriptures were given not just as a means of making individual lives better...Imagine what WE could do together."[3] I've found this helpful. I now seek to incorporate a "we" factor element into most of my messages.

Serving the Meal: Deliver the Message

In college I invested in a cheap tuxedo and got a job with an upscale catering company. It was an interesting job and gave me access to some very elegant black-tie events. Before the guests arrived, the head chef gathered the staff together. After giving some instructions for the evening, he would always conclude with these six words: "Remember—it's all about the presentation."

The chef was as concerned with the quality of the presentation as he was with the quality of the food. Each plate was a work of art masterfully designed. We were always to serve with our white gloves from the left of a person and pick up from the right side. And so it is with teaching—it's not just about the quality of the content, but also what you do with the presentation. It matters not only *what* you say but *how* you say it.

After drafting the message, it's time to plan and practice your delivery. Even though I've spoken to students hundreds of times, I still verbally and physically practice my messages. I usually find an empty room free from distractions and interruptions.

1. First, I begin on my knees (literally) with a time of prayer. I thank God for the Bible and its work in my life personally. I confess to God any known sin. I acknowledge my dependence on God. I pray for the needs of our group in general. As God brings specific students to mind, I pray for them. I ask God to burn his truth in my heart and give me passion and conviction. I pray for God's Word to penetrate students' hearts and God's Spirit to transform lives.

2. Next I read straight through the message without much expression or pausing. Then I go back and make notations in my mind and with my pen. I try to make sure I'm connecting all the dots with transitions. If the transitions are fuzzy to me, then I can guarantee the students will be lost. I've heard it said, "A mist in the pulpit is a fog in the pew." I'm also reviewing to make sure I'm thinking through a "commercial" every five minutes and intentionally planning times for interaction (more on that in the next chapter).

moving forward > by looking back

Three ways to grow as a communicator of God's truth:

> Listen to yourself on tape or CD after speaking. Perhaps this discipline has helped me improve as a communicator more than anything and helps me the next time I need to speak.

> Watch yourself on video twice a year to see your mannerisms and nonverbal communication. Take notes on whether your gestures enhance or distract from your communication.

> Be evaluated by a trusted volunteer once a quarter and genuinely seek her honest feedback on your strengths and areas you can improve.

3. Last, I speak the message out loud to myself as if to a room full of students—using voice inflections, mixing up my verbal pacing, gesturing, etc. It helps me actually to hear myself speak and allows me to adjust what looked right in print but doesn't sound right when spoken. After making some revisions, I go back and do it again. I review the stories several times until they feel very natural. However, I stop short of memorizing each word of the message. When I get up to speak, I want to be familiar with the message so as to refer to my notes as little as possible. But I also want to have the freedom to adapt. I find myself much more expressive and engaging if I'm not just trying to remember which word comes next. I have a friend who refers to this process as "memorizing the movements of the message."

You can find many other ways to prepare and practice before you speak. I recommend that you figure out a routine that best works for you.

Let me close with two thoughts.

First, take a deep breath. Exhale. Don't assume the pressure of changing students' lives. Look at your hands. Do you have holes in your hands? What does this tell you? You're not Jesus. We must trust that as we're faithful in teaching the Bible, God's Spirit will be working in students' lives—whether we see this or not. We need to approach most messages as food for the week. Few students remember what you talked about a couple of months ago. That's okay. And not all messages will evoke a life-changing response. That's okay, too. But as we're faithful in teaching students, we feed them for that week. And hopefully, they'll keep coming back for more.

Second, this chapter may evoke one of two responses—encouragement (I can do this) or discouragement (I can't do this). I trust this chapter has provided you with some practical ideas you can use this week as you teach students. My prayer is for you to press on in teaching students the Word of God so they'll grow up in their salvation. And if you feel inadequate for the task of teaching students God's Word, that's a good place to be. Remember what I said in the beginning: I have many insecurities and struggles related to teaching God's Word to students. But if God could speak through a donkey, maybe he can speak through us, too. God's always eager to use our offerings—even if we think our handful of loaves and few fish can't make a difference. May God guide each of us as we fully give ourselves to the work of God.

moving forward > questions

Questions for personal reflection and team discussion:

1. What do you enjoy most about teaching students? What do you find are some of the biggest challenges?

2. In what ways are preparing and serving a meal comparable to speaking to students? What are other examples of this analogy?

3. What's your routine for preparing to speak to students? Is it working? How can you improve it?

4. Why is it awkward for everyone if the speaker doesn't know how to end a message?

5. Of the 10 mistakes mentioned, what's an area of personal growth for you?

6. What are three practical things you can do to be more effective in teaching God's truth to students?

7. What aspects of this chapter do you want to discuss with others on your leadership team?

1. *Speaking to Teenagers* (El Cajon, CA: Youth Specialties, 2007), 110.

2. Ibid., 146-47.

3. Andy Stanley and Lane Jones, *Communicating for a Change* (Colorado Springs, CO: Multnomah, 2006), 129-30.

I stood at a whiteboard writing as quickly as possible.

I was training a group of student ministry pastors during a *moving forward > by looking back* seminar and asked this question: "What are some of the challenges of engaging students with God's truth?"

The answers were incessant. It was as if a lid containing the pressures they faced regarding teaching students was just now being unscrewed. Here are some answers I tried to scribble on the board:

> "Students think the Bible is just a big, old book that's irrelevant to real life."

> "The students themselves. They're more of a challenge than teaching the Bible."

> "Bringing relevant application from the text to their lives as students."

> "Students think the Bible is boring."

> "Sin in students' lives prevents the Word from taking root."

> "Few of our students actually bring their Bibles with them."

> "Students' attention spans are so short."

> "Students interrupt and ask tangential questions."

> "Getting students into the Word outside of our youth group time."

> "Students hear from others that the Bible isn't really God's Word and that it's full of errors."

> "There's so much to cover and so little time with students."

> "Helping students understand the relevance of the Old Testament."

> "Students distract each other."

What else would you add to the list?

Obviously teaching students God's truth can be challenging. Even the apostle Paul struggled to keep a young man named Eutychus from dozing off during one of his messages. (To see what happened to this guy, check out Acts 20:9-12.) But despite its challenges, teaching God's truth can be extremely rewarding when we overcome these struggles and engage students with the Bible.

The most common method of teaching is lecture style—the teacher speaks, and the students listen. But I'm not convinced this is the most effective method for youth ministry. Are you? I find it hard to focus when I'm listening to someone lecture for 30 minutes, and I sense I'm not alone. Obviously, we can't guarantee our students' attention, but through interactive teaching I believe we can increase the likelihood of engaging our students and keeping them engaged. Rather than speaking to students or at students, we'll help students be more receptive if we speak with them.

Interactive teaching is commonly understood as what happens when a teacher interacts with students during a lesson. However, that's only one aspect of interactive teaching. I believe we need to get students interacting in three distinct ways—hence I'll now refer to it as interactive teaching[3]:

1. Interacting with God's Word

2. Interacting with you (the speaker)

moving forward > by looking back

3. Interacting with other students

Varied contexts for teaching exist—including in small groups and larger groups. It's been my observation that the smaller the group setting, the more likely the teaching is interactive; and the larger the setting, the less interactive it is (if at all). This is understandable. But it doesn't have to be that way. I'd like to suggest it's possible and effective to be interactive even when teaching hundreds of students. It just takes some intentionality. In fact, most of the ideas in this chapter can be applied in larger groups, not just small groups. Because youth ministry settings vary, you'll need to contextualize the principles based on the size and setting of your student ministry.

Get Students Interacting with God's Word

The Bible is authoritative, sufficient, and effective. Therefore, we must strive to get students interacting with the Word. For that to happen, our teaching (whether leading a Bible study or delivering a message to a larger group) must be clearly rooted in and keep pointing students to God's truth.

My senior pastor, James MacDonald, has said, "Any word without the Word is just a bunch of words." The power isn't in our words, but in God's Word. Therefore, the most important level of interaction is between the students and their Bibles. Thus, what follow are some practical ways for getting students interacting with God's Word.

ENCOURAGE STUDENTS TO BRING THEIR BIBLES.

We expect students to bring their Bibles to our student ministries. We often say to our students, "If you don't have a Bible with you tonight, I don't want you to be missing out. It's not about what I say, but it's about what God says. So share the Bible with the person next to you." Students can be trained to bring Bibles if it's truly a value of your ministry. It may take some time, but it's possible if you're persistent. Because this is a value at Harvest Students, we have a high percentage of students bringing their Bibles—at most gatherings we have as many as 80 percent of students with Bibles.

A common dilemma in youth ministries is whether or not to provide stacks of Bibles for students who don't bring their Bibles. I recommend not having lots of extra Bibles available because students will realize if Bibles are readily available, then they don't need to bring their Bibles. However, it's always good to have new Bibles available for students who don't own Bibles.

ENCOURAGE STUDENTS TO WRITE IN THEIR BIBLES.

Several times in a message I encourage students to underline phrases, circle words, and write notes in their margins. Periodically, I'll say, "This truth is so important you may want to write it inside the front cover of your Bible." Sometimes when I'm speaking, I'll walk over to a random student to show her what I circled in my Bible—encouraging the rest of the students to do the same. Marking up their Bibles and taking notes are important practices to learn during the teenage years. As a student marks up her Bible, it becomes a much more meaningful and personal possession. If a Bible has personal notes in it, a student is less likely to lose or misplace it. Also, a marked-up Bible can be a great encouragement to chronicle its owner's spiritual growth.

Several years ago I built a clubhouse in the backyard for our children. The first day the clubhouse was open, I had each of our children stand with their backs to a wall, and Camille marked off the height of each of our kids. It's a simple-yet-wonderful history of their physical development. In a similar way, as students read their Bibles and come across passages they've previously marked up and noted, it can act as a history of their spiritual development. Their own Bibles can be personal journals of what they've learned and how they're continuing to grow up in their faith journeys. But this needs to be routinely reinforced when teaching students. As youth leaders we need to regularly cast this vision by reminding students of the benefits of marking up their Bibles.

LIMIT THE AMOUNT OF BIBLE VERSES YOU PUT UP ON THE VIDEO SCREEN.

In our zeal to capitalize on technology, many ministries project too many verses on video screens too often. Why is this negative? If a student can just read all the Bible verses on a screen, he'll be less likely to look at his own Bible. And if he's not looking at his own Bible, he won't be marking up his Bible and creating a spiritual journal of underlines and notes. Recently, I spoke to more than 400 students at a Christian school chapel. I was shocked when I discovered that fewer than 20 students and faculty members actually had Bibles with them. The assistant chaplain told me afterward most chapel speakers just put the verses on the video screen. That explained it. *The Christian school trained its students not to bring Bibles to chapel.*

At times it can be helpful to put words on a screen if you want students reading aloud from the same translation, or if you want to reinforce a specific point. But will you really be emphasizing a specific point if students are used to always seeing verses on the screen? A general rule of thumb I follow is to have students look up the primary passage in their Bibles and use the screens only to show supplemental passages.

GIVE STUDENTS REASONS TO USE THEIR BIBLES.

If you're going to train your students to bring their Bibles, your messages must continually point students back to the text. We should take students to the Word and not merely talk *about* the Word. Regardless of the size of the group we need to ask questions to get students looking in their Bibles. We need to ask questions such as "What does verse _____ say?" while being patient enough to let the students look and call out answers—without bailing them out with the answers. If students know we'll answer our own questions, then they won't answer. The smaller the group, the more open-ended your questions can be. The larger the group, the more specific your questions need to be. For example, if you're teaching a larger group of students and reading a verse such as Ephesians 5:15—"Be very careful, then, how you live, not as unwise but as..."—you can ask, "What's the next word?" Then pause and wait for students to shout out, "Wise!" Encouraging students to verbally fill in the blank provides a helpful emphasis in a large-group setting. It also allows students to interact verbally with the message. But let's not sell our students short when in smaller groups. Let's ask them questions to cause them to dig deep into the Word—and even allow them freedom to ask us questions.

GUIDE STUDENTS THROUGH THE TEXT—ESPECIALLY LONGER PASSAGES.

Students will lose interest if you read several long paragraphs in a row. Instead make brief comments as you read. Point out the interesting words, places, or facts along the way. If something sounds strange or unjust in the text, don't be afraid to point that out. If the text is a narrative, help students feel as if they're part of the story by imagining themselves in the text. Explain as you go but keep moving on.

I recently taught the story from Mark 4 about Jesus calming the storm. As I read through the passage, I paused to help students understand the physical context of the Sea of Galilee and imagine the emotions of being in a first-century boat in the middle of a serious squall with waves crashing in. I asked, "How would you feel?" and took the time to listen to a few students call out thoughts. I continued, "So the boat was taking on water, and what was Jesus doing?" Then I paused and waited for students to call out "sleeping" (to get students to look in their Bibles).

I think I shocked the students when I mentioned it didn't seem right to me that Jesus was asleep when his friends were in trouble. I continued, "Can you imagine how the disciples felt? They were ticked at Jesus. They felt as if he'd abandoned them in their need. Look at the text. The disciples said, 'Teacher, don't you care if we drown?' (Mark 4:38). How many of you have ever felt as if Jesus were asleep in the midst of a storm of your life?" After pausing to allow students to respond, I continued. Rather than reading a longer text straight through, it's usually more effective to guide students through the text in this manner.

ENCOURAGE A STUDENT VOLUNTEER TO READ A PASSAGE.

This can happen in smaller *or* larger groups. If the group is large enough to require a mic, just walk your mic over to a student and have him read the Scripture using your mic. Because not all students are at the same reading level or equally comfortable reading in public, you should always ask for volunteers instead of putting a student on the spot in front of others. Of course you can read the texts, but why not let students read them periodically?

moving forward > by looking back

If you're reading a longer narrative, try assigning reading roles. For example, if you're reading a story in the Gospels, you can assign students the reading roles of narrator, Jesus, Peter, the crowd, etc. For this to work, make sure every student is reading from the same translation. Involving students in role-playing keeps them better engaged and can be quite entertaining.

ASK, "WHAT DO YOU SEE IN THIS PASSAGE?"

This question would be dangerous if we asked students to interpret the passage. But this question is simply to encourage observation. This is perhaps the best way to get students interacting with their own Bibles in a smaller-group setting. This single question can revolutionize a small group Bible study. We train our small group mentors to ask this question weekly and to listen to the students' observations after reading a passage together. We believe this is an important question for engaging students in the Bible and training them to discover God's truth for themselves.

At first our small group mentors were hesitant to ask this question for fear of where the answers could go. But it didn't take them long to discover the value of the question and be convinced this is a key element to Bible study. I put our volunteers at ease when I tell them it's hard to go wrong with this question. The observations can be quite random. That's okay and even encouraged.

Of course, it's possible to get "I dunno" from students. But a little patience, persistence, and encouragement can go a long way. Let students know there are no right or wrong answers. Let them know random observations can be liberating. It's simply, "What do you see in this passage?" Encourage students to identify characters and settings. Encourage students to look for words or phrases that are interesting, significant, connecting, confusing, or repeated, or are comparisons or contrasts. Sometimes I liken the observation phase to being a CSI studying the crime scene from all sorts of angles. We've discovered most students appreciate this freedom to look into their Bibles.

After spending a few minutes hearing random observations from students, the small group mentor begins to go through the biblical text systematically and the lesson in a natural and interactive way. Rather than teaching a course on Bible study methods, we seek to regularly model Bible study methods for our students.

Get Students Interacting with You

Real communication is always two-way. If you're speaking but not connecting with your listeners, you're not really communicating. Therefore, *communicating with* students is much more than *speaking to* students.

Effective student ministry leaders speak *with* students more than *to* students or *at* students. It's possible to have a conversational approach to teaching even in a large-group setting. I like to think of teaching as akin to a structured conversation.

Building rapport with students is necessary for effective communication. Humor can build rapport with students, but it's not the only way. Students are drawn more to authenticity than to humor. Students are drawn to someone who's real—someone they can respect and trust. And respect and trust don't happen automatically because of your title. When you're new in a group, many students automatically give you a negative three on a respect-and-trust scale of one to 10. Respect and trust must be earned.

Before you get up to speak, you must have the logos-ethos-pathos thing going on. You'll always struggle to connect with students if you don't earn their respect and trust and engage them at these basic levels—no matter how funny or dynamic your personality or presentation.

MORE PRACTICAL SUGGESTIONS FOR SPEAKING *WITH* STUDENTS RATHER THAN *TO* STUDENTS OR *AT* STUDENTS FOLLOW:

Speak among the students.

Students rarely engage with a speaker who stands behind a podium while reading a manuscript. Even in a large-group setting it's possible to speak among your listeners. Walk among the students—off the stage, down the aisles, around the room, and even behind the

The Popular-but-Dangerous Question

"What does the passage mean to you?"

We remind our mentors several times each year to avoid this question because it shifts the authority of God's infallible truth to our personal and often fallible opinions. The Bible's truth isn't subjective to human opinions. Most often our intentions are right in asking the question—but nonetheless, it's a dangerous question to ask. Rather we need to train ourselves to ask these questions:

"What do you think the text means?"

"How does God's truth apply to your life?"

students. If possible, ditch the podium completely. Students are much more receptive if they feel as if you're talking *with* them versus *at* them by giving them a speech.

Speaking among the students communicates you care enough to reach out to them. I once served at a church where our high school group met in the church's chapel—a room with a balcony. On several occasions I spoke 80 percent of the message from the balcony so I could be among the students who weren't necessarily excited to be there in the first place.

To speak among the students, though, you should know your message well enough not to have to read your message. A technique I've learned is to use a small enough font to shrink my entire notes down to the front and back of a half-sheet of card stock paper I can tuck inside my Bible—allowing me to be portable and speak among students. I recommend you give this a try.

Interact with your eyes.

Did your mom ever say to you, "Look at me when I'm talking to you!"? It's because eye contact is important. When we don't make eye contact with the students we're speaking with, we communicate a lack of confidence and a lack of trust.

As you speak with students, be sure to make eye contact with them. Avoid a natural tendency to pace uncontrollably while looking all around a room. Instead train yourself to look individual students in the eye. In my early days of ministry I would sweep the crowd with my eyes, often looking over their heads and avoiding eye contact so as not to be distracted. I was speaking, but because I lacked eye contact, I wasn't communicating. This has been an area of constant growth for me.

Even if you're speaking to a room full of students, seek to speak to individuals through intentional eye contact. Pick out some students and directly talk to them for a few seconds. This will create a powerful connection not only with the individuals, but also with the whole group.

And if you're seeking to make eye contact, but students aren't looking at you, use that as a signal that you're not connecting—you should make some adjustments quickly to reengage them.

Encourage students to talk back to you.

This can seem impossible in larger-group settings, but it can be as simple as having students repeat the "sticky statement" (the central statement referenced in chapter 3.1), read a verse, shout a word for emphasis, or answer the question, "How many of you have felt this before?" You might make a point such as, "Without God's wisdom we're prone to foolishness." An effective way to follow up the point is to have students audibly say, "Without God's wisdom, *I* am prone to foolishness." Or if you're teaching on God's sovereignty, you might want to say, "Everything—say 'everything' [and wait for the students to say 'everything']—God wants to have happen happens." Getting students to repeat things back to you is a simple, effective interactive technique. I heard someone teach from the book of Exodus to students in a conference setting, and he cued students to say "What's up with that?" several times as they came to a part in the story that didn't make sense. For this to be effective interaction with a thousand students, this statement needed to follow the prompting of the speaker. But I wonder how huge and liberating it might be if our students felt the freedom to interject "What's up with that?" in smaller-group settings, too?

Allow students to call out answers.

This involves more than students repeating something back to you. Ask open-ended questions to solicit audible responses from students. In teaching on worship, I asked students to call out things students worshiped instead of God. I had my list, but I wanted students to participate. In the same message about worship I asked students to call out attributes of God and quickly wrote down as many as I heard on a large whiteboard on the stage. After collecting dozens of answers, I shared that most of God's attributes could fall under the broad categories of God's greatness and God's graciousness. We went back to the list the students had brainstormed. This time students called out whether the attribute was an example of God's greatness or God's graciousness.

In other words, I could've just read a list of attributes, but having students call out answers was more effective in keeping students engaged through interaction. It also helped students participate in and contribute to the message as I unfolded it.

Get students out of their seats.

This can happen at several levels. The simplest way is to have all students stand as they repeat a phrase, quote a verse, or read a definition. Just getting students to stand momentarily helps keep their interest and emphasizes a particular point. Beyond this, it's always good to invite a few students to get out of their seats as part of an object lesson.

If you're teaching a narrative passage, get students out of their seats briefly to act out part of the story. Use students to hold things for you or have students stand to represent things. When you have a student stand and get involved in the message, you will gain the interest of the other students because they're curious to see what's going on.

Periodically use a quick refocusing statement.

Statements such as "Listen up!" "Get this," "Hey, everyone look at me right now," or "Make a note of this" are effective for interacting with students if done with a sense of urgency and passion. These statements should precede a main point or idea. Make sure you're drawing students' attention to something worthwhile. However, these phrases should be used sparingly—certainly no more than one or two times in a message—or they'll lack effectiveness.

Arrange the physical environment to encourage interaction with you.

You can limit the ability of students to interact with you by the way you set up the chairs, the lack of overhead lighting, and an unnecessary sound system. The stalest room setup is folding chairs in straight rows. If you use free-standing chairs, set them up in rounded rows or even in the round. And better yet, change up your seating area from time to time. Encourage students only to sit in places where you can have eye contact with them and they with you. Turn your house lights on when you teach—even if you use only stage lights for other aspects of your program. If the room is dark, it's impossible for students to interact with their Bibles, and you won't be able to see the students' faces. This value can frustrate the tech team people who like the ambience of stage lights—but you'll see so many other benefits. Lastly, ditch the mic and sound system unless you absolutely need them. In my first year in ministry I used a mic all the time—even if there were only a handful of students who showed up—because frankly, I liked hearing myself on a sound system. But you're much more approachable if you're only amplified when necessary.

Some of these interactive ideas may seem simplistic. Teaching interactively is natural with a smaller group of students. But with a larger group, our tendency is to speak *at* students and expect them to listen quietly for 30 minutes. Yet it's possible to interact with hundreds of students in a message—it just takes some intentionality. And interacting with students helps them stay engaged and receive the message because they feel someone is speaking *with* them.

Get Students Interacting with Each Other

In addition to getting students interacting with the Bible and with you, it's good to get students interacting with each other around God's truth. And not just interacting with each other before and after the message—but during the message, too.

You may be thinking, "Hey! My kids are constantly interacting with each other during my messages—I'm trying to get them to stop. In fact, I've recruited some parents to be the 'shhhh police' to keep the peace. Why would I encourage students to interact with each other?" Well, we should encourage them to interact with each other in healthy ways. I believe it's cruel and unusual punishment to ask our students to sit through a 30-minute message without being given permission to interact with the students next to them.

Sometimes getting students to a healthy level of interaction with each other is as simple as adding another dimension to their interaction with you by having them turn to their neighbors to say something. In the example of encouraging students to talk back to you, I shared about getting students to audibly repeat: "Without God's wisdom *we're* prone to foolishness" then following up that statement by encouraging students to say, "Without God's wisdom *I am* prone to foolishness." To get to the level of students interacting with each other, have them to turn to someone next to them and say, "Without God's wisdom *you are* prone to foolishness." Obviously, we don't want to promote preachiness or get students' focus off themselves, but this statement helps get students interacting with each other in a lighthearted way. I've discovered students stay more engaged as a result of being encouraged to say some things to a neighbor. I seek to incorporate this method at least once per message.

Student interaction can also happen by getting them into random groups of three or four throughout the room. This can be done as an introduction to the message—or as a two-minute exercise within the message. Students can—

> read a passage together

> discuss a thought-provoking question ("Why do you think God allows pain in the world?")

> develop a one-sentence definition for a word (*integrity, compassion*, etc.)

> draw a picture (e.g., of students experiencing community with one another)

> brainstorm examples of a topic in the Bible (God's sovereignty)

> discuss a situation ("What advice would you give to a student in this dilemma?")

> create a top-10 list of things related to the topic ("Why don't students share their faith?")

> share personal stories related to the topic for the night

I recently had students get into small groups to share their "fish stories." Everyone has a fish story—whether it's the one that got away, catching their first fish, a memorable family moment, trying to get a fish off the hook, not understanding why people like to fish, etc. After two minutes of lively conversations throughout the room, I shared mine, which introduced a message from the Gospels.

Invite a couple of students to come to the front to debate an issue with one another. Assign topical role-plays. Encourage some students to act out a passage or do a spontaneous drama. Even if some students don't get picked, it'll still create a time of interaction between the students up front and the students who are seated.

When closing a message, occasionally have students turn to one other person to share their thoughts on the application of God's truth or one prayer request. This may require you to shorten your message by two minutes. Too often we dismiss our programs before allowing our students a few minutes to interact with each other around God's truth. Even if structured small groups follow the message, it can be effective periodically to allow students randomly to huddle with someone else before being dismissed to small groups. Not all students will focus their conversation on a follow-up to the message, but it can be worthwhile if this interaction is meaningful for some.

Obviously, lots of interaction between students should take place in small groups. Few things tank a group more than when an adult does all the talking. Healthy small group dynamics consist of more than a discussion between students and the leader. When a student asks a question, it's often best for the adult mentor to say, "That's a great question. What do the rest of you think?" Then give the other students the opportunity to try to answer their peer's question. Even if you have an answer, why not give other students the opportunity to offer their ideas? This is a simple way to get students interacting with each other and encouraging peer-to-peer ministry.

Laurie Polich has written a helpful book aptly called *Help! I'm a Small Group Leader.* She offers a winsome perspective of several student stereotypes in small groups, including the talker, the thinker, the church kid, the distracter, the debater, and the crisis producer (p. 86-87). Then she offers practical suggestions for engaging these students and getting them interacting in positive ways. This is a must-have resource for all small group leaders.[1]

Don't be afraid to encourage students to interact with each other in positive ways—both in small groups and larger-group settings. This brings variety to communication while breaking up the monotony of only listening to you. Other ways to get students interacting with each other abound, so don't be limited to just these ideas.

Before I could become a more interactive communicator, I had to first deprogram myself of some things I learned in the classroom and that had been modeled within the church. Effective communication with students doesn't involve flawlessly quoting a memorized script. Nor is it perfecting voice inflection and proper gesturing. Nor is it just downloading solid biblical content and hoping students pay attention and understand. To be effective in communicating God's truth, we need to engage students.

And this may be encouraging for some of us: It's possible to engage students without having the most engaging personality. Even if you feel limited in the humorous or dynamic or articulate or cool categories, it's possible to be effective as a communicator through interactive teaching[3].

As you prepare your next message for students, consider how you can make it more interactive. Think about this when you're studying the text and crafting your message. When you're reviewing your notes, identify the ways you'll be interactive with students. If you're speaking for 30 minutes, it's probably good for you to plan six times of interaction—that's an average of once every five minutes (or if you're speaking for 20 minutes, that's four times of interaction). This might seem impossible until you try doing it. Jot down on your notes where you plan to be interactive with the students—perhaps by getting students to underline something in their Bibles or repeat a phrase or imagine something or say something to a neighbor, or by soliciting answers from the group or discussing a thought-provoking question. Go back through this chapter and highlight interactive teaching[3] principles that you want to apply to your own ministry. Then try some of the ideas in this chapter—but not all at once. Pace yourself. Figure out what works for you and for your group. If a technique seems to work, incorporate it again at a later date.

Interactive teaching[3] may take intentionality at first, but in a short time it will become quite natural.

moving forward > questions

Questions for personal reflection and team discussion:

1. What are some of the challenges you face in engaging students with God's truth?

2. Describe the difference between speaking *to* students or *at* students and *with* students.

3. Why are the three aspects of interactive teaching[3] important?

4. What's the value of having students mark up their own Bibles?

5. What's the danger of asking, "What does this passage mean to you?" What are the two better questions to ask?

6. What are three practical things you can do to be more effective in interactive teaching[3] with students?

7. What aspects of this chapter do you want to discuss with others on your leadership team?

1.   *Help! I'm a Small Group Leader!* (Youth Specialties, 1998), pp. 86-87.

"Don't feed the bears!"

This is one of the first signs at the entrance to many of our spectacular national parks out west. Why? The answer is simple. Feeding the bears is harmful. It's harmful to people—and to bears, too. If bears get used to eating our nachos and sweets, they'll lose their instinct to eat the food God has provided for them through nature. To their detriment they'll become dependent on humans to feed them. Similarly, unfortunately, too many students have grown up in the church dependent upon adults feeding them God's Word.

"Give a person a fish, and you feed him for a day. Teach a person to fish, and you feed him for a lifetime." I'd like to amend this well-known phrase for ministry. "Teach a student the Bible, and you feed her for a day. Teach a student to study and meditate on the Bible, and you feed her for a lifetime."

I'm a dad of three young children—Jonathan, Micah, and Hannah. It's been a joy to celebrate each of their developmental milestones (e.g., sleeping through the night, first steps, potty training—yippee!—and learning to feed themselves). How wonderful it was when our family could sit down at the kitchen table for a meal and not have to spoon-feed each child dinner. Learning to feed yourself is a natural rite of passage. But imagine if I kept Jonathan dependent on me to feed him, never teaching him how to feed himself? Suppose this went on for many years. Imagine how embarrassing it would be for me to show up at Jonathan's middle school cafeteria to unwrap his PB&J sandwich, break it into bite-size pieces, and literally place the morsels in his mouth in front of all his fellow students? We need to move our students from being spoon-fed to being self-fed. In other words, we need to help our students learn how to explore God's Word and discover truth for themselves.

Although it might make us feel significant, it's unhealthy for students to be solely dependent upon us for their spiritual growth. Instead we must move our students beyond dependence toward interdependence, encouraging them to be in the Word personally. Isn't this really what we want—students growing in intimacy with God outside our ministry programs? More than getting students to show up at church, getting students into their Bibles throughout the week is really where it's at. Getting students into the Word on their own gives them spiritual nourishment now, but also develops a foundation for when they graduate from our ministries. Our vision of spiritual formation must include more than *teaching* the Word—we need to be *training* our students to master the Word, meditate on the Word, and memorize the Word.

Master the Word

Jesus was eating some Fish McMuffins with his disciples on the shore of the Sea of Galilee when he asked Peter pointedly, "Do you love me more than these?"

"Yes, Lord, you know that I love you," Peter answered quickly and emphatically.

Jesus said, "Feed my lambs."

Jesus asked Peter the same question again. And then again. Each time Peter replied, "You know that I love you." After each response from Peter, Jesus said "Feed my sheep" and "Feed my lambs" (John 21:15-17).

Jesus used this conversation with Peter in part to emphasize the importance of sharing the truth with others. But think more closely about the analogy. Does a shepherd feed handpicked blades of grass to each lamb in his flock? Of course not! What's the responsibility of the shepherd? He needs to get his sheep to the green pastures to allow them to graze. Similarly, our responsibility is to get our flock of students to the green pastures of God's Word and encourage students to graze in the truth for themselves.

Timothy was developing in ministry as he read these words from his mentor: "Do your best to present yourself to God as one approved, a workman who does not need to be ashamed and who correctly handles the word of truth" (2 Timothy 2:15). Paul's charge to young Timothy was to master the Word.

Think about it. Our students are our young Timothys. It doesn't get any more basic than helping them learn to study the Bible. But are we doing this?

One of the most critical things you can do as a student ministry leader is train students to master the Word by equipping them to correctly handle the Word of Truth. Let me offer three things we can do to encourage students to spend time in God's Word:

MODEL IT IN TEACHING.

The way we teach God's Word has a profound impact on how our students view the Bible. I wrote about this in the last chapter. Interactive teaching[3] promotes getting students interacting with their Bibles, digging into the text, underlining phrases, and circling key words. We can model how to study God's Word by a commitment to teach through Scripture instead of lifting a verse here and a verse there to fit what we want to teach. As we focus on insights from the text, we show our students how to dig into the depths of the Bible.

Our teaching pastor, Dr. Joe Stowell, shared this observation with me: "In my 18 years of being president of Moody Bible Institute, I saw an increase in passion with each incoming freshmen class while at the same time a decrease in biblical literacy." I'm not surprised; are you? I love that this generation of students has passion for God, but I'm concerned that they're not grounded in the Word. I'm not interested in developing Bible quiz champs, but I do want to graduate students who are grounded in the truth and have a hunger for God's Word. Can you imagine what God could do if we helped combine our students' passion along with being firmly grounded in God's Word?

EXPERIENCE IT IN COMMUNITY.

Students are more likely to study the Bible on their own if they routinely experience a form of Bible study in small groups. This is a reason I'm committed to small group Bible studies. However, just because a student is involved in a small group doesn't mean she's being empowered to master the Word. The tendency of many small group leaders is to teach students what to believe instead of training students to master the Word. Small groups should be communities where students are encouraged to discover truth for themselves. We train our small group mentors in a basic three-step Bible study method:

1. What's it say? (observation)
2. What's it mean? (interpretation)
3. Now what? (application)

Then we encourage them to follow this pattern in small groups. Students begin with self-discovery: They observe the text—characters, setting, interesting words, significant phrases, repetition, comparisons, contrasts, and even confusing things. And random is okay. Then leaders guide students through the text. They conclude by encouraging students to identify applications to life. Students are more likely to apply the text if they're given freedom to identify the application to their lives rather than having an adult communicate a prescribed application.

Beyond your regular small groups, students can be encouraged to lead Bible studies at their high schools. This is part of the 2 Timothy 2:2 multiplication process: "And the things you have heard me say in the presence of many witnesses entrust to reliable people who will also be qualified to teach others" (TNIV). As Bible study is modeled and students experience it personally, the healthy next step is to teach others. The reality is that a teacher always learns more than the students being taught. Therefore, if you really want your students to grow, encourage

moving forward > by looking back

them to find opportunities to teach inside and outside your group. Few things will catapult a student's spiritual understanding and maturity as much as having the responsibility of teaching others.

PROMOTE IT THROUGH RESOURCES.

I can't go fishing without the right resources. I need a fishing pole, bait, and a body of water. If you value students being in the Bible, then provide them with resources for personal growth:

> Bookmark—the text in the sidebar can be adapted for use in your ministry: Put the text on bookmarks for students to keep in their Bibles as guides for personal Bible study.

> Reading plans—one reason students don't read God's Word on their own is they don't know what to read. A reading plan helps overcome this common roadblock. Develop a half-page card listing verse references to read over the course of a month or semester. Periodically, you may choose to promote a "30 Days in the Word" challenge as an emphasis for a month (perhaps right after a retreat) to encourage students to get back on track. If students don't know where to start, I often encourage them to go to the chapter in the book of Proverbs that coincides with the day's date.

> Devotional guides—a number of good student devotionals are available. Some are short reads, some encourage journaling, and others are Bible studies. Find some appropriate for your group and promote them as resources for personal quiet times. To encourage our students to get into the Bible, some of our staff, adult volunteers, and ministry-minded students collaborated on a series of devotional journals for students. It's cool to get students writing devotionals for their peers. Perhaps this could be a project for your student ministry team.

> e-devos—some youth ministries send daily e-devos to students on a subscription list or post them weekly on their Web sites.

> Student Bibles—I was in a Christian bookstore recently and was amazed by (and grateful for) the assortment of some pretty cool student Bibles, so make students aware they can upgrade from their white vinyl-covered Bible they got at kindergarten graduation. If a student likes her Bible, she's more likely to use it.

Personal Bible Study Tips for Students

1. Begin with a simple plan. Most students are defeated before they ever start because they don't have direction. Pick a devotional or book of the Bible that's manageable. If you're just now trying to get into the Word, don't start with Ezekiel or Romans.

2. Mark your Bible with a pen. Mark up your Bible. Underline verses. Circle words. Write things in the margin of your Bible. Your Bible can become your spiritual journal. Marking your Bible helps you see how much you've grown and reminds you of what you've learned.

3. Be observant. It's amazing how many things you miss if you just quickly skim a passage. You'll discover so many things if you read a passage seeking to be observant of the text. Look for words, phrases, contexts, people, places, etc., that stand out to you.

4. Reflect on the passage. It's important to linger in a passage and meditate on the Word. You can meditate by praying Bible verses back to God. It's simple. Use the text of God's Word to guide your prayer.

5. Expect God to speak to you. Have you ever read a passage and wondered, "Now what? How am I supposed to apply this to my life?" Not all passages are going to have a clear "Thou shalt do this or that." However, God can speak to us in every passage. Perhaps this simple acrostic will help you better apply God's Word. As you read a passage, consider whether you see:

   Sins to confess
   Promises to claim
   Examples to follow
   Actions to take
   Knowledge to grow in

6. Tell someone what you're learning. Statistics tell us we remember more of what we write down than what we just read. But we remember a lot more of what we tell others than what we write down. And as you tell others what you're learning from God, you spiritually stir up others.

I've discovered many students are genuinely interested in developing the spiritual practice of quiet time, but they need resources and encouragement. And as you encourage students in this area, make sure you give them opportunities to share what they're learning from God's Word either in your small groups or whole-group setting. Each week our small group mentors ask, "What did you learn from God's Word this week?" The question is seasoned with grace, but it helps students

moving forward > by looking back

stay accountable. As students verbalize what God's teaching them, it encourages the other students in the group while solidifying what God is teaching them.

Meditating on the Word

There are two common types of meditation: Mystic meditation and biblical meditation.

Mystic Meditation	**Biblical Meditation**
Focus is on emptying the mind	Focus is on filling the mind
Implies you're one with God	Recognizes God alone is God
Seeks an inner resource within a person	Seeks illumination from the Holy Spirit
Detachment from the world	Attachment to God

We need to encourage students to meditate on the Bible—corporately and personally. The words for *meditate* and *meditation* are used 20 times in the Bible. If they're mentioned that many times, I'm guessing it's an important concept God doesn't want neglected:

> "Do not let this Book of the Law depart from your mouth; meditate on it day and night, so that you may be careful to do everything written in it. Then you will be prosperous and successful" (Joshua 1:8).

> "But his delight is in the law of the LORD, and on his law he meditates day and night" (Psalm 1:2).

> "For I meditate on your statutes" (Psalm 119:99).

> "Let the word of Christ dwell in you richly" (Colossians 3:16).

As the saints in previous centuries have demonstrated, meditation is an important aspect of the Christian life. But I'm concerned many Christians and youth ministries today are neglecting meditation. I'm equally concerned because some meditation practiced by Christians and in youth ministries is more mystical than biblical.

Meditation must allow us to be connected to the truth of the Bible. We don't meditate to practice an altered consciousness or empty the mind of content. We must not turn the Bible into a mystical device for personal revelation. God is the one who reveals and illuminates Scripture. We don't meditate to seek a mystical experience, to gain a special revelation beyond the text, or to give attention to all manner of interpretations. We meditate to commune with God, to gain a deeper understanding of the text, and to allow the Word to dwell in us and shape our lives.

Common forms of biblical meditation include contemplative reading, continual reflection, and imaginative meditation. Let's consider how we can model these practices in our ministries and encourage students to practice them as well.

CONTEMPLATIVE READING

Too often we speed-read the Bible and check it off our lists for the day. Instead we ought to read the Bible contemplatively to allow the Bible to get through to us.

> *Receive the Word.* Immerse yourself in a brief passage of Scripture—perhaps only a few verses. Ingest by reading slowly and deliberately several times. Reading the verses aloud helps you focus. Read to encounter God. Receive the words as if God is speaking to you in the present moment. Certain words may stand out to you; let them take root in your soul. Allow the Word not only to inform you, but also to shape you.

> *Respond in prayer.* After receiving from God, respond in a prayerful dialogue. Respond by personalizing the Scripture back to God using first-person language as an expression of your heart. Respond in confession, adoration, or thankfulness as the Spirit prompts you. Respond audibly or through a written prayer.

> *Rest.* Spend time in silence by basking in the presence of God: "Be still before the LORD and wait patiently for him" (Psalm 37:7). "In repentance and rest is your salvation, in quietness and trust is your strength" (Isaiah 30:15). Too often we rush in and out of God's presence. Take time to linger in the presence of God.

Depending on your group dynamics, you can follow this pattern for 15 minutes or more. This is best done by creating an environment

moving forward > by looking back

of silence, stillness, and solitude. Begin with a brief explanation of the steps in contemplative reading. Then encourage students to spread out—perhaps throughout the room, the building, or even outdoors. Give students a passage to meditate on and a blank piece of paper for journaling. After the time of meditation have the students get into groups to share about the experience, read their written prayers (if they feel comfortable), and discuss how they can practice contemplative reading on their own.

Obviously, this type of meditation presents many challenges within a whole-group program. This won't work if students are disinterested, the physical setting is distracting, or the time is rushed. If this kind of format doesn't work with your whole group, here are some other suggestions:

> Invite students to another night (or day) dedicated to contemplative reading. Only students who want to be there will come.

> Practice contemplative reading for the morning devotional time on a retreat instead of giving students handouts with prescribed Bible study questions that encourage students to look for answers to your questions.

> Incorporate contemplative reading into any extended ministry trip—especially if you're out in God's creation (e.g., a hiking trip, canoe trip, rafting trip, wilderness trip, etc.).

As we model contemplative reading, we help students get familiar with the practice and encourage them to practice it in their personal lives.

CONTINUAL REFLECTION

Do you know the background to the phrase "chew the cud"? It refers to a cow's eating habits. I lived in Wisconsin, so I know a few things about cows. When Millie eats her food, she chews on it and swallows it. Although the human process stops there, it doesn't for cows. After chewing and swallowing, Millie regurgitates her food back into her mouth, chews on it some more, and swallows again. Pleasant picture, huh? Believe it or not, this is a biblical understanding of meditation.

We have much to learn from Millie about savoring God's Word by reading, swallowing, meditating, and swallowing again. To meditate on the Bible is to linger on the truth and savor it—and let the savoring continue throughout the day and night. Rather than closing our minds to God's truth when we close God's Word, we need to encourage our students to pick something from a message or from their quiet times to "chew on" throughout the day.

IMAGINATIVE MEDITATION

This is a powerful way to engage students with a biblical narrative—especially when students have a tendency to tune out familiar stories. In a recent series in the gospel of John our high school students experienced imaginative meditation when we came to John 8—the story of Jesus' interaction with the woman caught in adultery. Because we desire students to experience and discover God's truth for themselves, we replaced our regular teaching time with a time of meditation. Our students were in smaller groups with adult mentors. The students read and reflected on the passage five or six times, following the outline given (see sidebar). Students discovered fresh insights from the passage as the Scriptures came alive through this meditative exercise.

We need to create time to quiet our students to meditate on God's Word. This demands periodically slowing down our ministries. Don't get me wrong: I'm all in favor of high-octane ministry. I love loud music, crazy games, and passionate teaching—and I believe these things connect with most students most of the time. However, our programs shouldn't always redline on the RPMs of energy. It can be powerful to create moments for biblical meditation.

And as we model meditation to students, we encourage students to slow the RPMs of their lives to commune with their Creator.

Memorizing the Word

When I was 28, I had a stark realization: I'd memorized more Scripture in the first 14 years of my life than the latter 14 years.

Think about all that's wrong with that picture. During the latter years I'd gone to Bible college, received my master's degree from a

moving forward > by looking back

John 8 Imaginative Meditation

Tell students, Tonight we'll not only hear God's Word, but we'll also experience God's Word through imaginative meditation.

I'll read a story from John 8:1-11 several times through, and each time I do, you're to put yourself in someone's "sandals." Imagine yourself inside the story. What do you see? Touch? Smell? Hear? Feel?

After students have closed their eyes, tell them to imagine being a Pharisee in the story. Read the story as a narrator with little inflection in your voice. Allow some stillness and silence before and after you read. Then pause to hear comments from the students' time of reflection. Now ask—

> What were you seeing and hearing in this story?

> As a Pharisee, what were you feeling?

> What did you want to say?

> How did you feel toward Jesus?

Next have students imagine the passage as the adulterous woman. Have them close their eyes and reread the story. Then have a time of reflection using the same questions.

Repeat these same steps of reading and sharing as a different character—a disciple, Jesus, and yourself. Encourage students to put themselves back in history to be part of these situations.

---

seminary, and been ordained as a pastor, yet I'd neglected the discipline of Scripture memory in my personal life. And because it was neglected in my personal life, it was absent in my ministry practice.

As a kid I was an Awana geek through and through. Gray shirt. Red scarf. And about as many patches and pins as a kid could earn. Because of Awana, I memorized hundreds of verses during my grade school years. Why is Scripture memory a priority of children's ministry in most churches but not in student ministry (or adult ministry, for that matter)? Do we actually think it's kid stuff?

Jesus demonstrated one of the values of Bible verse memory—standing strong in the midst of temptation. Three times Jesus said, "It is written..." and three times Satan was defeated (Matthew 4:1-10). David begged the question, "How can a young man keep his way pure?"

Then he answered his own question, "By living according to your word. I seek you with all my heart; do not let me stray from your commands. I have hidden your word in my heart that I might not sin against you" (Psalm 119:9-11).

Memorizing Scripture is like making a bank deposit. We deposit money in our account and return to the bank when we need to withdraw our money. So if we're to deposit God's Word in our hearts to help us in times of temptation, wouldn't we say the temptations are a bit more intense at 16 years old than they were at six years old? We mustn't grow lazy in our student ministries and neglect Bible verse memory.

We need to get over the mental hurdle of thinking students can't memorize things. That's simply not true. Most students have memorized (or will soon memorize) Newton's laws of motion, quadratic equations, the state capitals, and the square root of *pi*. Students memorize locker combinations. Fantasy football stats. Lines from movies. Song lyrics. Let's dispose of the myth students can't memorize. They can. You *know* they can.

Another reason Bible memory is neglected in most student ministries is because the only model we know is the kids' club approach with sticker charts and merit badges to motivate students to memorize. Obviously, this doesn't work with teenagers. So let's consider some ways to engage students in memorizing God's Word.

SMALL GROUPS

Small groups can be wonderful settings for memorizing God's Word. However, this doesn't happen without the willingness of the students and the intentionality of the small group mentor. If the small group mentor isn't memorizing the verses, you can guarantee the students aren't, either. Each week mentors can highlight a verse to memorize from the passage studied. Students can write the verse on a 3 x 5 card. A key to making memorization work is review—not only with the current verse, but also reviewing verses from previous weeks.

STUDENT MINISTRY TEAM

The student ministry team shouldn't be doing all the work of the min-

moving forward > by looking back

istry. Instead seek to invest in their lives and challenge them to deeper spiritual growth. Select a passage of Scripture to be your guide for the semester or school year. We recently finished a yearlong study of Romans 12. We dedicated 15 minutes of our meeting to digging into this chapter—studying, memorizing, and applying. By the end of the school year, many student leaders had memorized Romans 12—but they did so one verse at a time.

MISSION TRIPS

When students apply to be a part of a mission trip—whether to serve in a local setting or internationally—use the training and the experience to encourage them to memorize God's Word.

As a prerequisite for our missions trips, we require students to memorize a series of verses for sharing the gospel. The benefit isn't just for the trip—they can be depositing these verses in their lives to withdraw as needed in the future.

Also, we select a theme passage for all mission teams to govern our attitudes and mission. At our first training time we assign sequential phrases of the theme passage to each student on the team. Rather than taking attendance in meetings and on the trip, an adult leader is able to simply say, "Colossians 3:12-17," and each student then quotes his part of the passage in sequential order. If the passage abruptly stops, we know a student is missing. It doesn't take long for students to memorize their phrases. And because of the constant repetition, most students have the whole passage memorized by the end of the trip.

Toward Lifelong Devotional Practices

This section has been about truth. But there's more to engaging students in God's Word than teaching students the Word. Teaching students the Word must be a priority in our ministries, but so must training students to master, meditate on, and memorize God's Word. The latter takes greater effort and intentionality—but is necessary for discipleship.

It's one thing for students to sit in a chair and listen to a message. It's another for students to develop devotional practices in their personal lives. And if they can do so during their teenage years, it provides a pattern for spiritual growth after they graduate. After all, our goal in youth ministry must be more than getting students through their teenage years. Rather we must have a vision for helping develop lifelong convictions and disciplines to enable students to walk with Jesus long after high school graduation.

If we want these devotional practices to be a priority in our students' personal lives, then they should be modeled routinely in our ministry communities. A natural tendency is to offer a class or teaching series on spiritual disciplines. While this might be beneficial, I believe devotional practices are better caught than taught. More than teaching students how to master, meditate on, and memorize the Bible, let's provide constant environments for students to experience these practices. So when planning the next semester for your ministry, make sure you ask yourself in what ways you can incorporate some of these ideas within the rhythm of your regular ministry times.

moving forward > questions

Questions for personal reflection and team discussion:

1. Why should our vision for discipleship or spiritual formation be more than teaching students the Bible—and include training students to be *in* the Word on their own?

2. What do you think are some of the reasons students don't spend time in the Bible on their own?

3. What are some of the challenges in teaching students to feed themselves from God's Word?

4. What are some ways you can incorporate times of biblical meditation into your ministry?

5. Why do many student ministries ignore Bible memorization?

6. How can you be more intentional with modeling and encouraging students to master, meditate on, and memorize the Word?

7. What aspects of this chapter do you want to discuss with others on your leadership team?

moving forward > by looking back

(s)ervice

engaging students with
God's world

If students aren't reaching out to others, they'll become unhealthy and stagnant—and so will your group.

Can you guess what this is?

If you grew up in the church or went to Bible college, you may have guessed the bodies of water in Israel. And you're right. The top circle represents the Sea of Galilee. The line is the Jordan River. And the bottom oval is the Dead Sea. I've always wanted to walk where Jesus walked—perhaps someday I'll get to Israel. Among the things I'd like to do in Israel is the Dead Sea. That's right—"do" the Dead Sea.

But I don't just want to see the Sea—I want to float and read a newspaper in the Sea. Because of the high salinity, the Dead Sea is commonly referred to as the "Sea of Salt." It's unusually buoyant because the water is 30 percent saline, making it the world's second saltiest body of water. It's 8.6 times saltier than any ocean.

In contrast, the Sea of Galilee is Israel's largest freshwater lake and is popular for its fish supply. The Sea of Galilee flows into the Jordan River. And the Jordan River flows into the Dead Sea. But the Dead Sea doesn't flow out to another body of water, which makes it a dead sea.

Similarly, if our lives have no outflow, our faith will be unhealthy and stagnant. *Faith is formed not only from input, but also from output.* We need to engage students in God's world. Service involves reaching out to meet people's physical and spiritual needs in the name of Jesus.

Our Acts 2 snapshot (see the Introduction) includes several references to service. These early disciples cared for people's physical and spiritual needs. They sold their belongings and gave to anyone who was in need. And God kept adding new believers to their community.

So far we've studied adoration, community, and truth. A natural outcome of genuine worship, authentic fellowship, and teaching of the Word is an eagerness to reach out. And when the people of God get serving, it leads to more adoration, community, and truth. This cyclical pattern is seen in the book of Acts.

(s)ervice in Acts

It's all about the name.

The Acts believers had a singular purpose. They were about one thing. They literally gave their lives to one thing—the name. *Service* in Acts involved more than being a charitable or humanitarian organization caring for the needs of people. Their service stemmed from their commitment to the gospel. The ministry of the early church was all about the supremacy of the name of Jesus. Check out some of these references to the name in Acts (all italic emphases added):

> "And everyone who calls on the *name* of the Lord will be saved" (2:21).

> "Repent and be baptized, every one of you, in the *name* of Jesus Christ for the forgiveness of your sins" (2:38).

> "By faith in the *name* of Jesus" (3:16).

> "Salvation is found in no one else, for there is no other *name*" (4:12).

> "Then they ordered them not to speak in the *name*" (5:40).

> "Speaking boldly in the *name*" (9:28).

> "Everyone who believes in him receives forgiveness of sins through his *name*" (10:43).

> "Men who have risked their lives for the *name*" (15:26).

> "They were baptized into the *name*" (19:5).

> "And the *name* of the Lord Jesus was held in high honor" (19:17).

> "I am ready not only to be bound, but also to die in Jerusalem for the *name*" (21:13).

It was all about the name of Jesus. The believers spoke boldly of the name. They cared for physical needs in the name. They ministered in the name. They suffered in the name. They called others to the name. They risked their lives for the name. We, too, need to be all about the name.

Most people think service is volunteering in some capacity. I'd like to broaden our perspective of service to include any time we reach out to care for people's physical needs *and* their spiritual needs. Let's consider how the early believers engaged in service through caring and sharing in the name of Jesus in Acts 3-4.

CARING IN THE NAME

Acts 3 opens with Peter and John meeting a guy in need. He was in a desperate condition. He had no hope of overcoming the crippled condition he'd had since birth. In the morning he was picked up, carried to, and laid at the temple gate to beg for the day. Perhaps he hoped to capitalize on an act of kindness from someone seeking to earn the favor of God or the favor of others walking past. In the evening some people returned to pick him up and carry him home. The next day he repeated the same routine. He begged at the temple gate day after day. Week after week. Month after month. Year after year. For 40 years (4:22).

Can you imagine the rejection and the shame this guy must've felt? He recognized the regulars going to the temple, and they recognized him, but most avoided eye contact and hurried by. How often is this our response to those in need? And not just curbside beggars, but anyone with a need that inconveniences us? But compassion doesn't look away. Instead it starts with empathizing with someone else's pain and leads to acting on another's behalf. And on this particular day Peter and John gave this man much more than he was begging for.

In an act of compassion Peter stooped down and met the beggar in his need. Looking the guy in the eye, Peter said, "'Silver and gold I do not have, but what I have I give you. In the *name* of Jesus Christ of Nazareth, walk.' Taking him by the right hand, he helped him up, and instantly the man's feet and ankles became strong" (Acts 3:6-7). And I love what comes next: "He jumped to his feet and began to walk. Then he went with them into the temple courts, walking and jumping, and praising God" (Acts 3:8). How cool is this?

Can you picture the scene? The guy had never walked before. Never. But that day he was leaping (not limping) and hollering with excitement. Soon the crowd was caught up with the commotion. Some must've been doing the two-fisted eye rub in disbelief. Some were whispering to each other, "Is that the same guy who lies at the gate day after day?"

"It can't be."

"No. I think it is. Look. I tell you. It's that guy!"

"You're right. It's the same guy. How was he healed?"

Then people began to point fingers at Peter and John and give them the credit for the man's healing.

How do you handle personal attention for ministry success? Do you absorb the glory for yourself or reflect the glory to God?

SHARING IN THE NAME

Peter quickly reflected the glory to God. This man who, in a cowardly manner, denied his faith a few weeks before began to preach boldly to the crowd. Peter declared, "By faith in the *name* of Jesus, this man whom you see and know was made strong. It is Jesus' *name* and the faith that comes through him that has given this complete healing to him, as you can all see" (Acts 3:16, emphasis added). In case they didn't hear it the first time, he mentioned the name a second time. Is the name of Jesus on the tip of your tongue?

Peter and John continued, "Repent, then, and turn to God, so that your sins may be wiped out, that times of refreshing may come from the Lord" (Acts 3:19). What has happened to calling students to repentance? When was the last time you spoke of the need to repent at an outreach event? It might not be popular, but it's biblical. Today's outreach messages rarely vary from this theme: *If you place your faith in Jesus, God will give you _____ (joy, love, purpose, peace, eternal life).* So students respond because of what God can add to their lives. Instead of being used for God's purposes, students want to use God for *their* purposes. No one can truly turn *to* God without turning *from* something. The early church spoke truth by calling people to repentance (see also Acts 20:21).

And "many of those who had heard the word believed, and the number of the men came to about five thousand" (Acts 4:4 ESV). Not bad for a rookie preacher! The apostles were teaching the Word, and the Spirit was transforming lives. The church was exploding. And this growth was in addition to the 3,000 who responded to the Word in Acts 2:41. Make a note of this: Direct connection exists between teaching the Word and belief. This is true in the book of Acts (2:41, 4:4, 11:20-21, 12:24, 14:3-4, 15:35-36, 17:2-4, and 28:23-24). And the same is true today. I'm concerned that rather than potentially offending some students, some student ministry leaders choose not to teach the Bible. Instead God's Word is replaced by "extreme" this or "hot" that, curiously thought-provoking DVDs, or feel-good pep talks. As a result our ministries sidestep the transforming power of the Bible.

The Acts believers were filled with the Spirit. They taught God's Word with boldness. They proclaimed the name. And God transformed lives.

The religious leaders were about as happy as Bears fans at Lambeau Field after a Packers victory. In other words, greatly disturbed. So they seized Peter and John and took them into custody. Teaching the Word got Peter and John into trouble. Oops. Bad plan. Maybe they should've just softened the edges a bit. Perhaps they should've been more seeker sensitive and culturally relevant. What do you think?

I love the only question the religious leaders asked: "By what power or what *name* did you do this?" (Acts 4:7, emphasis added). Peter respectfully replied, "Rulers and elders of the people! If we are being called to account today for an act of kindness shown to a cripple...It is by *the name* of Jesus Christ of Nazareth, whom you crucified but whom God raised from the dead, that this man stands before you healed" (Acts 4:8-10). Peter and John truly believed their effectiveness wasn't due to a clever strategy or ministry model. Nor to their dynamic teaching ability. It wasn't due to a cool meeting place. God forbid we become full of ourselves and think any ministry success is due to anything we are doing. Instead we must remember it's all about the name.

Peter continued, "Salvation is found in no one else, for there is no other *name* under heaven given to men by which we must be saved" (Acts 4:12). It's all about the name. This statement is ridiculed by world religions, the media, and our culture. Sadly, some Christians are embarrassed by this statement. We must contend for this truth. While preaching about Acts 4:12, my senior pastor, James MacDonald, commented:

I don't delight in that. I'm not happy about this. I just know what God's Word says. Broad is the road that leads to destruction. Many people are going that way. Narrow is the road that leads to eternal life. Only a few are finding it. You might say, "I want everyone to go to heaven." Well, God does, too. God isn't willing that any should perish but all should come to repentance. God so loved the world that he gave his only Son so everyone who believes in him should not perish but have eternal life. It's only the arrogance of the human heart that insists on multiple ways. We understand narrowness in every other intellectual discipline...Why should it surprise us that it's the same in theology? God made the universe to operate on principles. *Truth* by definition is intolerant. All truth, real truth, is intolerant of error. And we're significantly damaging the church of Jesus Christ when we embrace the spirit of the age and pull tolerance into the center of it all.

Have you noticed spirituality is in, but Jesus is out? It's fashionable to be spiritual, but not Christian. You can mention God, but not Jesus. Why? Our pluralistic American society accepts any belief as an equal means to get to God. But Jesus clearly claimed to be *the* way to God, not a way to God. Ironically, Jesus isn't tolerated by people who pride themselves on being tolerant. But Jesus really isn't exclusive. Jesus is inclusive. He welcomes any and all who believe. The amazing thing isn't that Jesus is the only way. The amazing thing is—we have a way at all. All I know is what the Bible says: "Salvation is found in no one else" (Acts 4:12).

The more Peter and John talked, the more the religious leaders noticed something: "When they saw the courage of Peter and John and realized that they were unschooled, ordinary men, they were astonished and they took note that these men had been with Jesus" (Acts 4:13). I've heard this passage taught many times. It usually goes like this: Peter and John were ordinary guys—they were jeans and T-shirt kind of guys' guys. But what made them unique was they had spent time with Jesus, and Jesus clearly had rubbed off on them. Therefore, if you and I spend time with Jesus, we'll be like Jesus, too.

That's an accurate application of this passage, but I think we can find more. This understanding misses the context and the most important part of the verse. My pastor helped me see there was a particular way Peter and John were acting that got the religious leaders' attention. This verse is about their boldness. They addressed the religious leaders with respect and confidence. They weren't intimidated, and they spoke with genuine conviction. When the religious leaders saw this, they began to say to each other, "This is oddly familiar. Where have we seen this boldness before? Oh, yeah. They're just like the guy they are following. They're just like Jesus."

Before we move on, let me get this on the table about boldness. Boldness isn't about being mean, obnoxious, loud, or pushy. Boldness isn't about being harsh. It's not the bullhorn guy on the street corner. It's not the student standing on a cafeteria table and rebuking classmates. It's not wearing a "Turn or Burn" T-shirt. It's not I'm-going-to-shove-this-down-your-throat-whether-you-want-to-hear-it-or-not. At Harvest we talk about boldness as being gentle, kind, and loving. Boldness is being sincere and authentic. Boldness is just being convinced. It's not being afraid to share what Jesus has done in your life. Peter and John weren't afraid, and they spoke with boldness.

CARING SILENCES CRITICS.

Clearly, the religious leaders were agitated. As they deliberated about what to do, the healed guy was all smiles as he stood beside the apostles. And they were left with nothing to say. The kindness Peter and John had shown silenced their critics. Isn't this awesome? I long for this to be true of our lives and our student ministries. Let's not just share about the name—but let's care in a way so even our critics can't speak maliciously about our ministries. Perhaps Peter was reflecting on this exact moment when he later wrote these words:

> Who is going to harm you if you are eager to do good? But
> even if you should suffer for doing what is right, you are

*blessed...*But in your hearts set apart Christ as Lord. Always be prepared to give an answer to everyone who asks you to give the reason for the hope that you have. But do this with gentleness and respect, keeping a clear conscience, *so that those who speak maliciously against your good behavior in Christ may be ashamed of their slander."* (1 Peter 3:13-16, emphasis added)

The religious leaders couldn't deny the evidence. How could they harm Peter and John for their kindness? Peter and John weren't just about saying stuff; they were lovingly reaching out in the name of Jesus and caring for people. They were healing hurts and meeting people's needs.

Nonetheless, the religious leaders were jealous of the ministry competition in town. The new ministry was drawing attention away from their church. Have you ever felt this about another church or student ministry in your area? Jealousy is such a destructive thing in the church. Because their popularity was being threatened, the leaders ordered Peter and John "not to speak or teach at all in *the name of Jesus*" (Acts 4:18). Sounds like today, right? We have freedom of speech but lack the freedom to speak about the name—at least not without catching some flak.

CAN'T STOP CARING AND SHARING

Peter and John didn't heed the warning because they had a higher calling. Peter and John replied, "For we cannot help speaking about what we have seen and heard" (Acts 4:20). I love this. They couldn't stop speaking. *This* is boldness. When was the last time students couldn't stop speaking about what they'd experienced in Jesus? How would it be if this was true of kids in your group?

After being released, Peter and John found their friends. They shared a brief report and then got on their knees and prayed together. They praised God for his sovereignty and prayed for continued boldness. "And after they prayed, the place where they were meeting was

moving forward > by looking back

shaken. And they were all filled with the Holy Spirit and spoke the word of God boldly" (v. 31). The Holy Spirit filled their lives and their mouths.

Chapter 4 ends with these words about their caring and sharing: "All the believers were one in heart and mind. No one claimed that any of his possessions was his own, but they *shared* everything they had. With great power the apostles continued to *testify* to the resurrection of the Lord Jesus...there were no needy persons among them" (vv. 32-34).

This is a picture of missional living. The early believers were all on the same page. They were all committed to the same things. They had unity. And a tangible expression of their unity was caring through being sacrificially generous. They gladly sold and shared their possessions. They had a what-is-mine-is-yours mentality. And as a result they had "no needy persons among them." This fires me up. I long for this to be more of a reality in our student ministry.

Along with their caring, the apostles practiced sharing. Because they were filled with the Spirit, they had great power as they shared with boldness. And what exactly were they sharing? They were testifying to what they'd seen and heard. In other words, they shared their testimonies—specifically about the power of the resurrection. Have you or your students ever thought, "I don't know what to say" when it comes to sharing your faith? Well, why not start with your story? That's what the apostles did.

Perhaps Peter's testimony went this way: "I was on my fishing boat when I realized I was a sinful man and Jesus was the Son of God. I fell to my knees and surrendered my life to Jesus. And he completely changed my life. Then one day Jesus died. But three days later he rose from the dead. And because Jesus is alive, you can be alive, too." The apostles simply and sincerely shared their testimonies about the resurrection of Jesus. I'm guessing if the apostles shared their testimonies when sharing their faith, then maybe we should, too.

Throughout the book of Acts the believers were reaching out and serving through caring and sharing in the name of Jesus. Let's expand our study to consider a biblical theology of service.

a biblical theology of (s)ervice

God *is* compassion.

Any discussion about a biblical theology of service must begin with the character of God. And when we think of the attributes of God, we don't list adjectives about God. God doesn't *have* attributes; God *is* his attributes. God doesn't have love; God *is* love. God doesn't have holiness; God *is* holiness. God doesn't have compassion; God *is* compassion.

God isn't defined by compassion. God defines compassion. Compassion is more than an emotion. Emotions don't help people. To hurt when someone is hurting or feel sad when someone is sad is pity—not necessarily compassion. Todd Phillips writes, "Real, biblical compassion is not just taking pity on someone. *Feeling badly is not compassion.* You cannot simply say, 'I feel badly and I wish I could do something.' At best, this can be called sympathy; at worst, it is apathy."[1] Biblical compassion involves both emotion and expression.

Therefore, to say God is compassion means God suffers with people in need, and God's character stirs him to action.

As followers of Jesus Christ we should be the most compassionate people in the world. We should feel the pain of the poor, oppressed, marginalized, and victimized—and then be moved to action. Our motive for serving others is: We long to reflect the character of God in our lives—not because of a guilt trip or because it's fashionable among celebrities. Since God is a compassionate God, we must be compassionate people (see Luke 6:36).

Both Testaments reveal God's compassion for physical needs (body) and spiritual needs (soul).

GOD'S COMPASSION FOR PHYSICAL NEEDS

Ever wonder how God feels about the disadvantaged in society? The psalmist left no room to wonder when he wrote:

> The Lord is gracious and compassionate,
>
> slow to anger and rich in love.

moving forward > by looking back

The Lord is good to all;

he has compassion on all he has made...

The Lord is faithful to all his promises and loving toward all he has made. (Psalm 145:8-9, 13)

Then the psalmist moves from this general description to eight specific examples of God's compassion. He proclaims that God—

> Upholds the cause of the oppressed
> Gives food to the hungry
> Sets prisoners free
> Gives sight to the blind
> Lifts up the humble
> Loves the righteous
> Watches over foreigners
> Sustains the fatherless and widows (Psalm 146:7-9)

If these things matter to God, shouldn't they matter to us as well?

I recently attended the memorial service for Joe Stowell II. He was the father of our teaching pastor, Dr. Joe Stowell, and the grandfather of two friends. Anyone who knew the elder Stowell knew his life passage was Isaiah 58:10-12. This passage is a powerful statement about how God views the oppressed and disadvantaged:

And if you spend yourselves in behalf of the hungry and satisfy the needs of the oppressed, then your light will rise in the darkness, and your night will become like the noonday. The LORD will guide you always; he will satisfy your needs in a sun-scorched land and will strengthen your frame. You will be like a well-watered garden, like a spring whose waters never fail. Your people will rebuild the ancient ruins and will raise up the age-old foundations; you will be called Repairer of Broken Walls, Restorer of Streets with Dwellings. (Isaiah 58:10-12)

God *is* compassion. God feels the pain of the needy and is stirred to action.

God's compassion is seen most clearly in the life and ministry of Jesus. In the past God spoke through Isaiah and other prophets. But God has also spoken to us through his Son, who is God's "exact representation" (Hebrews 1:2-3) and "the image of the invisible God" (Colossians 1:15). Truly, what Jesus did on earth is equal to God's character, and God's character is equal to what Jesus did on earth.

The Gospels are packed with other examples of Jesus being deeply concerned for people's physical needs. Late one afternoon when Jesus was teaching a crowd, he saw famished faces. He stopped his message and said to his disciples, "I have *compassion* for these people; they have already been with me three days and have nothing to eat. If I send them home hungry, they will collapse on the way" (Mark 8:2-3, emphasis added). So he multiplied a few loaves and fish to feed the 4,000 men until they were satisfied.

In another instance, when Jesus "saw a large crowd, he had *compassion* on them and healed their sick" (Matthew 14:14, emphasis added).

Lepers were among the most neglected in Jesus' day. They were unattractive, unwelcome, and unloved. One day a man with leprosy came to Jesus begging on his knees: "Filled with *compassion*, Jesus reached out his hand and touched the man" (Mark 1:41). Jesus could've healed him through a spoken word. But his compassion compelled him to tenderly touch the very skin of the leper.

Jesus fed the hungry. He healed the sick. He cured paralytics. He gave sight to the blind. He protected people by calming a storm. He cured the mute and the deaf. He restored a sick woman to health. He healed "every disease and sickness" (Matthew 4:23). Jesus didn't see those with physical needs as an inconvenience. He didn't avoid their suffering—rather he met them in their suffering.

As was his custom, Jesus went to the synagogue on the Sabbath. On one particular Sabbath he stood up before the congregation and read from the scroll of the prophet Isaiah. He unrolled it to a particular place and began reading: "The Spirit of the Lord is on me, because he has anointed me to *preach good news to the poor.* He has sent me to *proclaim freedom for the prisoners* and *recovery of sight for the blind,* to *release the oppressed,* to proclaim the year of the Lord's favor" (Luke 4:18-19, emphasis added). Jesus was the fulfillment of this Scripture. These words were a summary of his earthly ministry. Should it surprise us that Peter and John took time to minister to the lame beggar in Acts 3? They did exactly what their Master would've done.

GOD'S COMPASSION FOR SPIRITUAL NEEDS

Jesus cared deeply for people. Beyond having compassion for physical needs, he felt compassion for souls. "When he saw the crowds, he had *compassion* on them, because they were harassed and helpless, like sheep without a shepherd" (Matthew 9:36 emphasis added).

What is a sheep without a shepherd? Lost. Two kinds of people live in the world—lost and found. The only difference between lost people and found people is—found people have acknowledged their sin and placed their faith in Jesus Christ. Some people feel uncomfortable about the word *lost*—but this word is used in the Bible. Still, let's not forget how Jesus felt toward the lost—he had compassion. Jesus felt something deep in his spirit. His heart was stirred with emotion. He felt tenderness.

Are you filled with tender compassion when you see spiritually lost students in your community or in your church? How much do you really care? Recently, I was at the mall, and a group of six students was walking toward me. The kids were decked out in black with low-riding pants, some tats, facial rings, and studded chains. Some hair was dyed a dark red, some was dyed black, and one guy had a shaved head. The guys were vulgar and loud. The girls were hanging on the guys. I'm ashamed to admit rather than being filled with compassion, I was filled with pride and judgment. Rather than seeing these students as sheep who were harassed and helpless, I viewed them as a pack of wolves. God, forgive me for stereotyping based on outward appearances. God, replace my judgmental and self-righteous spirit with tenderness and compassion.

I wonder how many lost sheep walk into our churches only to leave feeling even more harassed. Have we lost our compassion for the lost?

Jesus told a story to show God's compassion for the lost. It was about a teenager who basically said to his dad, "I don't care whether you're dead or not. I want my inheritance. And I want it now." Can you imagine the pain in the father's heart?

The boy took the money and ran. It was now party time—alcohol, women, gambling, and maxing out his credit on stuff. He lived for everything the world offered. But one day he had no more money. He'd squandered all of it on wild living.

In desperation he looked in the want ads for a job. But because he was a high school dropout the only job he was qualified for was feeding pigs for a farmer. He hit rock bottom when he realized the pigs were living and eating better than he was. He began to think about life back home. Even the workers on his dad's farm were treated better than he was being treated. He was full of regret and ashamed of all he'd done. But he chose to make a change. He got up and headed for home.

As he was walking, he thought about what to say to his dad. He rehearsed his speech over and over again: "Dad, I was wrong to disrespect you. I don't deserve to be your son, but I'd like to be your servant."

Jesus described what happened next: "But while he was still a long way off, his father saw him and was *filled with compassion* for him; he ran to his son, threw his arms around him and kissed him" (Luke 15:20, emphasis added). What an incredible picture of God! The father was watching for his wayward son, hoping he would return. And when the father saw him, he wasn't filled with anger. Instead he was filled with compassion. And he ran to his son and hugged him.

At first the son didn't get it. He nervously stuttered his way through his rehearsed speech as if he could earn his dad's favor. But the dad called for a robe, sandals, and a ring. Then they celebrated with a party in the son's honor—because he'd been lost, but now he was found.

This is a story about God's compassion for spiritual needs—but it's not the only such story in Scripture. In fact, the entire Bible is a redemptive story, from Genesis through Revelation. The big picture—or metanarrative—of the Bible is *God redeeming the world.*

The story begins with God and his creation of the world. Everything was perfect in the garden of Eden. Adam and Eve had it all—health, happiness, companionship, and an incredibly close relationship with their Creator. But not long into the story they chose to disobey God. The fall brought sin and its consequences into the world. As a result we have crime, death, pain, broken relationships, war, and all the other junk that comes with sin. Even though people turned their backs on God, God made a covenant promise through a relationship with Abraham and his descendants. Throughout the Old Testament the people of Israel struggled to remain faithful to God. Nonetheless, God remained faithful.

Two thousand years ago God came to Planet Earth to redeem humankind. The Gospels give details about how Jesus lived a sinless life, died a horrific death, and rose victoriously over the grave. Now all who receive Christ can have a relationship with their Creator while on earth and for eternity. The majority of the New Testament is about how we can be witnesses of and witnesses to this redemptive story. And we see how God will one day restore creation completely in the book of Revelation.

Today you and your students are invited to join in this redemptive story by reaching out to meet people in their physical and spiritual needs in the name of Jesus.

Because God is a God of compassion for people's physical and spiritual needs, we are to reflect his character by caring and sharing. Our theology must directly impact our lives. The next three chapters move forward to show how to be a practical theologian about service.

Imagine If...

Imagine if our ministries were less about our ministries' names and more about *the* name. Imagine if our students were actively involved in compassionate service outside the walls of our groups. Imagine if, because of our service in our communities, no one could speak a bad word about our groups without being ashamed of their slander. Imagine if the statement "There were no needy people among them" were true of our ministries. Imagine if our students had genuine compassion for lost souls. Imagine if our students couldn't help but speak of what God has been doing in their lives. Imagine if our students understood the redemptive story of God. Imagine if God were to increase our compassion for the needy, oppressed, and marginalized in our world. Imagine if we had a greater compassion for the spiritually lost in our lives. Imagine if our hearts were in tune with the heart of God.

Would our ministries be any different? Might we see God transforming lives?

moving forward > questions

Questions for personal reflection and team discussion:

1. "God is compassion." What does this statement mean to you?

2. How would you describe the role of service (caring and sharing) for the early believers in the book of Acts?

3. How is service an outflow of adoration, community, and truth?

4. Is there a difference between meeting needs and meeting people in their needs?

5. If your students aren't reaching out, do you notice their faith becomes stagnant? If yes, why do you suppose that is?

6. Would your ministry be any different if you were to renew your commitment to the ministry of service? If so, in what ways?

7. What aspects of this chapter do you want to discuss with others on your leadership team?

---

1. Todd Phillips, *Get Uncomfortable* (Nashville, TN: Lifeway Press/threads, 2008), 32.

God has placed your student ministry in a specific community for a reason. Have you ever thought about why you're in the community you're in?

Before organizing service trips to another city, think about how you might be able to serve in your own community. In *A New Kind of Youth Ministry*, my friend Chris Folmsbee tells a story about how he bumped into another youth group at a fuel stop in Paducah, Kentucky. Chris was returning home to the Twin Cities with his youth group after a missions trip to Nashville. His group had spent the week serving the homeless by feeding them, passing out clothes, and interacting with them. As he stood next to the gas pump, he noticed the name on the other church van. The other youth group was from a United Methodist church in Nashville. Chris struck up a conversation with the other youth pastor and learned they were coming home from serving the homeless in Minneapolis. This gas-station encounter caused both youth pastors to question what they were doing.[1]

Have you taken the time to know your community—the city or county where God has placed you? Do you know the needs in your own community? Do you know the homeless rate or how many families are living under the poverty line? And more than knowing facts about your community, do you feel the pain of your community? Beyond knowing about the people in your community, have you entered into the lives of people—individuals and families outside your church body? What plan does God have for your community? Are you up for being part of that plan?

Serving Locally

My older brother has asked these questions for our church. In his role as pastor of compassion ministries, Kent has sought to engage our congregation with caring and sharing in the name of Jesus within our immediate geographical community.

Across the street from our Rolling Meadows campus is Arlington Park, the premier horse track in the Chicagoland area. It's home to the nationally televised Arlington Million each August, boasting a million-dollar purse. During the horse racing season of May through September, more than a thousand immigrants move onto the racetrack property and live in the dorms behind the stables. The dorms are cinder-block spaces no bigger than motel rooms. Most units don't even have a private bath. It's not unusual for parents to have four or five children living with them in these rooms as their dads and moms clean the stables and the highbred horses. Each summer more than 200 children and youth move to the property with their parents. The activities and opportunities are limited—and many never leave the property for the entire summer. We believe this is one reason why God has placed our church in our community.

We personally invite these kids into our church for youth activities and offer Spanish translation in our services. But more than this, we enter their turf. Each summer our students and adults partner together to provide day camps—including games, crafts, music, and Bible lessons—for the children and youth living at the racetrack. And we sponsor a day trip to Six Flags to culminate the summer. We're just seeking to love our neighbors and shine the light of Christ for them.

Not far from our Elgin campus is the Mulberry Court apartment community consisting of 600 units in a dozen buildings. This housing complex is known for its high crime and gang activity. It used to be one of the most unreached neighborhoods in the Elgin area. But police officers, schoolteachers, social workers, and city officials have noticed a change since our church began to rent a two-bedroom apartment in the heart of this complex. Harvest House is a prayer-empowered, relationship-based, neighborhood-focused ministry providing after-school mentoring, ESL classes, youth outreach, and a food pantry. This ministry is year-round, including a weekly summer barbecue and day camps. Rather than handing out gospel tracts, we're living the gospel through entering into these people's very lives. Many public officials are encouraged that a church would be intentionally invested and impact so many individuals and families. This ministry is a tangible expression of the gospel as we seek to love our neighbors by building a bridge of connection between our church and community. Some of our students volunteer weekly with Harvest House, and our student ministry supports this outreach several times during the year through various partnerships.

Your community is different from our community. God has placed us where we are. And God has placed you where you are. What plan does God have for *your* community? How will your student ministry (and your church) be incarnational expressions of Christ in your community?

Living Incarnationally

Living incarnationally begins with having God's perspective. We need to see beyond the immense challenges within our community and see the harvest field. We need to see beyond hard-hearted youth and see the harvest field. We need to see beyond the struggling immigrant family and see the harvest field. We need to see beyond generational sin and see the harvest field. We need to see beyond the racial divides and see the harvest field. As Jesus was, so we must be gripped with compassion for those around us.

The problem is, we can be so independent of our own community. Our culture promotes a lifestyle disconnected from neighbors. And our churches have allowed our culture to create a gap between us and our neighbors. But Scripture says to "love your neighbor as yourself" (Galatians 5:14). We need to reach across the divide. We need to be part of our community. Since Jesus entered our world, he knows what we go through and our struggles. In the same way God desires for us to enter into lives around us—not just do lots of things, spreading ourselves thin in many directions. This may mean choosing fewer activities to devote more intentional time with fewer people. Are you willing to do that? Beyond caring for people in general, we need to care for individuals.

Paul writes, "For it is by grace you have been saved, through faith—and this not from yourselves, it is the gift of God—not by works, so that no one can boast. For we are God's workmanship, created in Christ Jesus to do good works, which God prepared in advance for us to do" (Ephesians 2:8-10). We aren't saved by good works. But we are saved for good works. And we must never separate the good news from good works. We must do the works God has prepared for us to do.

We're to do good works because that's what we were created to do in Christ. The reason we do good works isn't just to create goodwill in our communities, but because of who God is. God is a God of compassion. The more we learn about God and the more we love God, the more we want to reflect him in all we do. This is what it means to practice our theology. Paul writes, "For Christ's love compels us...So from now on we regard no one from a worldly point of view" (2 Corinthians 5:14, 16). Our motive is nothing less than Christ. And as we fall in love with Christ, we begin to see people from a wholly different point of view.

What would a community of students look like if they were truly compelled by the love of Christ? One thing is certain: It wouldn't have a *serve us* attitude but rather a *service* mentality. Titus 3:14 states, "Our [students] must learn to devote themselves to doing what is good, in order that they may provide for daily necessities and not live unproductive lives." None of us wants our students to live unproductive lives, right? Therefore, we need to provide opportunities for students to experience serving others outside the walls of our churches and in our communities. And this is where evangelism begins—serving through caring for people.

This chapter offers practical examples for moving students from *serve us* to *service*. But don't just do ideas. Don't just fill your calendars with activities. Instead make sure students understand the theology of service. And consider the needs of your particular community and the ministry partnerships possibly already available. Ask yourself these questions:

> How can we partner with what our church is already doing in our community?

> How can we partner with an existing ministry or agency in our community?

> How can we offer one-time opportunities to expose students to service?

> How can we promote genuine partnerships for students to experience the benefits of investing in ongoing relationships?

Serving through Actions

SECRET SERVICE

We've mobilized our high school students to serve through "Secret Service." Students arrive at the church and hop on buses knowing they're going to serve—but not knowing where or how. Buses go on a variety of routes, and each bus has several stops where some of the students unload. Some of the destinations include—

> Nursing homes—provide bingo, play table games, lead music, make crafts, visit the elderly in their rooms

> Salvation Army—help clean a retail store or organize donations in a warehouse

> Children's hospital—make cards and visit children

> Park district—pick up trash or remove graffiti at a park

> Inner-city organization—play games with neighborhood kids or serve food
> Crisis pregnancy center—assist with a donor mailing
> Local food depository—sort food donations
> Habitat for Humanity—help with a home-building project
> Red Cross—serve in whatever way is needed

Students experience the joy of one-time serving and are exposed to opportunities they may not otherwise experience. After serving, students are eager to share their stories and hear about other stories and destinations from the others in the group. Secret Service can work for any size group. Actually, if a youth group is small, Secret Service is easier to implement because it involves fewer sites and fewer vehicles.

SECRET SERVICE LEADERSHIP OVERVIEW

Thank you for being willing and available to serve at Secret Service. Below is a summary of your responsibilities:

Arriving and connecting with leaders

> We need all our mentors to arrive by 5:30 p.m. We'll gather as needed outside by the curb. We hope to check in some students and get the first bus rolling by 5:45 p.m.

> Each bus will be going to multiple destinations, so you need to gather cell phone numbers of the other leaders on your bus. If you have a cell phone, please bring it with you. Also, see if the bus driver has a cell phone and trade phone numbers if so.

> In addition to your cell phone, please bring a digital camera because we'd love to see pictures of how all our teams are serving God and people.

Loading the bus

> You need to be standing outside the school bus in the parking lot. We have multiple buses, so go to the bus with your project number.

> Do not tell the students where the bus is going—hence, "Secret" Service.

> As students arrive, we'll direct them to bus 1. After bus 1 is loaded, we'll load bus 2, etc. We want to encourage students just to load and get to know other students tonight. Please help us with this. You don't have to try to keep all your students in your home group on the same bus or on your particular bus.

> Before students get on the bus, you need to confirm they've submitted their parental release form for the school year and give them wristbands. The wristbands indicate which stop each student should get off the bus at.

> Once a student gets on your bus, he can't get off until you arrive at his destination.

> We want our buses to pull out between 5:45 and 6:10 p.m. We'll have staggered departures. As a bus is full, it will pull out.

THANKSGIVING GROCERY RUNS

While the traditional Thanksgiving food drive can generate some food, it usually comes at no sacrifice to the students. You know how it works. Students are challenged to bring some food items to youth group for the inner-city mission, so what do they do? They raid Mom's kitchen cupboards as they walk out the door and fill a plastic grocery bag with

En route to location

> While driving, you can play 20 questions. Students can ask up to 20 yes or no questions and try to guess the destinations. Remember: only yes or no questions. If students can't guess, tell them.
> After students guess locations, briefly describe how you'll serve at the locations (see your Secret Service mission).
> Remind students they're to serve in action and attitude tonight.
> Pump up your students to serve God and people tonight!
> Get to know the students and encourage them to get to know each other.

Arriving at the location

> Have students get off with you and look for the contact person at your site.
> Have the contact person do a brief orientation with the students—explain background, who they are serving, and why.
> Your main role is to keep students focused and encourage them.
> You should arrive at your destination between 6:15 and 6:45 p.m. You'll have a limited amount of time to serve based on the drop-off and pickup schedule.
> If you have time before you get picked up, take some time to debrief with the students:

-What did you see, hear, and feel tonight?

-Did you learn anything tonight?

Leaving the location

> Before you leave, have each student sign the thank-you sheet.
> Your pickup time will be determined by drop-off time: The first group dropped off is first to be picked up. The bus captain needs to coordinate details with the driver.
> Please have your group ready to load when the bus arrives.
> Your goal should be to return to the Harvest campus by 9 p.m. or sooner.
> If you didn't have time to debrief at the site, do so on the bus ride home.

a few soup cans and some boxes of mac 'n' cheese. Once at church the students stack their items into a giant food tower, and the next day it gets delivered to the organization. The whole thing is totally impersonal and has little, if any, impact on students.

Why not replace the food drive with a grocery run? This will give students an opportunity to—

THANKSGIVING GROCERY RUN
Sunday before Thanksgiving

Here's what you do:

1. Tell students to bring $5 (or more) on the Sunday before Thanksgiving. Determine and communicate in advance where your group is meeting.

2. Travel to a grocery store.

3. Divide students into groups of two to four and give them shopping instructions.

4. Hand out premade 3 x 5 cards:

   > List parts of the Thanksgiving meal grocery list (e.g., one card might list lettuce, tomatoes, cucumbers, baby carrots, and salad dressing). The team is responsible for picking out the items and buying them; OR

   > Simply tell the students to go to aisle 4 or 6 or whatever. Students then pool their money to buy a variety of grocery items in that aisle. The toiletry and paper aisles are fine because people need these items, too. Note: This option is best if you want to provide a variety of groceries beyond a Thanksgiving meal.

5. Adult mentors should pool their money for the turkey. It's usually best to give only turkey breasts, as a whole 15-pound turkey can be overwhelming to a family who doesn't have the means to cook it. Or contact the grocery store in advance. Perhaps you can get a small turkey donated for this service project.

6. Students go through the checkout line as a group and pay for their groceries on their own. Then all the groups combine their grocery items. Drive to the family's residence. Introduce the team, deliver the food items, hand the family a signed card from your group, and pray with the family.

7. End the evening by reflecting as a group about your experience and praying for the families.

This is a great project to serve families in need. It's also a fabulous way to help students understand how much groceries, diapers, and paper products cost. Students get to spend their own money and work from a budget in the store.

> Sacrificially give

> Understand the real cost of paying for groceries—this helps students understand the financial hardship it can be for families with little or no income to do something they (the students) take for granted (eating)

> Realize families in your own community have needs—single moms, dads who've been laid off, families with unexpected medical bills, etc.

moving forward > by looking back

> Put real faces and circumstances with their donations
> Have fun getting out of the church to go shopping with friends
> Be witnesses to the grocery store employees

You can adopt one needy family for every 15 to 20 students in your group. Depending on the size of your group, you might combine two small groups. While many ways to find needy families in your own community are available, I suggest you start by talking with the benevolence or compassion ministry in your church. Each Thanksgiving, Harvest Students works in partnership with Harvest House and our single-mother ministries. Further details for the grocery run are given in the sidebar.

THE AMAZING (FOOD) RACE

Most cities or counties have a food depository serving those in need—perhaps your own church has a food pantry. This activity is a fun and competitive way to get your students out of the church building to interact with your church's neighbors, encouraging them to join in serving the needs of others. Below are some sample instructions:

Join the High School ministry on Wednesday, July 11 at 7:00 P.M. as we race to collect as many food items as we can in an hour for the Harvest food pantry. Bring some food from home and some money to donate.

1. Collect the food students bring from their homes.

2. Collect money donated by students. Choose two students to go with a leader to the grocery store to spend the team's money.

3. Collect food by going door to door in assigned neighborhoods. Only leaders are allowed to drive students in cars.

> Guidelines for door-to-door collection

1. Students must be in groups of two with a minimum of eight students per block—we want groups of students within eyesight of each other.

2. Knock on the door.

3. What to say: "Hi. My name is _____, and this is _____. We're from _____ Church. (Hand person the card.) We're trying to collect food for a community food pantry through our church. Do you have any nonperishable items you'd be willing to donate?" (Don't go inside homes.)

4. Thank people regardless of their response.

5. Groups must stop going door to door at 8 p.m. sharp.

> Return to the church with the food

1. Count your food items.

2. Sort food items into correct categories.

3. Get students to move the food to the pantry area.

The grade with the most food items wins.

CHRISTMAS PROJECTS

The Christmas season is a wonderful time of year to get students to consider the needs of others. Rather than having your annual Christmas party with a white-elephant gift exchange, why not do something to serve others outside your church building? What kind of statement would this make to your students about the value of serving others? Many project opportunities appear at this time, such as—

moving forward > by looking back

> *Operation Angel Tree—a ministry of Prison Fellowship*
  Did you know that 2.3 million children, including some in your own area, have moms or dads in prison? Angel Tree reaches out to children of inmates and their families with the love of Christ. Angel Tree will connect you to children and families in need so you can provide Christmas gifts from the inmate parent for the children.

> *Operation Christmas Child—a ministry of Samaritan's Purse*
  Through Samaritan's Purse, you can give gift-filled shoe boxes to needy children from Malawi and Kazakhstan and Liberia to the ends of the earth.

> *Operation Joshua*
  Provide Christmas gifts and care packages to military personnel in your church or community stationed overseas during the holidays.

Students can bring gift-filled shoe boxes to youth group or their small groups and have a wrapping party as part of the project. Or use your small group time to go shopping together.   Another   Christmas idea is to divide your group into teams and scatter throughout the community to sing and ring the Salvation Army bells at local grocery or department stores. (Of course, you'll need to sign up for a time slot with your local Salvation Army branch). Many shoppers are inspired to see teenagers caroling and tend to give more generously as a result. This can be a bonding time for your group—especially if you can end the night at a pizza place or at someone's home. If your group is large, scatter by grade or small groups to several stores at the same time.

30-HOUR FAMINE

This is an international youth movement through World Vision to fight hunger. Did you know that 28 children die every minute from malnutrition or diseases that could easily be prevented? That's 1,667 children every hour, 40,000 children daily. Students are encouraged to go without food for 30 hours—generally from lunch on Friday through a later dinner on Saturday. This experience allows students to feel a small sense of the hunger people experience every day and to support the cause of World Vision by seeking Famine sponsors. In addition to supporting this worthy cause, the Famine can unite your group through extended time together.

Each year that I've led a 30-hour Famine, we've had students spend Friday night together. On Friday evening we invited some guest speakers to expand our students' local and global perspectives. We worshiped together and prayed in stations for needs around the world. Then on Saturday we mobilized our team to serve in various projects throughout the community. Before breaking the fast on Saturday night, our students sat together and were recognized during the Saturday evening worship service. When breaking the fast, World Vision suggests surprising students with two meals by placing them in one of two rooms—each with a different meal. The majority of the students receive rice, black beans, and water (the most common meal around the world). But a randomly selected percentage of students is taken to another room to eat pizza, chicken wings, garlic bread, salad, assorted beverages, and a dessert. This can be a teachable moment for both groups of students as a reminder of how a majority of the world still only eats rice and beans while most Americans have many varied meal options every day. (Important note: Be sensitive to students in your group who may have eating disorders or other medical reasons for non-participation. Consider if this activity will work for your group under the latter circumstances and ways you can modify participation or parameters.)

A GREAT DAY OF SERVING

A church in our area sponsors an annual Great Day of Serving. What I like about their event is that it's intergenerational—allowing students to serve alongside their parents and other adults of the church. It's really a great time for the church to be the church and not be segregated by age. The Saturday event starts with a morning rally for all who are serving. Then the volunteers deploy throughout the community to do various work projects serving those in need. The day ends with an evening celebration of worship and testimonies from the day.

LOVE OUT LOUD

Mobilize your students to be a blessing to others in your community by spending a Saturday afternoon just giving stuff away—either in an impoverished area or in your own community. Go to an apartment complex and set up a folding table in the courtyard to give away "bags of love" with assorted groceries, paper products, light bulbs, and toiletries to each family. Take a few balls with you because chances are you can quickly get a game of kickball or foursquare going with the children. Or take your students to an area where homeless people gather. In addition to a smile and a handshake, give out sack lunches, socks, and knit caps (in winter) or extra fruit and water bottles (in summer). Seek to engage in conversation, listen to stories, and pray together. Or go to a place in your community where people gather or pass by as pedestrians. Hand out bottled water and snacks. I know a student ministry that has a free hot chocolate station in the park across the street from their church. Or take your students to places like a local strip mall to offer free services such as cleaning bathrooms, picking up trash, washing windows, etc.

These are just some small ways to show a watching world how God loves them. Before you start, prepare the students with the questions you'll discuss at the end of the experience:

> What did you *see*?

> What did you *hear*?

> What did you *feel*?

> How will you apply this experience in your everyday life?

BREAKING DOWN THE URBAN-SUBURBAN WALL

I know a church that sends a different middle school small group to their city's rescue mission to serve each Tuesday evening. Tuesday is when the middle school ministry meets as a large group. And each week one small group is always missing from the regular program. The rescue mission can count on about 10 students each week to serve. Once all the small groups have participated one time, the small groups rotate again. This rotation allows each small group to serve two to three times each school year. I think this is a wonderful idea for providing an ongoing connection and still getting lots of students exposed to this inner-city ministry.

But let's be careful not to perpetuate a common stereotype: The suburban church is giving and the urban center is in need and receiving. Many urban churches and ministries are capable and frankly, more effective at ministering to the people in their community without students being bused in from the suburbs to save the day. Instead suburban churches need to take students simply to assist and observe what's already happening. Maybe the suburban church is the one in need—and should be humble enough to allow the urban ministry to give to them. When I was ministering in the suburban Milwaukee area, I was active in a youth pastors' network including urban and suburban churches. Through the network I struck up a friendship with Bill, an urban youth pastor. Together we dreamed about ways to bring our students together—including several times on each others' turfs. The goal wasn't to give to the other ministry, but rather to learn from each other and be visible expressions of the body of Christ. Our students were greatly impacted by each of these experiences.

Serving through Giving

Another way to get our students serving and caring for needs is through challenging them to give sacrificially and cheerfully of their finances. Of course, you can always pass an offering basket during your regular ministry gathering. But you have other ways to challenge students to step up and give.

SELL-YOUR-POSSESSIONS CHALLENGE

Jesus challenged the rich young ruler to "sell everything you have and give to the poor" (Luke 18:22). Rather than reading this passage, why not experience it? Challenge your students to bring in a personal item of value to donate to sell in order to give the proceeds to the poor. After all, isn't this what the early church did in Acts 4:32-34? Select a student or adult volunteer who's proficient on eBay to post items on the Internet or take your items to a local eBay store. Determine three needs your money can support and let your students have some ownership by choosing which of the three needs your group will support through your eBay profits. This challenge serves a two-fold purpose: It generates cash to serve the poor, and it helps students purge themselves of their own possessions. This can be a timely challenge in January after a season of plenty. Repeat this challenge periodically.

THE 20-BUCKS CHALLENGE

Randomly select five students or more and give them each a $20 bill (or more). But there's a catch. If a student accepts the $20 bill, she understands the money doesn't belong to her but to God. Each student must agree to steward the $20 to bless and serve other people over a two-week period. As in the Parable of the Talents in Matthew 25, students are encouraged to seek to increase this investment to serve even more people. Then in two weeks each student comes back to your group to share ways they served others. This exercise can inspire others to do the same—but with their own money.

CLEAN-OUT-YOUR-CLOSET CHALLENGE

Challenge your students to bring clothes from their closets to a designated student ministry night. Have some students arrive early to create various sorting piles for pants, shirts, sweaters, jackets, and shoes at the front of the room. Dedicate some time in your program to affirm students and celebrate how their donations will serve others. To make this project more personal, select some students to take with you when you drop off the donations at the selected organization that will distribute these items to those in need. Take a camera along to get video or pictures of the organization or people being served. Show the pictures at the following ministry night.

LUNCH-MONEY CHALLENGE

Did you know that 2.8 billion people live on less than $2 per day? That's nearly half the population of our planet. And 1.2 billion of these people have to get by on $1 per day. Many students spend $5 or more per day for a hot lunch at school or fast-food restaurants. Select one month to challenge students to go without lunch on a designated weekday. Instead encourage students to donate their lunch money to an offering for a relief organization like World Relief or Compassion International. When others ask why they're not eating, it can become a conversation starter about global needs and students' faith.

COMMON-CAUSE CHALLENGE

Many students are eager to respond to a compelling challenge to donate specific items to a common cause. Highlight a ministry in need of a specific item, then encourage students to bring the item to donate the following week. Ideas include diapers (or baby food) for a crisis pregnancy center, school supplies for an after-school tutoring program, towels for a home for refugees, socks for a homeless shelter, or toys for an orphanage. Don't just presume what a ministry needs. Call and ask, "How can we help support you?" And if they say, "We really need socks," be okay with socks. It's cool to see the joy students have as they rally around a cause and give beyond dropping a few coins in an offering basket. Additionally, students tend to respond best when another student is the one sharing about a common cause challenge rather than the adult youth leader.

Now What?

Results from a recent survey by Fuller Seminary's Center for Youth and Family Ministry indicated the top thing graduating seniors would have wanted more or much more of in youth group was—can you guess? Service opportunities. Yep. Not games. Service. I'm encouraged by this; how about you?

This chapter contained some service examples for engaging students with God's world beyond the walls of the church. But they're just that—examples. Some of the ideas require more planning and time than others. Some are one-time acts of service; others are meant for ongoing ministry. But even with one-time opportunities, seek to see how they can be developed into follow-up opportunities.

The rhythm that seems to be working in our ministry is to do at a least one whole-group service activity and one donation focus per semester. But this is our rhythm. You need to develop a rhythm for serving that works in your ministry and your community.

moving forward > by looking back

After taking the time to know and feel the needs in your community, you might be overwhelmed because the challenges are immense. You may find many opportunities for engaging students in service in your community. Therefore, it's imperative to seek God's power by bathing this element of your ministry in fervent prayer. Don't just do something to do something. What has God prepared in advance for you to do? Ask God to give you eyes to see the needs in your community. Ask God for a heart of compassion. Ask God to reveal how he wants to use you and your students in the plans he has for your community. Ask God for perseverance when it gets tough.

As you engage in compassionate service in your community, you can "let your light shine before men, that they may see your good deeds and praise your Father in heaven" (Matthew 5:16).

moving forward > questions

Questions for personal reflection and team discussion:

1. What are some of your challenges for moving your group from *serve us* to *service*?

2. What would your community of students look like if it were compelled at all times by the love of Jesus?

3. Why do you think God has placed your student ministry in the specific community you're in?

4. What ministries can you partner with for ongoing service with your students?

5. How can your ministry better reflect a heart of compassion and meet others' needs?

6. How is caring for others a necessary part of your reaching out?

7. What aspects of this chapter do you want to discuss with others on your leadership team?

1.   *A New Kind of Youth Ministry* (Youth Specialties, 2006).

"You are one cent."

We were in our first team meeting after having landed in San Jose, Costa Rica, just a few hours before. Mark Edwards, a personal mentor to me and the director of Sonlife Latin America, had given each student on our team a U.S. penny.

The words "one cent" bore significance. With a grin at the play on words, Mark said, "You are one sent. You are one sent by your church and the people who are supporting you. But more importantly, you're one *sent* by God to reach students and help make disciples in this Latino culture. After this trip you'll return to the States as one sent to make disciples in your culture back home." Being a missionary isn't just something students *do* on a trip or in another culture. Instead we're all missionaries in our own cultures, schools, families, and workplaces.

Displaying a penny between his thumb and index finger Mark continued, "I want you to keep your penny in your pocket throughout this trip as a reminder of your mission. Whenever you reach into your pocket, remember you are one sent.

After you return to the States, anytime you see a penny it's my prayer that you remember you're one sent by God to make disciples." It's been many years since Mark cast this vision for missional living, but the illustration is indelibly etched into my mind. Jesus cast the same missional vision to his disciples. It was a Sunday morning, and the disciples were gathered behind closed doors. Jesus was crucified and buried a few days before, but he was now standing among them. They could hardly believe it.   Jesus said to them, "Peace be with you! As the Father has sent me, I am sending you" (John 20:21). This is a directive to the church in its earliest days. The disciples weren't to hide behind closed doors: They were to take the gospel to their community.

This same directive is relevant and authoritative for our lives and ministries today.

For each of us is "one sent."

Soul Conversations

Living out this mission of being "one sent" involves entering into soul conversations. It's not enough to just care for the poor or establish friendships with non-Christians. We're called to share the good news of Jesus Christ. This was a primary topic of prayer for the apostle Paul as he wrote a letter to the early church in Colosse from a prison cell:

> And pray for us, too, that God may open a door for our message, so that we may proclaim the mystery of Christ, for which I am in chains. Pray that I may proclaim it clearly, as I should. Be wise in the way you act toward outsiders; make the most of every opportunity. *Let your conversation be always full of grace, seasoned with salt*, so that you may know how to answer everyone. (Colossians 4:3-6, *emphasis added*)

Being full of grace doesn't mean avoiding truth. Nor does it mean sharing only part of the truth. As followers of Christ, we need to be like our Master, who was "full of grace and truth" (John 1:14). Jesus was 100 percent grace and 100 percent truth. Soul conversations are about sharing the truth in love.

Salt serves several purposes, including flavoring, preserving, and purifying. We don't know exactly which meaning Paul had in mind, but we do know this: Salt was made to impact *something else*. I've never had a late-night craving for a handful of salt; but I have craved some salt with bland French fries or a buttery ear of corn. Jesus said, "You are the salt of the earth" (Matthew 5:13). And let's clarify here: Jesus doesn't suggest that believers should be salt. He says we *are* salt. In the same way salt is made to impact something, we're made to impact our world.

We're salt in our everyday conversations when we:

Show Jesus—through caring for people by meeting them in their need

Ask Questions—by encouraging people to think about things they might otherwise ignore or keep silent about

Listen—with genuine interest and caring attention

Talk about Jesus—by sharing our stories and the story of the gospel

Sharing our faith begins with *showing Jesus* to others. Since this was the focus of the last chapter, this chapter will look at *asking questions*, *listening*, and *talking about Jesus*.

Jesus routinely entered into soul conversations. One day while Jesus was with his disciples passing through Samaria on a road trip between Jerusalem and Galilee, he stopped at a rest stop outside of Sychar. The disciples went into town for carryout, but Jesus chose to rest at the local well. He was flat-out tired from the long journey. But rather than take a nap, Jesus initiated a conversation with a woman (who had come to draw water) by asking a question: "Will you give me a drink?" (John 4:7).

The conversation flowed naturally and covered several topics including an analogy between water and living water, the woman's sinfulness, the true identity of Christ, and comparative religions. His soul conversation with the Samaritan woman in John 4 provides several significant insights for us today.

moving forward > by looking back

First, Jesus was on his way between Jerusalem and Galilee. This is "in between" time. This should be a challenge to us and our students; when we're involved in a service project, missions trip, or outreach event, it's easy to put on the ministry "hat" and look for opportunities to reach out to others. But when these events are over, we put these hats on the shelf until the next event. Instead we should live missionally by seeing the "in between" moments as opportunities to enter into soul conversations.

Second, Jesus asked a question—and listened! Many Christians need to grow in this area. When we listen a couple of things are *happening*: We know better what's happening in others' lives and what's *lacking* in their lives, which helps us know how to better introduce and talk about Jesus. And if we're asking questions and listening, others will be more likely to ask us questions and be ready to listen. When people ask, they provide an opportunity for us to talk about Jesus.

Third, Jesus moved the conversation from the known (water) to the unknown (living water). You've probably heard the tongue-in-cheek theory that every actor in Hollywood is within six degrees of separation from starring in a movie with Kevin Bacon. I'd like to suggest that sharing our faith in Jesus is always within six degrees of every conversation. We can season lots of everyday topics with soul conversations.

Fourth, Jesus didn't shame the Samaritan woman because of her sin. Her lifestyle was an aspect of the conversation, but not *the* aspect. Jesus didn't guilt her into feeling worse about her sin. Jesus modeled truth and grace. Jesus treated her with dignity and respect. There's no one beyond the grace of the gospel.

Fifth, Jesus kept bringing the conversation back to the most important topic: His true identity. It's not enough to be a spiritual person; one must have a correct understanding of who Jesus is. The woman was looking for the Messiah. Jesus declared, "I who speak to you am he" (John 4:26). Jesus is the fulfillment of the messianic prophecies—"the Lamb of God, who takes away the sin of the world!" (John 1:29).

But this isn't the end of the story.

Most of the time our outreach observations end with Jesus. But we can learn from the example of the Samaritan woman herself. Convinced that Jesus was the Messiah, she went back to the town and shared her testimony. It was that simple: Her story of life transformation was so compelling that many wanted to experience what she had experienced—many Samaritans sought out Jesus and later told her, "We no longer believe just because of what you said; now we have heard for ourselves, and we know that this man really is the Savior of the world" (John 4:42). How cool is that? And how simple is that?

We, too, can *share our story* and *share the gospel story*. The rest of this chapter will look at these two essential elements for engaging in soul conversations.

Sharing Your Story

THE *WHY* STORY

Before you can share your story, you need to have a story. The Samaritan woman shared her story because she had experienced something for herself. Have your students ever thought about *why* they are Christians? Perhaps the main reason why students don't share their faith more often isn't because of inadequate evangelism training, but because they may be uncertain about their own faith.

Before we equip our students to share their faith, it's essential that we help students wrestle with this question: "Why is the Christian faith *my* faith—not just my parents' faith, church's faith, or friend's faith?"

I like to ask students, "Tell me, *why* are you a Christian?"

"When I was seven years old..." begins the common reply.

At this point I politely interrupt, "Not *when* you became a Christian—*why*?"

"Oh, okay. I was at camp and..."

"No, that's *where* you became a Christian."

"Umm...I realized I was a sinner. I believed that Jesus was the Son of God and that he died for me. I prayed a prayer expressing my faith in him."

"That's great! But that's *how* you became a Christian, not *why* you are a Christian."

"Okay. I guess it's because I love God and I want to live my life for him."

"Fantastic. But that's *what* it means to live as a Christian. *Why* are you a Christian?"

Many students (and adults) struggle to answer the "Why?" question—to realize their reasons for their faith. Here are some other common responses to the "Why?" question:

"Because I was brought up that way."

"Because influential people in my life are."

"Because a speaker called me to convert at a camp or conference."

"Because I find _____ in my faith" (joy or fulfillment or peace or meaning).

"Because I believe it's the way to heaven."

"Simply because I believe."

But couldn't all these statements be made in regard to embracing Islam, Buddhism, Mormonism, Hinduism, Scientology, Baha'i, or whatever other faiths? Students' *why* stories must get beyond personal experience; we must help them process their *why* stories at two levels:

1. "Why are *you* a Christian?" Personal faith, narrative experience—not the Christian faith of others

2. "Why are you a *Christian*?" Personal convictions, objective truth—not any faith of others

This process looks different from conventional apologetics. Most apologetics training engages the head, not the heart. (I think I've read somewhere that knowledge puffs up.) Now I believe knowledge is essential, but it must be connected to personal convictions. And most apologetics training focuses on the objections of unbelievers. It's reactive training. The emphasis is, "How will you respond if someone asks you these questions?" Then the training proceeds to equip students with a mental database of propositional truths and practical illustrations to download to someone if they ask certain questions.

I believe we miss Peter's heart if we emphasize the first part of 1 Peter 3:15 to the neglect of the last three words: "Always be prepared to give an answer to everyone who asks you to give the reason for the hope *that you have*" (emphasis added). Our focus should be on developing a hope within our students—not just equipping them to answer someone else's questions. Our primary concern should be developing our students' faith ("Do you believe _____? If so, why?")

Do you believe there is a Creator God? If so, why?

Do you believe the Bible is the Word of God? If so, why?

Do you believe Jesus is the Son of God? If so, why?

Do you believe Jesus died and rose again? If so, why?

Do you believe salvation is by grace through faith in Jesus alone? If so, why?

Do you believe you were created to live for God's glory? If so, why?

We need to challenge our students to wrestle these questions to the ground—and for themselves—not just to formulate an answer for somebody else. Why not use the latter questions as an outline for your next small group series? Rather than the standard format of starting with teaching and ending with discussion questions, why not start with a question? After students have entered into a discussion, you can then offer logical evidence for objective truth but in a way that challenges students to solidify their own personal convictions. As students genuinely believe something for themselves it will be easier for them to share it with others.

One of my ministry goals is that all Harvest high school graduates can tell their *why* stories—including details of their faith experiences (*Why I am a Christian*) and convictions about at least one compelling objective truth (*Why I am* a Christian). The compelling objective truth is important because it can be an anchor if a student drifts into a sea of doubt during the college years, as so often happens.

A primary focus of our weeklong Spring Break Senior Trip is to help students wrestle through questions of their faith while participating in small group research and projects. At the end of the trip, all the seniors are encouraged to identify and verbalize their compelling truths. These vary from student to student—as well they should. Some include evidence for a Creator God, the reliability of Scripture, the identity of Jesus, the resurrection, and other things. It's a cool thing when students can get to the point of thoughtfully sharing their own *why* stories.

And let me clarify, the why story isn't just about knowing evidence about the Christian faith. It's about identifying personal convictions—because part of our personal story is when it moves beyond head knowledge. The next kind of story is the 'what' story. This story emphasizes the personal narrative experience.

It's what Paul did in Acts 26 as he stood on trial before King Agrippa.

THE WHAT STORY

The next page is a worksheet to help students process their what stories.

Your Story

Your Life before Christ

> What was your life like before Christ—struggles, longings, trying to "have it all together," needs, doubts, fears, broken relationships, peer pressure, not wanting to give up something, hardship, etc.?

> What were some of your misconceptions or hesitations about a relationship with God?

> If you grew up in a Christian home, was there ever a period when you resented the Christian faith? Explain.

How You Came to Christ

> What made you realize your need for a personal relationship with God?

> How did the Christian faith become meaningful to you? What were the circumstances?

> Was there a crisis (physical, relational, spiritual) that brought you to faith in Christ?

Your Life Since Trusting Christ

> Share how God has helped you with any of the above. What does a relationship with God mean to you?

> How is Christ changing your life?

> How is a personal relationship with God different from religion? What are the benefits of a relationship with God?

> What have you discovered to be true about God?

> What are some ongoing hardships, doubts, fears, etc., God is working through in you?

moving forward > by looking back

Your Life before Christ (B.C.)	How You Came to Christ (+)	Your Life since Trusting Christ (A.D.)

Tips for Storytelling

Explain the following to students in words they'll understand:

> Your story doesn't need to answer each question (on the worksheet). These are some sample themes to consider when processing your before-and-after story.

> Your story doesn't need a timeline outline. Too many testimonies emphasize "when" (e.g., "When I was four years old...when I was eight years old...then when I was 13..."). Instead we need to encourage students to share "what" was happening and "what" has happened in their lives. Most people couldn't care less about someone's timeline, but they do connect with feelings, doubts, crises, life changes, etc.

> Your story must be authentic. Share who you really are. Don't exaggerate or make something up. Share *your* story. Resist the temptation to be envious of someone else's story. Be willing to share the good and the bad. But make sure your story glorifies God and God's grace rather than your past or present sin.

> Your story should not include confusing "Christian-ese." Instead use simple language that people who don't yet believe in Christ can identify with.

> Your story shouldn't be a memorized speech to recite word for word—rather it should help you identify elements of your story that you can adapt naturally to an everyday conversation.

Once students have identified their Why and What stories, encourage them to share them with others. It's that simple. It's what the woman from Samaria did. It's what the blind man did in John 9:25—"One thing I do know. I was blind but now I see!" It's what Peter and the other apostles did in Acts 4:20—"we cannot help speaking about what we have seen and heard."

If you're in a training context, have students role-play with one another. Or encourage your regular small groups to have one student share her story each week as part of the group time. Or elevate the priority of storytelling in your large-group time.

moving forward > by looking back

Encouraging students to process their stories is primarily for their benefit. As they reflect upon their stories, their faith is rooted more deeply in their own lives. And as they understand their stories, they can more naturally share them with others in soul conversations.

Sharing the Gospel Story

People need to hear more than our stories. Our stories can create an interest, but they lack the power to save. The gospel is "the power of God for the salvation of everyone who believes" (Romans 1:16). The power is not in a story, apologetic, or presentation. The power is in the gospel itself. We must share the gospel story. The apostle Paul writes, "faith comes from hearing the message, and the message is heard through the word of Christ" (Romans 10:16).

If your students are in soul conversations with friends, do they know the essence of the gospel story well enough to naturally season the conversations with salt? Would your students know what to say if they had a Philippian jailer experience and a non-Christian friend asked, "What must I do to be saved?" That's not a ball that I want to fumble if it's handed off to me. And it's not one I want my students to drop due to my neglect.

I'm concerned that many Christian students are ignorant of the essentials of the gospel. More than this, I'm concerned that many student ministry leaders are confused about the essentials of the gospel.

Recently a respected church drafted a statement to clarify the essence of the gospel. The senior pastor wrote a short paper summarizing what the church has believed for 2,000 years about how one becomes a child of God. The statement was forwarded to some leading theologians and pastors around the country soliciting their input and critique. Several well-known Christian leaders agreed about the accuracy of the drafted statement. The pastoral staff at this particular church was asked to read the statement and sign a document of agreement to the essence of the gospel message.

Each pastor signed it, except one—the youth pastor. Why? Because he was no longer certain that this was what the gospel was really all about. This dilemma led to this youth pastor abruptly resigning in the middle of the school year, and the students were left disillusioned and confused.

A few years ago a young couple rode with Camille and me to our middle school winter retreat in Michigan. As we neared our camp the woman asked from the backseat, "Craig, I should know this, but what if I'm talking with a student who's ready to become a Christian this weekend—what should I say to her?" I was shocked by the question, but I was grateful she asked. After talking it through together, I realized others might be wondering the same thing. The next morning we reviewed some essentials with our entire group of retreat volunteers.

If some youth pastors and adult volunteers are unclear about the essentials of the gospel story, how can we expect our students to be clear?

We need to help students not only understand the gospel for themselves, but also in a way that they can share with others.

The Gospel Message

There has been some confusion about what the gospel is and is not. It's been widely debated within the Christian community in books, conferences, and blogs. The discussion has caused an internal wrestling in my own heart. I've read the books and entered into the conversation. This is a critical theological cornerstone that I don't want to leave to "this is what I think" or to the opinions of others.

Compelled to see what the Scriptures teach about the gospel, I read the opening chapter in the Gospel of Mark: "Jesus came into Galilee, proclaiming the gospel of God" (v. 14 ESV).

Now I know the word *gospel* means "good news." But what *is* the "good news"? What exactly was the gospel Jesus was proclaiming? Mark continues, "'The kingdom of God is at hand; repent and believe in the gospel.'" (v. 15)

The word *gospel* is used 77 times as a noun in the New Testament. The verb form of "preach the gospel" is also used 77 times in the New Testament. Most of the references don't explain what the "gospel" is—instead its meaning is assumed.

In Mark 1, the gospel is connected to "the kingdom of God is at hand." Theologian William L. Lane writes, "Jesus is declaring that a critical moment has come. God begins to act in a new and decisive way, bringing the promise of ultimate redemption to the point of fulfillment."[1] The promises of the past are finding fulfillment in the present. Jesus has come to secure our redemption. This is truly good news!

The essence of the gospel is: Jesus is Lord. When Jesus says, "The kingdom of God is at hand," he means, "Here I am. Exhibit A. I am the Lord." Because Jesus is the Lord, he came into our world as Redeemer. But why do we need a Redeemer? It all starts with a living Creator God who's the ruler of the world (Genesis 1-2). But humans rejected the ruler in order to be their own rulers (Genesis 3, Romans 3:10). Thus, humans are now under condemnation and separated from their Creator (Hebrews 9:27). Creator God sent Jesus, God's one and only Son, into our world (John 3:16). After living a sinless life, Jesus died as the atoning sacrifice for our sin (2 Corinthians 5:21, 1 Peter 3:18). Jesus rose from the grave as Lord and ruler of all (1 Corinthians 15:2-7, 1 Peter 1:3). God has now exalted Jesus to "the highest place and gave him the name that is above every name." One day every knee will bow and every tongue will confess that Jesus Christ is Lord, to the glory of God the Father (Philippians 2:9-11). This is the essence of the gospel.

THE GOSPEL CALL

Jesus was proclaiming the gospel of God, therefore "*repent* and *believe* in the gospel." Then Jesus said to Simon and Andrew, "Come, *follow me*" (Mark 1:15, 17 ESV). Once we understand the good news of who Jesus is, it demands a response of repentance, belief, and following. Both aspects (the message and the call) are necessary parts of the gospel.

Like those in Jesus' day, we have an opportunity to respond by repenting, believing, and following:

Repent

The Scriptures are clear that there's no forgiveness of sin without repentance. Repentance may not be popular; but it's biblical. "[God] commands all people everywhere to repent" (Acts 17:30). Repentance involves our intellect, emotion, and will:

> Intellect—recognizing one's sin is wrong before a holy God

> Emotion—godly sorrow, not just being sorry (see 2 Corinthians 7:9-10)

> Will—desire to turn from sin and turn to Jesus Christ

Peter proclaimed, "Repent, then, and turn to God, so that your sins might be wiped out, that times of refreshing may come from the Lord" (Acts 3:19). Students don't need to clean up before trusting Christ—that will happen as God sanctifies them. A changed life is not repentance, but the *result* of repentance. The apostle Paul states, "I have declared to both Jews and Greeks that they must turn to God in repentance and have *faith* in our Lord Jesus" (Acts 20:21). This leads to the second response. Biblical repentance includes *turning from* sin and *turning to* God.

Believe

Saving faith isn't hopeful wishing. Instead it's rooted in the person and promises of Jesus. Saving faith involves knowledge and active trust. One must have a basic understanding of Jesus, his atoning sacrifice on the cross, and his victory over the grave. Christianity isn't a blind faith; it's rooted in the truths of Jesus. But believing is more than understanding facts. Even demons know who God is and facts about Jesus (see James 2:19). Saving faith involves active trust. (It's one thing to believe a chair is strong enough to hold you up; it's another thing to decide to have active trust and sit in the chair. Suppose there are three frogs on a log and two decide to jump off—how many are left on the log? The answer is one, right? No. Still three. Just because two *decided* to jump off didn't mean they went through with it.) To truly believe involves acting on a decision by trusting in Jesus Christ for salvation.

Follow

The fruit of genuine repentance and belief is following Christ. It's important that when we call students to repent and believe that we also call them to follow Christ with their lives. Jesus is not only the way and the truth—Jesus is the *life* as well. And not just our life in eternity; Jesus is our life *now*.

Repent and believe, then follow. This is the essence of responding to the gospel story. But the Bible also teaches that repent, believe, fol-

moving forward > by looking back

low must become *repenting, believing, following.* Saving faith results in one's sanctification. And one's sanctification involves ongoing repenting, believing, and following.

Do your students understand the essentials of the gospel message—the true identity of Jesus as Redeemer and Lord? Do your students understand the essentials of the gospel call—repent and believe, then follow? If so, are they personally convinced about these essentials? If so, can they share these essentials of the gospel story clearly?

One Size Fits All?

The gospel is one-size-fits-all. The gospel is a universal truth for all people regardless of race, socioeconomic status, gender, age, or religious background.

But sharing the gospel story is *not* one-size-fits-all.

Let's consider various examples in the book of Acts:

> Because the audience in Acts 2 was Jewish, Peter spoke of Jesus as the Messiah and referenced prophecies from Old Testament passages.

> When Philip saw an Ethiopian reading the Scriptures, he entered into a soul conversation by *asking questions.* After *listening* to the man's confusion about a passage in Isaiah, Philip explained the passage, then *talked* about the "good news about Jesus" (Acts 8:35).

> Paul "reasoned in the synagogue with the Jews and the God-fearing Greeks, as well as in the marketplace day by day" (Acts 17:17).

> But later in Acts 17, Paul changed his approach as he engaged with the philosophers in the Areopagus by beginning with the known, then moving to the unknown.

> When Paul was on trial in Acts 26, he used courtroom terminology (e.g., *defense, testimonies,* and *witness*).

The gospel is one-size-fits-all, but there can be many approaches to sharing the gospel story. A good deal of evangelism training teaches a readily memorized presentation. But our goal is *not* to get through a canned speech—rather we should enter into a discussion by asking questions, listening, and talking about Jesus.

Before we get to some examples for sharing the gospel story with clarity, we should acknowledge that there are many New Testament references to the "mystery" of the gospel. Yet in the same context in which the apostle Paul talks about proclaiming the "mystery" of the gospel, he also talks about sharing the gospel "clearly, as I should" (see Colossians 4:3-4).

Mystery and Simplicity

The mysteriousness of the gospel and the necessity to share with clarity has divided some Christians. Those who embrace the "mystery" of the gospel often embrace a messy gospel that can never be articulated clearly. Those who embrace a "clear" gospel often articulate a packaged gospel void of marvelous wonder and mystery. This inner tension between a mystery and clarity need not lead to division.

The eye is one of the most complex members of your body. It's a scientific mystery to comprehend the symmetry of complexities continuously working together for you to read these words. Even though the eye is incredibly mysterious, it can be explained in simple terms. Just the other night I was reading a book about the body to my first-grader. Several pages were devoted to explaining the eye in ways that a grade school student (and his dad) could understand. Because the eye can be explained simply does not mean that the eye is any less complex. A simple understanding does not diminish its mystery to me—if anything it enhances the mystery. Yet I can explain the eye to others in a simple way they can understand, too.

In a similar way, the gospel is an incredible mystery, yet there is a simplicity to it we can understand and explain to others. We must help our students understand this. *We should not let the simplicity of the gospel get lost in the mystery of the gospel. Nor should we let the mystery of the gospel get lost in the simplicity of the gospel.*

Training Students to Share the Mystery of the Gospel with Clarity

The gospel story shouldn't be reserved only for large-group messages at winter retreat. Nor should it be reserved only for adult youth leaders to share with students. In fact, students are usually more effective at sharing the gospel story with students than are adults. Therefore, we must train our students to share the gospel story conversationally—including both the gospel message and the gospel call.

I believe students are capable of leading their non-Christian friends to faith in Christ—because I've seen it. I find more joy in a student leading a friend to Christ than me leading a student to Christ. There are a lot of benefits, including that more students "stick" because of a natural relationship for follow-up. And students learn early on in their faith that they can share their faith with other friends because that's the way it was modeled to them.

We need to encourage students to develop friendships with non-Christians in their worlds—on their teams, in clubs, classes, workplaces, and neighborhoods. We need to encourage them to be salt by Showing Jesus, Asking Questions, Listening, and Talking about Jesus. But if we're going to help them talk about Jesus, we need to equip them with the essentials of the gospel story.

As I noted, some evangelism training prides itself in helping students memorize the gospel message so they can tell it in two minutes or less—but we must make sure we're not training our students to regurgitate a memorized speech for a friend. Nor am I in favor of a "hit-and-run" approach to evangelism. That doesn't mean God's Spirit doesn't prompt us to share the gospel with a stranger on a plane or in a park. But most often our conversations are with people we know. The goal is not to get through a sales pitch—but to engage in a soul conversation.

The next few pages give examples for training students to share the gospel story. As you read, keep these three things in mind:

1. This isn't an exhaustive list. There are many more approaches to sharing the gospel story.

2. The examples are varied because there's no one-size-fits-all way to share the gospel.

3. Each example seeks to describe the wondrous mystery of the gospel in clear language students can understand and explain to others.

Bible Stories

The chart on the opposite page details four mega themes when sharing the truth of the gospel. It was developed my friend Eric Liechty. The four mega themes of God, us, Christ, and life can be shared in various ways through asking questions, telling Bible stories, talking about personal experiences, and using short sound bites. This chart is helpful for understanding different parts of the gospel. Since non-Christians are at different points in their faith journeys, this chart explains which things to share at different points along the way. It also includes the appropriate biblical responses to God's truth as part of assessing the process.

G.O.S.P.E.L.

Jesus didn't always start with himself when sharing the gospel story. Often he went back to the Old Testament—including once while in a soul conversation with two men on the road to Emmaus. Jesus began "with Moses and all the Prophets, [and] explained to them what was said in all the Scriptures concerning himself" (Luke 24:27).

When Paul engaged in a soul conversation with the philosophers at Mars Hill, he started with creation. He didn't start with Jesus. Nor did he start with Genesis 3. He started at the beginning of the story. The Bible doesn't start in the Gospels, but in Genesis. Too often we start at the end of the story when people need to understand the beginning of the story first.

Paul then shared about a benevolent God. Writing about Paul's Mars Hill message, Greg Stier observes—

MEGA THEMES	GOD	US	CHRIST	LIFE
CLASSIC DISCIPLINES	Theology	Anthropology	Christology	Missiology
EPIC TRUTHS	**Great and gracious**	**Marked**—God's image (evidenced by desire for greatness and graciousness) **and marred**—by sin (evidenced by hiding and blaming wrongs)	**God and us** without sin (way, truth, and life)	**Glorify God** (loving God and others by making disciples)
QUESTIONS (for listening)	Describe God	Describe us	Describe Christ	Describe life
BIBLE STORIES	Creation, flood, Abraham and Isaac	Created in God's image, rebelled	Born of virgin, fulfilled God's promises	Jesus' followers left everything to follow him
MY EXPERIENCES (for sharing)	Describe when God has been great and gracious	When did you realize you were wrong?	When did you start trusting Jesus?	How has living for God's glory impacted you?
SCRIPTURE SUMMARY OF EPIC TRUTHS (for sharing)	"One thing God has spoken, two things have I heard: that you, O God, are **strong**, and that you, O Lord, are **loving**" (Psalm 62:11-12).	"Then God said, 'Let **us make man in our image**, in our likeness.'" (Genesis 1:26) "For all have sinned and fall short of the glory of God." (Romans 3:23)	"For **in Christ** all the **fullness of the Deity lives in bodily form.**" (Colossians 2:9) "Jesus answered, 'I **am the way and the truth and the life.** No one comes to the Father except through me.'" (John 14:6)	"Whatever you do, **do it all for the glory of God.**" (1 Corinthians 10:31) "**Love the Lord your God … and Love your neighbor** as yourself. (Matthew 22:37-39) "**Make disciples.**" (Matthew 28:19)
ONE-VERSE GOSPEL (for sharing) "For the wages of sin is death, but the gift of God is eternal life in Christ Jesus our Lord." (Romans 6:23)	God [Gift / God / Eternal Life]	Man [Wages / Sin / Death]	Christ (cross)	Man | Christ | God [Wages / Sin / Death] [Gift / God / Eternal Life]
10-SECOND "SOUND BITE" GOD'S MESSAGE	God made us.	We blew it.	Christ paid for it and we must trust him	and share his message of love with others.
EPIC RESPONSES TO TRUTH	**Seeking** (pursue getting to know God)	**Repenting** (ready to admit "I'm wrong")	**Trusting** (Jesus is the way, the truth, and the life)	**Following** (live life to God's glory)
IMPACT OF OUR RESPONSES TO TRUTH	Finding God	Being forgiven	Being saved	Experiencing lifelong pleasure and purpose

Paul paints the gospel as a love story. He preaches a loving God who is patiently waiting for humanity to return to Him...When sharing the gospel with students, we must keep in mind that the Bible is a love story, filled with all the elements of a good novel...romance, tragedy, broken hearts, sacrifice, second chances, and happily-ever-afters. The difference is this: The Bible is nonfiction.

Greg has summarized the biblical meta-narrative with this helpful acrostic:

SCENE	SCRIPT	POINT
Sacred romance	*Genesis 1-2*	**G**od created us to be with him.
Broken heart	*Genesis 3*	**O**ur sins separate us from God.
Devastating separation	*Genesis 4-Malachi*	**S**ins can't be removed by good deeds.
Climactic sacrifice	*Matthew-Luke*	**P**aying the price for sin, Jesus died and rose again.
Second chance	*John-Jude*	**E**veryone who trusts in Jesus alone has eternal life.
Happy ending	*Revelation*	**L**ife that's eternal means we will be with God forever.[2]

At the end of his Mars Hill message Paul makes an apologetic point: "He has given proof of this to all men by raising him from the dead" (Acts 17:31). Even though he had solid proof, he chose not to start with logical evidence. Instead he shared the gospel story and concluded with supporting proof.

ABCs of the Christian Faith / Romans Road

My youth pastor trained me in this summary of the gospel when I was a teenager. I underlined each verse in my NIV Student Bible and wrote the reference of the next verse in the margin so the verses were linked together. I remember stumbling through several soul conversations with my non-Christian friends, but it was helpful to have this outline as a reference point in my mind. Since becoming a student ministry pastor, I've passed on this three-point outline to countless students:

> **A**dmit you're a sinner—you can't save yourself, and you desire to turn from sin to God.

"For all have sinned and fall short of the glory of God" (Romans 3:23).

"For the wages of sin is death, but the gift of God is eternal life in Christ Jesus our Lord" (Romans 6:23).

> **B**elieve in Jesus—he's the Son of God who paid the penalty for sin in his death and rose again.

"But God demonstrates his own love for us in this: While we were still sinners, Christ died for us" (Romans 5:8).

> **C**onfess your faith—choose to let God lead your life.

"That if you confess with your mouth, 'Jesus is Lord,' and believe in your heart that God raised him from the dead, you will be saved" (Romans 10:9).

"For, 'Everyone who calls on the name of the Lord will be saved'" (Romans 10:13).

I received an email today from a student who reminded me it's his first spiritual birthday. Scott came on a retreat a year ago with his friend Daniel. The cabin times were a struggle throughout the day because Scott was pretty obnoxious. But God was working in his heart. Not only was he engaged in the cabin conversation, but he also asked how he could become a Christian. Since I wanted some students to experience the joy of leading someone to Jesus, I opened the question to the guys. I was so proud of Grant and Chris' leadership as they walked Scott through the ABCs in a very natural way. It's been a year since, and Scott is still walking with God.

Tell Gospel Stories

Jesus was a master of telling the gospel story through telling gospel stories. We know these stories as *parables*. Mark writes, "With many similar parables Jesus spoke the word to them, as much as they could understand. He did not say anything to them without using a parable" (Mark 4:33-34). Another way for students to share the gospel story is through equipping them to tell gospel stories that illustrate biblical points. Among the many modern-day parables, one of my favorites is about a great and generous king.

Imagine a great and generous king. In the midst of his benevolent reign, he hears that his subjects have revolted. He sends messengers to investigate. The rebels kill them. So he sends his own dear son, the prince. They murder him viciously, hanging his body on the city wall.

What would you expect the king to do now? Send his armies and take revenge, right? *Kill those rebels! Burn their villages to ashes!* That king certainly has both the power and the right to avenge his son.

But what if the king turned around and offered these criminals a full pardon?

"I will accept my son—whom you murdered—as the payment for all your rebellion. You may go free. All I require is for you to admit your transgressions and embrace my son's purchase of your forgiveness."

We'd be stunned—blown away—to hear this, wouldn't we? But the king's not finished.

"I invite any of you to come live in my palace, eat at my table, and enjoy all the pleasures of my kingdom. And I will adopt you as my own children and make you my heirs, so everything that's mine will be yours forever."

Incredible.

Then he says, "I won't force you to accept my offer. But the only alternative is spending the rest of your life in the prison. The choice is yours."

Can you imagine someone responding, "How *dare* the king send anyone to prison? What a cruel tyrant!"? This is God's grace to us.

moving forward > by looking back

Suppose you worked hard, saved up money, then came to the king and said, "Here. I'm paying you back."

Imagine the king's response. You couldn't *begin* to pay him back. The very attempt is an insult. It cheapens his son's death.[3]

Training Students to be Storytellers

As student ministry leaders, one of our primary roles is to prepare students for works of service—including engaging in soul conversations through *sharing their stories* and *sharing the gospel story*. Let me suggest a few contexts for equipping your students with some of the content in this chapter:

> *Whole-group teaching series.* Dedicate a four- to six-week series to equip students to share their lives, share their stories, and share the gospel.

> *Workshop format.* The size, format, or spiritual interest of your group may make it difficult to use your large-group time to train students in soul conversations. If so, consider dedicating a Saturday to training students in a one-day format. Only students who want to come will come, and your workshop can be more interactive than a large-group meeting. You can train each session or enlist others to train one session each. Partner with another student ministry in your area to shoulder the load together. Or make it a retreat by doing an overnight in your church building.

> *Elective class.* Instead of offering one-day training, perhaps it would work better in your ministry to offer this training as a four- to six-week elective (at an optional time for students).

> *Ministry team training.* If you have a student ministry team, dedicate some time each year to train them and hold them accountable for engaging students in soul conversations.

> *Retreat or camp theme.* If it's difficult to find additional time to train students, devote one of your already scheduled retreats or camps to the theme of training students to have soul conversations.

> *Missions trip training.* Before taking students on a service project

in the States or on an international mission trip, use your training meetings for more than sharing information about the trip. Instead utilize these sessions for training students to share their stories and the gospel story.

> *Conference.* Take your students to one of several national conferences, such as Youth Specialties' DC/LA or Dare2Share, which are dedicated to training students to share their faith.

Why do we care and share? Because that's who God is. God has compassion for people's souls. We reflect the character of God when we have compassion for people's souls.

Think of all the prayer requests Paul could've included in his prison letter to the Colossian church. He could've asked for prayer for his release. He could've asked for prayer for his comfort. He could've asked for prayer for justice on his behalf. Instead this was Paul's request: "That God may open a door for our message, so that we may proclaim the mystery of Christ, for which I am in chains. Pray that I may proclaim it clearly, as I should" (Colossians 4:3-4). I'm challenged by Paul's example.

As we seek to live missionally and enter into soul conversations, let us remember the importance of prayer. As Paul did, we have three things to pray for:

> *Open door*—opportunity to show Jesus, ask questions, and listen

> *Open mouth*—boldness to talk about Jesus

> *Open heart*—for God to draw the lost to himself

But reaching out to others isn't limited to soul conversations. The final chapter will help us rethink outreach as we move from living missionally to having a missional ministry.

moving forward > by looking back

moving forward > questions

Questions for personal reflection and team discussion:

1. What are some things that hinder students and adults from entering into soul conversations?

2. Describe the last soul conversation you had.

3. What are some ways you can encourage students to be "saltier" in their everyday conversations?

4. Why is the question, "Why are you a Christian?" such a significant (and often difficult to answer) question for students?

5. How do you summarize the essence of the gospel story? What is the gospel call?

6. How will you train your students with some of the content in this chapter? With what will you train them?

7. What aspects of this chapter do you want to discuss with others on your leadership team?

1. *The Gospel of Mark* (Grand Rapids, MI: William B. Eerdmans, 1982), 64.

2. *Outbreak* (Chicago: Moody, 2002), 195.

3. Randy Alcorn, *The Grace and Truth Paradox* (Colorado Springs, CO: Multnomah, 2003), 34-35, 82.

We need to rethink outreach and start thinking about reaching out.

Most student ministry leaders associate outreach with large-group evangelism where success is defined by the number of students in attendance and the number of first-time professions of faith in Jesus. Our limited understanding of outreach has led many to rent inflatables and invite students to bounce around to pretty mediocre music and hear a speaker they don't know tell them they're going to hell. Why do we do this to non-Christian students? Why do we do this to our Christian students? I'm not against inflatables. And I'm not against large-group events. But we must rethink outreach as more than primarily a big event with an activity and a message. Instead we need to start thinking about reaching out.

Because the early Christians loved God and people, they were all about reaching out. Rather than being attracted to an event, people in the book of Acts were attracted to these new Christians and to their God. And the church was engaged in reaching out missionally to their culture. The early church was about attractional living and missional ministry.

We practice our theology when we reach out. We reach out because God reaches out and because we desire to reflect God's character in our lives and in our ministries.

We need to create a ministry culture that encourages reaching out every time we gather as a community of believers and as we scatter to our schools and relationships. Reaching out must not be confined to an event; it must be a lifestyle. Does this mean we shouldn't offer special events for reaching out? Not at all. We do need variety in our ministries and "side doors" for new students. But we need to view reaching out as more than an event.

I want to encourage us toward a five-spoke, holistic approach to reaching out.

Think about the spokes on a five-point tire rim. All five spokes on the rim are necessary. If one's missing, the tire becomes imbalanced, and the ride gets bumpy. In a similar way our ministries are imbalanced without all five spokes in our reaching-out methodology.

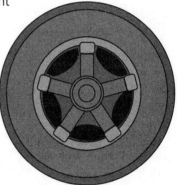

	ACTS Priority	Chapter
Spoke one regular ministry gatherings	A, C, T	1.0 to 3.3
Spoke two serving opportunities	S	4.1
Spoke three soul conversations	S	4.2
Spoke four programmed reaching out	S	4.3
Spoke five nonprogrammed reaching out	S	4.3

Before you panic about the chart telling you to create an even busier ministry filled with even more activities, feel free to breathe a sigh of relief: I'm not suggesting you add any more activities than you're already sponsoring. I'm simply saying we need to be more strategic with our ministry programming. Here's what I mean:

Spoke 1—*your regular youth group night.* Hanging out with the same students each week is comfortable. But God never calls us to a life of comfort. We must help our students catch the vision that our regular gatherings are weekly opportunities to reach out. This can and should happen during our regular ministry times where students gather for worship (adoration), the teaching of God's Word (truth), and small groups (community). What better way to introduce non-Christian students to Jesus than by letting them observe other students passionately worshiping God and hearing God's Word being taught? This can shatter some stereotypes while creating a curiosity that God might not be distant and boring but very real. Further, small groups can provide a context for students to experience Christian community before they believe in Christ. They also provide a safe setting for students to explore Christianity, ask questions, and share doubts.

Spoke 2—*serving.* Why not devote one of your regular nights a semester to whole-group serving and collect a special offering on another Sunday night? In addition to these times, students can be encouraged to engage in ongoing serving opportunities through a ministry of your church or a community organization.

Spoke 3—*soul conversations.* Reaching out primarily happens in the context of relationships outside ministry events as students live missionally and enter into everyday conversations full of grace and seasoned with salt. After training your students to tell their stories and the gospel story, routinely encourage them to enter into soul conversations and be S.A.L.T.:

> **S**how Jesus
> **A**sk questions
> **L**isten
> **T**alk about Jesus

Spoke 4—*programmed reaching-out gatherings.* These can include several events strategically placed throughout the year to replace your regular gathering time. This adds variety to your programming and provides students with opportunities to reach out by inviting friends to participate in a special event, program, or activity.

Spoke 5—*nonprogrammed reaching-out gatherings.* Reaching out can happen in smaller, more casual, and sometimes even spontaneous gatherings. Some of these times may appear on a ministry calendar, some not. These gatherings are usually either relationship-based (sharing life together) or activity-based (sharing an experience together).

Since earlier chapters of this book have already addressed spokes 1, 2, and 3, this chapter will focus on spokes 4 and 5.

Within the rhythm of our ministry calendar we need to plan special events—programmed (spoke 4) and nonprogrammed (spoke 5)—focusing on reaching out. These vary from regular ministry gatherings, and support—not replace—relational reaching out. Sometimes the gospel is verbally shared—sometimes it's not. Reaching out needs to be seen as a process. Sometimes the goal is to have new students come and see by being introduced to other students and to your student ministry. Yet at the same time we need to be balanced and have times throughout the ministry year when the gospel is clearly shared simply and succinctly with students, who are then given an opportunity to respond with repentance and belief.

So if reaching out can happen through regular ministry gatherings (spoke 1) and missional living (spokes 2 and 3), then why the need for special gatherings (spokes 4 and 5)? Here are three benefits:

1. *Introduce new students to the ministry.* New students may not be eager to come to a normal youth group night but willing to come to a special event. Special events allow students to come and see a larger group of believers in action when the focus isn't on new people in the room. Plus some students need to belong to a Christian group before they'll believe in Jesus. In addition, you may have new students attending your weekend church services who'll first get connected with your group through a special event. As student ministry leaders, we need to take responsibility to create "side door" gatherings to provide entry points for new students in our ministries.

2. *Model reaching out.* Many youth leaders encourage their students to share their faith—and even train them to do so. But even after receiving training, many students don't know how to share their faith. Reaching out can't only be taught; it must be *caught.* If reaching out is a priority in your personal life, it will likely be a priority in your group. And if it's a priority in your group, it will likely be a priority in your students' lives. We must, however, avoid communicating that outreach is an event.

3. *Provide tag-team support.* Mark shares in his gospel a story about how a paralyzed guy had some friends who cared enough for him they literally picked him up, carried him across town, and cut a hole in the roof to get him to Jesus (2:1-5). How cool is that? This was a tag-team effort. These friends needed each other to reach their friend. And they used an event to get their friend to Jesus. Shouldn't we encourage our students to act in the same way?

Rethinking...

Although no one way of reaching out through spokes 4 and 5 is the correct way, some ways are wrong. Some approaches to reaching out create unnecessary collateral damage. In some ways the following points are confessions of personal outreach mistakes that have caused me to rethink the process at five different levels:

RETHINK BAIT AND SWITCH—INSTEAD BE AUTHENTIC.

The bait-and-switch tactic is one of my biggest pet peeves. Not long ago I retrieved a glossy oversized postcard mailer from my mailbox. It declared in bold letters: "CRAIG STEINER HAS WON A 60-INCH PLASMA TELEVISION + A COMPLETE SURROUND SOUND SYSTEM." Then I read the fine print. The reality was, I'd won a *chance* to win the television if I purchased a bunch of products and disclosed all my personal financial data. I ripped up that mailer. Oh yeah, there's the one with telemarketer who offers you a party promising free vacation vouchers and a buffet—only to be required to endure a three-hour, high-pressure sales pitch about a vacation condo. And if you say no after all of that, then your party host will get the manager to talk with you. Then the associate manager. Then the senior manager. What's up with that? Or you sign up for a free three-month magazine trial and later discover your trial obligates you to a 36-month subscription at the newsstand price. The only people who enjoy bait-and-switch tactics are the ones running the scams.

So why is student ministry notorious for bait and switch? We say, "Come for the _____!" And you know the bait—food, fun, free stuff, games, concert, friends, etc. But then we turn down the lights and abruptly switch to a gospel presentation.

By the way, why do we refer to the greatest story ever as a presentation? I've tried to purge this overused term from my ministry vocabulary. I don't like it because it sounds too close to a *sales* presentation. Paul said, "We do not peddle the word of God" (2 Corinthians 2:17). We don't hock or pawn the gospel. God forbid we're used-car salespeople who put on the obnoxious personality and say, "Have I got a deal for you!" We don't need to sell the gospel. We need to share the gospel story with authenticity and sincerity.

Because we don't want to bait and switch, our ministry includes words about our relationship with God on all our promotional materials. This is clear either in the tag line or in the description of the event. We don't hide the fact that God is most important to our group. And we encourage our students to be up-front about this when inviting friends: "Hey, I want you to come to my church with me. It's pretty cool. You can come have fun, learn about God, and meet some other students." This is part of being authentic witnesses.

RETHINK ONE OUTREACH METHOD—HAVE A VARIETY.

Some churches emphasize a skater outreach. But what about nonskaters? Some emphasize coffeehouse outreach. But what about the more active students? Some emphasize sports-centered outreach. But what about the students who aren't into sports? Some ministries appeal only to extroverted students. But what about introverted students?

Does your ministry offer variety? Do you have a balance of programmed gatherings (moving students from element to element) and nonprogrammed gatherings (casual and relational or active)? Students grow tired of overprogrammed events all the time. But nonprogrammed gatherings do need to be balanced with more organized times together. Some students are attracted to sharing life in a casual, relational setting. Other students are attracted to an activity where they can share an experience together. We should offer variety.

Reaching out can take on many forms, including activities, events, and programs. Reaching out can happen at the church or away from the church. It can be a coffeehouse night. An open gym. An overnight lock-in. A capture the flag night. A special large-group program. A battle of the bands. A ski day. A fifth-quarter get-together. A small group event. Variety allows for programmed and nonprogrammed gatherings. Variety allows for some times to be come-and-see events and others when the gospel story is shared.

Retreats and other trips add variety and can be some of the most fruitful ministry contexts for reaching out. Students are removed from the temptations and distractions of everyday life while experiencing extended time in Christian community and hearing the Word of God. Many non-Christian students who are hesitant to go to youth group are willing to go to camp or on a special trip.

And bigger isn't always better. Often we associate outreach events with trying to get the biggest crowd to show up. Part of having a varied approach to reaching out involves realizing smaller contexts are effective, too. Luke 5 details Matthew's house party outreach. Since Matthew had been a tax collector, most of his friends were tax collectors. So Matthew invited a bunch of his tax collector buddies over to his house to a social gathering to meet Jesus (Luke 5:27-32). What if your students caught a vision that outreach isn't just done at big events at the church? What would it look like if a few of your students brainstormed together about reaching a group of common-interest friends— such as sports teammates or the play cast or members from a school club? Perhaps students could reach out to their own friends through hosting their own Matthew house party or another activity together.

Variety also encourages students to assess their relationships with their non-Christian friends and choose which gatherings are best for bringing specific friends. Just because students don't bring friends to every event doesn't mean they don't care about all their non-Christian friends. This may actually be a sign they really *do* care—they care

moving forward > by looking back

enough to think about which gatherings are best, given their friends' personalities and interests. Some non-Christian students need to be introduced to a community of believers through the closeness of a small group. Others need activity. Others need the connection of a relational gathering. And others need the attraction of a program. Offering variety throughout the calendar year provides students with various opportunities to reach out.

RETHINK ADULT-LED EVENTS—LET STUDENTS LEAD.

If you value an outreach ministry that's *of* students and *by* students—versus an outreach ministry *to* students, where the ministry is done for them—then provide your students with opportunities and resources for peer-to-peer ministry. When was the last time you asked students, "What can we do together to reach your friends?" Have you asked that question in the last 12 months? Rather than having students support your ideas, here's a thought: Why not support *your students'* ideas? I'm not advocating letting students do whatever they want, but you'd do well to listen to their ideas. Once you've landed on something you can do together, why not empower students to lead? After all, this is *student* ministry, right? A ministry *of* students and *by* students allows them to be part of the planning, promoting, and leading for special outreach events.

RETHINK ONE-TIME EVENTS—BE COMMITTED TO A JOURNEY.

It's extremely rare for a student to make a genuine decision to follow Christ as a first-time guest. It just doesn't happen that way—even biblically speaking. We can't set ourselves, or our students, up to think that way. Conversion usually happens through a series of planting and watering. And planting and watering. And more planting and watering. And then a lot more planting and watering. Paul writes, "I planted the seed, Apollos watered it, but God made it grow. So neither he who plants nor he who waters is anything, but only God, who makes things grow" (1 Corinthians 3:6-7).

One of the reasons we do special events is to plant seeds and water them. We don't control the harvest. God does. God gives the growth. But we can be faithful to plant and water.

There are many ways to describe the faith journey that ends with the decision to follow Jesus. I view the journey as students sitting in one of six chairs.

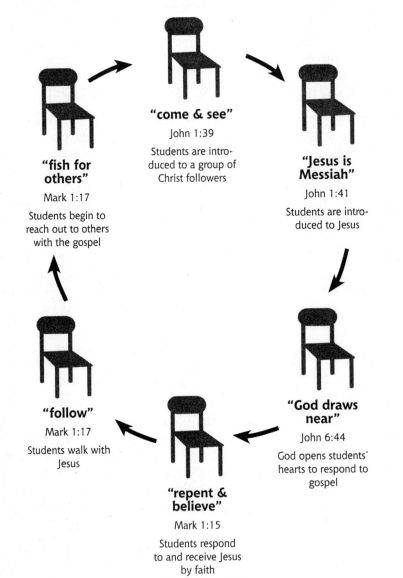

"come & see"

John 1:39

Students are introduced to a group of Christ followers

"fish for others"

Mark 1:17

Students begin to reach out to others with the gospel

"Jesus is Messiah"

John 1:41

Students are introduced to Jesus

"follow"

Mark 1:17

Students walk with Jesus

"God draws near"

John 6:44

God opens students' hearts to respond to gospel

"repent & believe"

Mark 1:15

Students respond to and receive Jesus by faith

We should have faith to believe God could be drawing a student anytime we gather with students, but we must avoid manipulative schemes and expectations that new students will respond each time the gospel is shared. Students usually respond to God if a trusting relationship with a friend has been built or if they've been seeking truth— very rarely do they respond to the gospel the first time they hear it or see it.

Think about some students you know in your group. Which chair is each sitting in? How can you be intentional in helping each student move to the next chair in the sequence?

The final chapter of the book of Acts ends with these words: "Some were convinced by what [Paul] said, but others would not believe" (Acts 28:24). Even though Jesus attracted crowds (at times thousands of people), he was never about entertaining crowds. Jesus was clear he didn't want people following him for "food that spoils, but for food that endures to eternal life" (John 6:27). When Jesus spoke about being the bread of life, many in the crowd said, "This is a hard teaching. Who can accept it?" (John 6:60). A few chose to believe and follow. This was a defining moment for people. Jesus never compromised the truth to manipulate and inflate a conversion number. In fact, Jesus was okay with the fact that some were offended and chose to walk away. If students don't always respond to the gospel, take heart—you're in good company with the apostle Paul and Jesus.

Over the years I've had to wrestle with and assess my own heart and ministry. Am I guilty of merely entertaining students to attract a bigger crowd? *Am I willing to provide defining moments for students by challenging them to repent, believe, and follow? Or do I compromise the truth by softening the message and ignore speaking the name of Jesus? Am I driven by the harvest or the opportunity to plant and water? Am I too insecure if students choose to reject the truth and walk away?*

RETHINK COUNTING CONVERTS—CARE FOR NEWBORN BELIEVERS.

If a student comes up to me and says, "I just gave my life to Jesus," I extend a high five or a hug and say with enthusiasm, "That's awesome!

Tell me more." It's important for the student to verbalize her new faith, and this helps me understand if she comprehends what she says she is believing.

No greater joy in ministry exists than seeing students respond in faith to Jesus Christ. It's not only about the six students who trusted Christ at an event, but about what happens inside those students after the event. Don't just count the students; care for the students. Our job isn't done once students make the decision to follow Jesus. At that point it's time to help students develop as disciples of Christ. We need to help students grow as newborns in their faith.

I didn't realize until I had my first child how much stuff newborns need. Jonathan needed a Pack 'n Play, a three-in-one travel system, a crib, and a diaper disposal system, just to name a small portion of what's needed to care for a newborn. But more than needing stuff, he was dependent on love, attention, and help. The developmental needs of a newborn baby are similar to the developmental needs of a new Christian:

Drinking milk	Learn how to feed on the Word of God
Dressing	Learn the importance of Christian community
Talking	Learn to pray
Walking	Learn to walk by faith in obedience

More than a new believers' class or a "your first 30 days as a new believer" book, new converts need to learn about these things through life-on-life time. And they need support from other Christian students, not just the adult youth leader.

One of my fondest ministry moments was baptizing dozens of students in our weekend worship services in August as a testimony of the Spirit's work in students' lives through our summer ministry. As I was baptizing Philip, his grandmother sat in tears in the front row. The fact Philip was even standing next to me was a testimony of an elderly woman's faithful prayers.

moving forward > by looking back

For 17 years she'd prayed for the salvation of her grandson. She encouraged Philip to attend camp—and actually registered him. He got on the bus for summer church camp not knowing anyone. A few days into camp, Philip's cabin leader was struggling with what to do about Philip's vulgar tongue and rebellious attitude, which were negatively influencing the other guys in the cabin. What would you have done? It wasn't until later we realized these were outward signs of a spiritual battle going on for Philip's soul.

Four days into our camp Philip surrendered his life to Jesus. I met up with Philip minutes later. I could sense his heart pounding, and he had a hard time breathing at a normal rate. His new life in Jesus was so evident. As a newborn, Philip needed support from other students. That night I moved him to another cabin with some spiritually strong guys who could help with the follow-up process. Philip continues to be a sponge and is soaking up all he can about his faith in Christ. Philip is now active in a small group with the same guys, who've become some of his closest friends.

Let's not be guilty of counting converts without providing care for newborn believers.

Rethinking Your Ministry Calendar

Our ministry calendars model what our real ministry priorities are.

When planning your ministry calendar, I encourage you to consider ministry rhythms, variety, and sustainability. I recently met with a youth pastor who was exhausted. Rob's ministry calendar included weekly Sunday school, Sunday night youth group, Wednesday night small groups, and the occasional weekend retreat or service project. And this was only the high school schedule. He was responsible for middle school, too. Middle school had Sunday school and Tuesday night youth group. If this wasn't crazy enough, he was trying to add outreach events on occasional Friday nights. How would you advise Rob?

I encouraged him to drop at least one weekly high school program and add variety to his regular night rather than adding an additional night. He'd only considered adding programs and never thought about periodically changing the focus of the regular nights.

You know your ministry context—community, students, ministry programs—best. Yours is different from ours. You need to seek the God of the harvest for vision and direction for how you and your students can faithfully reach out to and disciple students in your community.

It's time to rethink outreach and start thinking about reaching out. May we be overflowing with the Holy Spirit and so compelled by the love of Jesus that we're reaching out every time we gather as a community of believers and as we scatter throughout the week. May we be committed to planting faithfully and watering in a variety of ways—and letting God control the harvest.

moving forward > by looking back

moving forward > questions

Questions for personal reflection and team discussion:

1. How is your reaching out a part of your being a practicing theologian?

2. Do you see your regular ministry gathering as a holy huddle or an opportunity to reach out? Describe.

3. This chapter detailed six specific areas to rethink related to reaching out gatherings. Do you agree with these? Why or why not?

4. What are some of the dangers of an imbalanced approach to reaching out?

5. What's the current outreach temperature of your group? Explain.

6. In what ways do you need to rethink your ministry calendar to better reach out?

7. What aspects of this chapter do you want to discuss with others on your leadership team?

CONCLUSION

"The End."

These are the familiar words on the last page of many books that I read to my young children. Even though there are only a few pages left in this book, this is *not* the end. Instead, it's the commencement of another chapter. *Your chapter.*

I've listened to dozens of commencement addresses and have been honored to deliver the commencement address at area Christian schools on several occasions. I've concluded that there are three characteristics of a good commencement address: It's brief, it's memorable, and it reflects on the past, present, and future.

Jesus gave a commencement address to his disciples in Matthew 28. And it was a fantastic commencement address. It was brief: Matthew records only 60 words in three sentences. It was memorable: The fact that we can read them two millennia later attests to that. It speaks of the past, present, and future: This was not the end of ministry. It was a true commencement—an act marking the beginning of the disciples living out what they'd learned and experienced as they lived with their Master. Jesus sent his disciples on a mission.

They were to commence with making disciples themselves.

But the story doesn't end with the conclusion of the four Gospels. Instead it's the beginning of another chapter. The Book of Acts details how the Church emerged as the disciples faithfully embraced their mission to make disciples. They were devoted to adoration, community, truth, and service—and God empowered their ministry.

Now the baton has been handed to us. We have the opportunity to faithfully embrace the same mission: To make disciples among this generation of students. The story is not over. The story continues to be written.

I'm excited for you as you commence with your mission to make disciples in your youth ministry context. What a privilege that God has given us to invest in this generation of students—who knows how the story will unfold as our students grow up and reach the next generation.

Allow these words of benediction to encourage your spirit:

May the God of peace, who through the blood of the eternal covenant brought back from the dead our Lord Jesus, that great Shepherd of the sheep, equip you with everything good for doing his will, and may he work in us what is pleasing to him, through Jesus Christ, to whom be glory for ever and ever. Amen. (Hebrews 13:20-21)

Let's begin *moving forward > by looking back*...for the glory of God.

With Bible studies for just about any youth ministry audience or setting, the Digging Deeper Series gives you everything you need to draw
your students deeper into God's Word.

See, Believe, Live
An Inductive Study in John
Barry Shafer
RETAIL $19.99
ISBN 978-0-310-27498-8

Rock Solid Faith
An Inductive Study of 2 Timothy
Barry Shafer
RETAIL $19.99
ISBN 978-0-310-27499-5

Hear and Do
An Inductive Study in James
Barry Shafer
RETAIL $19.99
ISBN 978-0-310-27623-4